SOCIAL CONFLICT AND THE POLITICAL ORDER IN MODERN BRITAIN

Social Conflict and the Political Order in Modern Britain

EDITED BY JAMES E. CRONIN AND
JONATHAN SCHNEER

RUTGERS UNIVERSITY PRESS
NEW BRUNSWICK, NEW JERSEY

First published in the USA by
Rutgers University Press, 1982

Library of Congress Catalog Card No. 81-85438

Cronin, James and Jonathan Schneer
Social Conflict and Political Order in Modern Britain
    New Brunswick, NJ; Rutgers University/
    Croom Helm
    224 p.
    8206   811103

    ISBN 0-8135-0956-4

First published in Great Britain by
Croom Helm Ltd. Publishers, 1982

CONTENTS

1 SOCIAL HISTORY AND POLITICS IN BRITAIN

James E. Cronin and Jonathan Schneer

In 1971 Eric Hobsbawm wrote that it was a good time to be a social historian, for social history had become not only a recognised discipline within the profession, but also seemed to be its most lively and interesting branch, attracting the best students and generating the best research.[1] Since then, social history has continued to prosper, and nowhere more than in Britain.

Success generates its own difficulties, however, and there is evident among practitioners a sense that the mushroom growth of the field has produced a certain confusion regarding aims, methods and findings. The most obvious symptom of the problem is the fragmented character of the growth that has occurred.[2] When Hobsbawm surveyed the terrain he concluded that the next step was to move beyond the various narrow specialties that then made up social history to the production of an integrated, total 'history of society'. In fact, the development of social history has been in precisely the opposite direction, towards a further specialisation and fragmentation. Indeed, one could say that social history as a general study of the social totality has rarely been attempted, and that what has flourished instead are the various and shifting sub-fields normally grouped under the more general rubric. For just as the impetus towards social history in the 1960s derived from the interaction between a long-term dissatisfaction with a social types of analysis and the intellectual climate of the period, so more recent developments stem from the combination of dissatisfaction with academic social history as practised hitherto and the concerns of a very different decade. Not surprisingly, the major growth areas in terms of substance have been women's and family history, while the major advances in method have involved a democratising of technique through the increasing turn to oral and community history.

This kind of work is about as far removed from the 'totalising' history of society as it can be, and presents a genuine dilemma for many academic social historians, who need and deeply desire synthesis and interpretation, as well as for the new local and oral historians whose very interest in 'people's history' springs from political concerns that seem to get lost in the minutiae of their own local studies. The dilemma is felt acutely, for example, by those active in the History

Workshop movement, whose commitment to oral methods, studies of small groups and localities, and to women's history, often seems to conflict with their general political outlook. In a characteristic complaint, Jerry White, author of two detailed studies of an East London street and of a single block of flats, has argued that 'recent developments of . . . "the new local history movement", though in their time beneficial and corrective, need a new radical change of direction . . . if they are to give us a socialist local history'. Though rooted primarily in a personal political viewpoint and justified largely on that ground, White's argument implies a serious methodological and theoretical critique as well, for as he explains, 'the autobiographical mode reinforces a superficial historical consciousness and by doing so actually distorts reality'. In White's view, local, oral testimony is essentially uncritical and therefore unanalytical. The task of social, and especially socialist, historians is to ground it in some sort of critical social and political theory.[3]

One can sympathise with White's concern, even if one does not share his immediate political priorities. Much of the 'new, local oral history' *is* relatively unprocessed and unreflective. It *does* tend to be romantic and antiquarian because of its often autobiographical, subjective and private character. Links with the public and the 'significant' *are* often obscure. Moreover, its very silences can be more revealing than its apparent contents, its unspoken assumptions more telling than its assertions. These difficulties make the recent trends in social history problematical, and progress extremely convoluted and frustrating.

Nevertheless, social history continues to attract interest and attention among people who are neither antiquarians nor without theoretical sophistication. Stephen Yeo has summarised some of the features that make it so attractive, especially in Britain: its accessibility; its link with ongoing forms of working-class self-activity in WEA classes, community publishing groups and so on; its capacity for encouraging direct involvement with its subjects; its immediacy, rootedness and relevance; and its value not only as history but as literature (since it often consists of poems, stories, songs and life histories). These traits have made it both a different practice from established modes of historical production, and an increasingly popular one. Equally, they have important intellectual and political implications. As Yeo argues, 'The assumption underpinning virtually all of this work is that for working people to speak for themselves, about their own history *is* somehow a political act in itself.' Yeo goes still further in his defence of the new work in suggesting that the critique of it is inherently elitist and smacks 'of party/class thinking'. In his view, it is reactionary even to attempt to relate the findings of the new history to the traditional concerns of professional historians. The new products, he claims, 'cannot simply be annexed to the history industry, right, left or centre'. Nor should they be seen, as they are 'by many historians as being good "raw material" for that industry, as being "useful" "on that level"', for to imagine that the value of the new work lies merely in its having unearthed evidence concerning certain previously inaccessible levels of the social totality is to assume that one can discover whole new levels of reality and still explain them in the terms and concepts elaborated at an earlier time and on a much narrower basis. To treat the new history in this way would thus be a form of conceptual imperialism on the part of professional scholars.[4]

The ultimate defence of the new local, oral history against the charges both of political ambiguity and of historical narrowness, is that both the old ways of thinking about politics and of writing history are simply inadequate to its methods and findings.[5] Or, to put the matter more positively, the new history, itself a product of new political and social orientations, will generate in turn new ways of thinking about history, society and politics, new theoretical questions and insights, and thus will transform the terms of any new analytical synthesis. Viewed in this context, current calls for the reintroduction (largely from outside, it would seem) of theory, synthesis and politics into the new forms of historical work are a positive danger, for they would most likely lead to a premature closure of research and conceptualisation, and would produce merely syncretistic solutions to the intellectual problems raised by the new research.

Perhaps the main virtue of the interchanges under the auspices of History Workshop was to elucidate the political complexities of the debate over social history. In the initial stages, the critique of social history came from explicitly Marxist historians, like Elizabeth Fox-Genovese and Eugene Genovese. Following their lead, some younger Marxists sought to portray the argument as one that arrayed the left, with a proper sense of the importance of politics, against those simple-minded historians who had been taken in by the techniques and concepts of bourgeois social science. With the accession to the critics' camp of scholars like Lawrence Stone, this picture became blurred. With the counter attacks by Yeo and, in a slightly different context, by Edward Thompson, it has become clear that political perspective is no sure guide to assessing the debate.

Since the debate has had its sharpest expressions in the context of American, French and Germany historiography, it might be useful to

look quickly at the main points at issue. We may start with the
Genoveses' article of 1976. They sought to counter a reading
(misreading in their opinion) of the daily life and culture of the
oppressed which seemed to them to exaggerate its autonomy and self-
sufficiency. Though they were identifying a rather general trend in
American social history, particular animus was directed at Herbert
Gutman for his book about the strength and resiliency of the black
family under and after slavery. To them, this emphasis, by leaving out
or minimising the power and violence directed against black Americans,
grossly underestimated the oppression and tragedies that have so
marked the Afro-American experience.[6]

Since that intervention, the claim that social history leaves out
politics has become a common refrain, echoed by Lawrence Stone.
Tony Judt, Geoff Eley, Keith Nield, William Sewell and many others.[7]
Two common themes recur in most arguments. One is the criticism
of quantitative methods. For a time it seemed, at least in the United
States, that virtually all of the next (now current) generation of
historians would be trained in, and occasionally use, statistical
techniques. That prospect, if ever it was real, has now disappeared and
some of the earliest enthusiasts, like Stone, are major doubters. The
reasons seem clear: expectations of quantitative methods were
unreasonably high and the difficulties and complexities of quantitative
analyses poorly understood; also, as the quantitative revolution
proceeded in other social sciences, the methods normally employed in
those areas became increasingly complex and beyond the reach of most
historians.

So the retreat, by some, from statistics is comprehensible. What is
less easily understood is the vehemence with which those who
continue to use them have been criticised. Here the prime example is
Tony Judt's diatribe against social history, 'A Clown in Regal Purple',
which appeared in *History Workshop* in 1979. Judt's main complaint
was against the pernicious influence of American social science upon
social historians. He detected the sociologists' positivism in the mindless
use of numbers; functionalist orthodoxies behind the most innocent
use of terms like 'modernisation'; reductionism and one-dimensionality
at the root of the alleged neglect of politics and ideology. All these sins
were held to be inherent in the models necessary for quantitative
analysis. More extreme and strident than other contributions to the
discussion, the tone and character of Judt's argument suggest a
motivation deeper than the merely historiographical. His position,
however, is not significantly different from that elaborated by Geoff

Eley in his critiques of German social history. Between them, Eley and Judt (whose specialty is modern France) have criticised probably the majority of social historians presently writing about those two countries for various 'reductionist' and 'sociologistic' errors.

Their arguments also exemplify another common theme running through many of the criticisms of social history. They appear to view the detailed investigation of social structure and daily life undertaken by social historians as a diversion from the really important (and properly Marxist) study of politics and ideology. They seem to believe the study of politics to be more consistent with socialist or Marxist concerns than the apparently non-political elements of history. To this is added the contention that previous social history has been not only too narrowly social, but also too theoretically flaccid. They themselves seek to reintroduce theory into historical writing by more regular theoretical 'interventions' and 'critiques' of other social historians, and by utilising in their own work the latest insights derived from Althusser, Poulantzas and Gramsci.[8]

Fortunately, the debate about the problems of British social history has been somewhat less polemical, possibly because from the outset British social historians have not so much ignored politics as sought to determine its relationship to their discipline. The main issue at stake has been the relationship between social structure and the politics of the labour movement. Ordinarily, the problem has been phrased in terms of the apparent contradiction between Britain's social and economic precocity and her political backwardness. That is, although Britain was the first country to undergo an industrial revolution, and the first to become a truly urban, modern society, it has not witnessed a political upheaval of major proportions since the seventeenth century. This disjunction was the subject of a series of articles by Perry Anderson and Tom Nairn during the early 1960s, which in turn inspired Edward Thompson's *tour de force* in defence of 'The Peculiarities of the English'.[9]

The problem addressed by Anderson, Nairn and Thompson necessarily involved the linking of social history and politics, and its posing reflected the existing predisposition in Britain to keep these two sorts of concerns in tension and guaranteed that much further work would remain centred on the interaction. On the other hand, the particular solution offered by Anderson and Nairn was, in its own way, highly reductionist and set an unfortunate precedent in its too easy slippage from society and economy to politics and ideology. Part of the difficulty derived from the gross theoretical assumption upon which they based their work. They took as given the notion that a 'modern' society, of which Britain is supposedly an exemplar, should inevitably be marked by a 'modern', class-based and sharply polarised politics. Further, the type of politics they deemed fitting for a modern society was further to the left than has actually existed in almost any Western nation during the twentieth century.

By posing the question as they did, Nairn and Anderson could not but narrow the scope of their own inquiry. Their method was suitably simple: to isolate one (allegedly) peculiar aspect of British social structure and locate the source of Britain's political moderation there. More precisely, they argued that the roots of what they considered to be the present political impasse lay in the lengthy symbiosis in England of aristocracy and bourgeoisie. This had ensured that Britain's bourgeois revolution in the seventeenth century would be refracted through the thick, obscuring lens of religion, that its bourgeoisie would never be pushed into developing a coherent and thoroughly rationalistic ideology of its own, and that, therefore, its working class would be confronted with a nebulous but ubiquitous opposition against which it was especially difficult to struggle wholeheartedly.

The same flawed style of argument with its atrophied sense of the mediations between structure and conjuncture, society and politics, also informed other solutions to the problems posed by Anderson and Nairn. The most common of these was the theory of the labour aristocracy, which came to be seen by many historians as the 'peculiar' aspect of British social structure responsible for its reformist and parliamentarist politics. The notion has a longer, and a distinctive, lineage as well. Marx and Engels first suggested it and Lenin developed it in conjunction with his theory of imperialism. The classic modern formulation was Eric Hobsbawm's essay on 'The Labour Aristocracy in Nineteenth Century Britain' first published in 1954. Hobsbawm argued that the aristocracy of labour was a distinct stratum at the upper level of the working class which did not readily and naturally identify with the aims and interests of the bulk of the working class beneath them. Labour aristocrats were relatively more secure, better paid, more highly skilled and more likely to belong to a union than other workers, and developed a different lifestyle and outlook as a result. Though often at odds with their employers and with the establishment in general, their radicalism was socially and culturally limited and was easily absorbed within a non-class-based liberal reformism.[10]

Though the specifics of Hobsbawm's argument differed from the Anderson/Nairn positions, the form was remarkably similar and, because they both addressed important contemporary questions and seemed to make sense of both politics and social history, each has enjoyed a remarkably wide currency among labour historians. The labour aristocracy thesis, in fact, has been worked over several times by historians who have generally found it convincing and who have thus sought to strengthen it in various ways.[11] One point of friendly revision, for example, has been the attempt to stress the cultural creativity and autonomy of labour aristocrats who, according to Gray and Crossick, did not simply accept the standards of bourgeois society and carry them into the ranks of the workers, but rather have engaged in a sophisticated process of negotiation, accepting some and rejecting other 'bourgeois' notions and in the end fashioning their own unique constellation of beliefs, attitudes and behaviours. It was probably inevitable, given the gradual progress of research which almost always forces us to qualify generalisations and allow for greater degrees of complexity, that the labour aristocracy thesis should sooner or later be subjected to a more hostile critique. Because the hypothesis represented the main theoretical bridge between social and political analysis, the critique has broadened out to encompass the basic relationship between the two. Criticism has therefore moved quickly from empirical to theoretical grounds. To start, it has been argued that there was no cohesive stratum to whom the label could be usefully applied and that, instead, the working class throughout the nineteenth century was divided in a much different and more complicated fashion. Rather than a simple split between labour aristocrats and all other labourers, the Victorian working class, according to Musson and more recently Reid, was divided into a multiplicity of sections and groupings along lines of skill, residence, nationality, religion and sex. This structure made working-class organisation and politics highly sectional and class-wide allegiances and movements extremely difficult. According to this view, it makes little sense to invoke the development of a distinct labour aristocracy, complete by about 1850, to explain Britain's political stability.[12] Empirically, therefore, the new critics find the labour aristocracy thesis wanting.

However, they do agree with the proponents about the political reality that the thesis was designed to explain — that is, the apparent easing of social tensions in the third quarter of the nineteenth century or, as Harold Perkin expresses it, 'the rise of a viable class society'. But because the most tenable social explanation appears, to them, to have failed, they have turned increasingly to arguments of an explicitly political character and, consequently, to the bolder assertion that social analysis is inherently incapable of explaining political phenomena.[13]

The logic operative in the debate is significant and common to the larger discussion of social history. One begins with a problem of politics and proceeds to a social cause. Doubts are then raised about the usefulness of the *particular* social explanation. A return to political analysis is proposed. The circularity of reasoning is especially troubling, for there is nothing about the way it is framed to suggest any genuine synthesis or even any genuine learning process. One fears that the end result may well be a simple return to political history of an old-fashioned type, with nothing learned from the detour through social history except perhaps the need to avoid that route in the future.

As with the 'peculiarities' debate, the argument over the labour aristocracy illustrates both the strengths and the weaknesses of British historiography in the light of current debates about social history and politics. Unlike the situation in American, French or, to a lesser extent, German history, there is virtually no justification for arguing that social history in Britain has left out politics, for the interrelationship has long been central to research. At the same time, the long symbiosis between social description and political analysis has probably led to a lack of sophistication on both fronts, and to a lack of theoretical clarification about the ways by which these different levels of the social totality are articulated with one another.

The specific crisis in British social history must therefore be defined in rather different terms from the discussion of social history in other national contexts. For even if some of the arguments appear similar and even if, as with the state of oral history and community studies in Britain, the style of current social historical research seems fragmented and far removed from politics, the historiographical tradition is very different. Clearly it is not a matter of simply putting politics into social history, as some would wish, for it has really never been left out. Even in the newest local and women's history, politics is mostly implicit rather than absent. The task is really a rather different one: it is how to build upon the tradition of British social history so as to make our reading of social structure and daily life more subtle in its political implications, how to think about politics in ways that allow for its complexity, and how to understand and study the linkages and mediations between the two realms. From this perspective, it would seem that the main obstacle to overcome in the next phase of social history is the sheer difficulty of conceptualising and demonstrating the connections between society, economy, politics and ideology. The difficulty stems from a variety of causes unrelated to any alleged 'reductionism' on the part of social historians. Most importantly there are no, or at least very few, models available showing how to go about constructing the link.

Despite the absence of truly successful models that can be emulated, there are three relatively straightforward lines of inquiry whose pursuit could help to bridge the gap between social history and politics. The first is to attempt to fill in the space between the two with the analysis of culture and political attitudes. The second and third options involve working within social history to expand its analysis and findings towards politics and within political history to extend its reach in social terms. For various reasons, the greatest amount of effort has been directed towards the study of culture. Indeed, there has been a noticeable trend in Britain and elsewhere towards the abandonment of traditional political history in favour of various types of cultural or ideological analysis. There appear to be at least three reasons for this shift. First is the development of Marxist theory in a direction which places increasing emphasis upon the study of culture as a semi-autonomous sphere of social activity, thus rejecting the crude determinism which formerly characterised much Marxist scholarship in this area. The impact of Gramsci and Althusser has been significant here in sparking vigorous research into both 'high' and 'low' culture. Somewhat more advanced among students of culture than historians, this move is grounded on the implicit notion that issues about control and political order are often engaged primarily at the level of culture, and that this struggle is crucial in the overall attempt to constitute class hegemony.

The second reason for the attraction of cultural analysis is that the field has itself experienced a major reorientation in recent years. The change is most evident in the practice of intellectual history, where that old genre, the biography of an important figure in the history of ideas, is virtually extinct, replaced by studies of groups and movements, of schools of thought, of mentalities, of intellectual projects and paradigms. Here the attempt has been to demonstrate that intellectual history itself can be socialised by rejecting the old linear approach and substituting an attempt to 'contextualise' ideas.

The third factor adding to the lure of cultural studies has been the substantial achievement of historians of popular culture. Building upon the extensive collections of folksongs, ballads, oral traditions and descriptions of daily life by eighteenth- and nineteenth-century enthusiasts, historians have been able to piece together convincing pictures of the mental worlds of ordinary people in the past. In some ways this work is best understood as a side-effect of the general progress of social history undertaken by those most interested in culture. It also has been aided by the inspired work on 'mentalités' among French social historians.

We should argue, however, that although such work has great merit, further progress in connecting social history and politics requires theoretical and empirical work of a rather different sort involving the recasting of political and social history from within. The main achievement of social history has been to provide a massive increase in our knowledge of the patterns of everyday life of ordinary people. What is missing, however, is a theory of the political significance of these patterns, of how certain aspects of daily interaction have political effects. Rather, in most treatments, daily life is studied as an end in itself, or on the implicit and economist assumption that its structures will provide a map of the interests that contend in various sorts of politics. There is no self-conscious theory of just what difference daily life makes to people's desire and ability to involve themselves in political activity.

There are presently two extant theoretical perspectives which might be developed further as a means to provide such a reading of the significance of everyday life. One is embodied in a tradition of analysis which focuses upon the way the structure of daily living produces types of personality, of interaction and hence of discourse, with certain political consequences. Examples of this sort of argument and analysis can be found in the work of Richard Sennett, Henri Lefebvre, Norbert Elias, Habermas and others.[14] A second, and perhaps more useful, perspective derives from the work of various American social scientists, particularly Charles Tilly, whose first major work on Britain appears in this collection. Tilly and his followers seek to create an alternative model of politics and collective action to the reigning functionalism within American sociology.[15] The functionalist perspective on social movements tends to view the actions of disenfranchised groups in terms of their dissatisfaction with and alienation from established institutions. Discovering the roots of disaffection thus becomes equivalent to understanding the dynamics of collective action. For Tilly and others, this is not only inadequate, but incorrect. To view those who resist authority, or who attempt to change the existing distribution of power and property as malcontents, is to conduct the analysis entirely on the terms of those in authority. In their view, such work contains an inherent bias towards stability and against insurgency.

In place of this, Tilly would propose a 'resources' or a 'mobilisation' model for analysing collective action and, by implication, the state as well. He sees the mobilisation of groups not specially favoured within existing arrangements as being primarily a matter of the resources they command. Thus, he would treat the structure of daily life by examining how it effects the balance of advantages between contending social groups. Different techniques of production, different patterns of residence and types of social networks, as well as different political formations, all have an impact on the capacity of various groups and movements to organise and press their grievances.

By following either of these approaches to the 'politics of everyday life', it should be possible to move beyond the mere descriptions that characterise so much of current social-historical writing and to infuse such work with a sense of its meaning for politics and collective behaviour more generally. Still, half the problem remains: the elaboration of a new, broader type of political history. The major weakness of contemporary political history is not, as some contend, that it deals only with the activities of the elite, for in fact a good deal of analysis concerns the social status of elites of various sorts. This side of political history has been socialised, as it were. What has not been treated socially is the structure of politics itself. We need to know more about how political ideas, interests and leaders interact with forces and movements outside the charmed circle of high politics. We need to understand how 'publics' are constituted, how groups and interests are represented or excluded from representation, how in broad terms participation is determined and how power is mediated and legitimised. This again would require theoretical work directed at clarifying what lies behind such notions as 'legitimacy', 'citizenship' and 'representation'.

In order to develop a more socially aware understanding of politics it is also necessary to elaborate a theory of the impact of politics and the state on everyday life. At present an enormous amount of political research remains fixed upon the analysis of what policy makers intended to do, what assumptions guided their thinking, and what political realities determined their compromises. There is surprisingly little, however, on how effective and significant their policies were for ordinary people.[16] The evidence is there in court records, marriage and birth registers, the files of social service departments and in the collective memory of the objects of state actions. What is lacking in this instance is not theory, but rather the archival research necessary to prove or disprove various hypotheses.

In sum, we feel strongly that the way forward in social history is not some retreat into still more detailed, apolitical history, nor a move away from social analysis back towards a study of the purely political. Rather, it seems to us that the most fruitful path to follow is to build upon the strengths and achievements of previous social history with a view towards theorising its political significance while struggling to create a new kind of political history that will be more integrally social. This type of an agenda, we believe, best accords with the current status of social-historical research in Britain, and offers a route forward without abandoning the advances made to date. Moreover, it reaffirms the methodological and theoretical stance of that long line of British social historians who have always sought to avoid the fragmentation that is so commonly deplored today.

It is in that spirit that we offer the following collection of essays. As even the most casual reading will show, they represent a selection of work on British social history done by scholars working in a distinctly American context.[17] We have all either studied in America or have taught in American universities. This does not, of course, guarantee a unity of outlook or even of approach, but it does mean that most of us, being somewhat removed from the intensity of debate in England, are less committed to any particularly narrow or partisan conception of how to do social history. One happy result is that, as is evident from the essays themselves, we all have tried to orient our research towards the intersection of social history and politics. We do not pretend that our formulations are therefore inherently superior to any others, but we do feel that they make substantial contributions to our understanding of the complex interactions that occur between economics, social structure and politics.

Notes

1. E.J. Hobsbawm, 'From Social History to the History of Society', *Daedalus*, Winter 1971, pp.20-45.
2. Perhaps the most useful review of recent developments is contained in Raphael Samuel, 'History Workshop, 1968-80', in R. Samuel (ed.), *People's History and Socialist Theory*, (London, 1981) pp.410-17.
3. J. White, 'Beyond Autobiography', in R. Samuel (ed.), *People's History and Socialist Theory*, pp.33-40.
4. S. Yeo, 'The Politics of Community Publications', in R. Samuel (ed.), *People's History and Socialist Theory*, pp.42-8.
5. Graham Dawson and Richard Johnson, 'On Popular Memory: Theory, Politics Method', unpublished paper, 1981, argues for this aggressive defence of the new work.
6. Elizabeth Fox-Genovese and Eugene Genovese, 'The Political Crisis of Social History', *Journal of Social History*, X (1976), pp.204-20.
7. Lawrence Stone, 'The Revival of Narrative', *Past and Present*, November 1979, pp.3-24; W. Sewell Jr., *Work and Revolution in France* (Cambridge, 1981);

T. Judt, 'Clown in Regal Purple', *History Workshop*, Spring 1979, pp.66-94; Geoff Eley and Keith Nield, 'Why Does Social History Ignore Politics?', *Social History*, vol. 2, (1980), pp.249-71; Keith Nield, 'A Symptomatic Dispute? Notes on the Relation between Marxian Theory and Historical Practice in Britain', *Social Research*, XLVII, 3 (Autumn 1980), pp.479-506.

8. See also the discussion of the importance of 'theory' in the debate sparked by Richard Johnson, 'Thompson, Genovese and Socialist-Humanist History', *History Workshop*, Autumn 1978, and continued by R. Johnson, E. Thompson and Stuart Hall in R. Samuel (ed.), *People's History and Socialist Theory*, pp.378-408.

9. Perry Anderson, 'Origins of the Present Crisis', *New Left Review*, Jan./Feb. 1964, pp.26-53; 'The Myths of Edward Thompson', *New Left Review*, Jan./Feb. 1965, pp.2-42; Tom Nairn, 'The Nature of the Labour Party (I)', *New Left Review*, Sept./Oct. 1964, pp.38-65; 'The Nature of the Labour Party (II)', *New Left Review*, Nov./Dec., 1964, pp.33-62; Edward Thompson, 'The Peculiarities of the English', *Socialist Register 1965*, pp.311-62. The continuing importance of the debate is suggested by Nield, 'Symptomatic Disputes?', pp.479ff.

10. E. Hobsbawn, 'The Labour Aristocracy in Nineteenth Century Britain', reprinted in *Labouring Men* (London, 1974), pp.272-315.

11. For a summary of the discussion see John Field, 'British Historians and the Concept of the Labour Aristocracy', *Radical History Review*, Winter 1978-9, pp.61-86.

12. A.E. Musson, 'Class Struggle and the Labour Aristocracy, 1830-60', *Social History*, I, 3 (1976), pp.335-56; A. Reid, 'Politics and Economics in the Formation of the British Working Class', *Social History*, III, 3 (1978).

13. Hence the renewed popularity of arguments about political deference and narrowly political arrangements in explaining the 'quiescence' of the mid-Victorian era and, by implication, the limitations of subsequent radicalism. See, for instance, P. Joyce, *Work, Society and Politics: the Culture of the Factory in later Victorian England* (Brighton, 1980) and, more symptomatically, Keith McClelland's review in *History Workshop*, no.11 (Spring 1981), pp.169-73; as well as A. Reid, 'Labour, Capital and the State in Britain, 1880-1920', paper presented at the Conference on the Development of Trade Unionism in Great Britain, France and Germany, 1880-1914, Tutzing, Germany, May 1981.

14. The most recent statement is R. Sennett, *The Fall of Public Man* (New York, 1976). See also Oskar Negt and Alexander Kluge, *Öffentlichkeit und Erfahrung: Zur Organisationsanalyse von bürgerlicher und proletarischen Öffentlichkeit* (Frankfurt am Main, 1972) and, of course Henri Lefebvre, *Everyday Life in the Modern World* (New York, 1971). For a useful critical discussion, see M. Poster, *Existential Marxism in Postwar France* (Princeton, 1975), pp.238-60. The ideas of these theorists have had an obvious influence upon the work of Christopher Lasch, whose *Culture of Narcissism* (New York, 1978) illustrates both the potentialities and some of the pitfalls common to this social-psychological approach.

15. The most theoretical statement is C. Tilly, *From Mobilization to Revolution* (Reading, Mass., 1978); but see also Charles, Louise and Richard Tilly, *The Rebellious Century* (Cambridge, Mass., 1975).

16. Again, Charles Tilly's work provides a starting place. See, in addition to the works cited above, his collection on *The Formation of National States in Western Europe* (Princeton, 1975).

17. We do not wish to imply that this selection is either random or that it represents our view of what is best in current American work on British social history. Indeed, American scholars have made quite notable contributions to the study of the family, women, crime, leisure, housing and social policy and

education which are not at all represented in this collection. However we do feel that this volume groups together those who are working most directly on the interaction between social theory and politics and within the context of labour history and collective action, where most of the debates about this interrelationship have taken place.

2 BRITAIN CREATES THE SOCIAL MOVEMENT

Charles Tilly

Historical Anniversaries

The year 1980 marked the 200th anniversary of London's Gordon Riots. Just over two centuries ago, in 1780, Lord George Gordon organised his Protestant Association; it was his means of broadcasting the demand for repeal of the Catholic Relief Act which Parliament had passed two years earlier. After a massive march of Gordon's supporters from St George's Fields to Parliament, the marchers' presentation of a giant anti-Catholic petition, and Parliament's refusal to deliberate under pressure, some of the great crowd who had passed the day in Parliament Square rushed off to sack Catholic chapels. On the following days, more Catholic places of worship fell, as did the houses of prominent Catholics and of officials who had gained the reputation of protecting them. Eventually the orderly destruction of buildings spiralled into looting and arson. The 9,500 troops who entered London to end the affair killed 285 people in the clean-up. The courts hanged another 25. It was eighteenth-century Britain's bloodiest confrontation between troops and civilians, and one of the century's most costly popular attacks on property as well.

The Gordon Riots are well known to British historians. Charles Dickens's *Barnaby Rudge* lodged Lord George, his Protestant Association, and the fearsome days of anti-Catholic action in English literature as well. But no commemoration, so far as I know, marked their bicentennial. Attacks on religious minorities — rightly — do not call up proud recollection in Britain. Furthermore, Lord George Gordon died in Newgate Prison, where he had gone for libelling the Queen of France, the French Ambassador, and the administration of justice in England; those are not exactly the credentials of a candidate for civic beatification.

The year 1982, in contrast, will most likely bring more than one historical festival. For we approach the sesquicentennial of 1832's Reform Bill. Just about 150 years ago began the renewal of popular agitation for parliamentary reform which finally brought Commons, Lords and King to undertake a broadening of the franchise, a reduction in the number of boroughs under control of a family or a clique, and an extension of representation to many towns which had previously been excluded from direct participation in the national electoral process. The two years preceding the Bill's passage in 1832 witnessed one of the greatest national mobilisations Britain had ever seen, and the Bill itself altered irreversibly the character of routine politics in Britain.

Between the 1780s of the Gordon Riots and the 1830s of Reform, large changes occurred in the way the British did their everyday political business. Back in the 1780s, we find outselves in the world, not only of Lord George Gordon, but also of John Wilkes. Seventeen years before, the rakish Member of Parliament had stirred the British public with his *North Briton*'s publication of an article (in its famous no. 45) offering an indirect attack on the King's speech. Wilkes's brief imprisonment, the burning of no. 45 in Cheapside, and Wilkes's later republication of the offending issue as well as a pornographic *Essay on Woman* had launched a sensational public career: new prosecution, flight to France, secret return to Britain, failed appeals for clemency, new incarceration, successful campaigns for re-election to Parliament repeatedly rebuffed by the Commons, great crowds outside Wilkes's new prison, mass celebrations of his electoral victories, equally vigorous displays of anger at his legal defeats, huge marches through the streets. In short, the trappings of a momentous movement around a popular hero. By the time of Lord George Gordon's rise to prominence, Wilkes's great days as a demagogue had passed; during the Gordon Riots, in fact, he lined up squarely on the side of order. Nevertheless, in 1780 he still symbolised mass action and popular sovereignty. He was still prepared to trade on his reputation as a reckless political innovator.

Before Gordon's Protestant Association, Wilkes's followers had pioneered the mass petition march. They had created a widely-based special-interest association; Wilkes's Society of the Supporters of the Bill of Rights was already a formidable political force, making and breaking candidates for Parliament, by the end of the 1760s. The Wilkites had perfected the display of symbols which simultaneously identified people as supporters of a cause and summed up the theme of that cause. The deployment of the number 45, recalling the issue of Wilkes's *North Briton* which the hangman had burned as seditious in 1763, is a good example. It worked so well that the lighting of 45 candles, the marching of 45 men, or the setting out of 45 bowls of punch became standard ways of signifying opposition to the royal government not only in Britain, but also in the far-off colonies of North America. Aside from his channelling of popular anti-Catholicism, Lord George Gordon's innovations were minor; they consisted of extending the social base of his special-interest association, and then joining a a mass-based special-interest association to the public display of symbols, numbers, and determination on behalf of the cause.

Nevertheless, establishing the association as an instrument of popular collective action opened a new pathway through British politics. As Eugene Black states it:

> Association made possible the extension of the politically effective public. Discomfited country gentlemen could move against the increasing power of the territorial magnates (which concerned them as much as the increasing power of the crown) with Christopher Wyvill through political association. In the same way powerful, discontented manufacturers and merchants were ready to join Joseph Parkes, even Francis Place, in the Political Unions and the struggle for the great reform bill. Modern extraparliamentary political organization is a product of the late eighteenth century. The history of the age of reform cannot be written without it (Black 1963: 279).

Thus association, according to Black, covers the gap between our two anniversaries: from Lord George Gordon to the Reform of 1832, we witness a great increase in the scope and effectiveness of deliberately-formed, specialised, manifestly political organisations as instruments of collective action.

That much is true. By the 1820s, special-interest associations were carrying out a far wider range of activities than those of middle-class societies for the promotion of good works and useful knowledge; working-class Owenites and old-line Radicals were creating organisations to deploy and display their strength at the same time as they brought a new, cheap, popular press into wide circulation. The rising prominence of associations, however, did not amount to a 'taming' of popular politics. 'The postwar radical movement,' as John Belchem remarks, 'secured a mass mobilisation resonant with confrontationist fervour' (Belchem 1981: 5).

More was to come. In the years immediately preceding Reform, for example, the increasing visibility of O'Connell's Catholic Associations in Ireland and Britain stimulated the creation of the anti-Catholic Brunswick Clubs. Reminiscing about Edinburgh in his memoirs, the Scottish Whig Henry Cockburn described a characteristic sequence:

> In March 1829 we had a magnificent meeting in the Assembly Room to assist Wellington and Peel, in their tardy and now awkward

Emancipation necessity, by a petition in favor of the Catholics. A shilling a head was taken at the door, and about 1700 shillings were got. As from the confusion several passed untaxed, there must have been about 2000 present; and there were at the least double that number outside, who could not get in ... No meeting could be more successful; and the combination of persons in general so repugnant, gave it great weight over the country. It must have suggested a striking contrast to those who remembered that it was in this very city that, only about forty years ago, the law had not strength to save the houses and chapels of the Catholics from popular conflagration. There were, as there still are, some who, if they could have done it, would have thought the repetition of that violence a duty; and there were many even at this meeting who had no better reason for their support of emancipation than that it implied the support of ministry. Those, whose religious horror of Catholicism made them think the application of the principles of civil toleration to that faith a sin, did not appear; but procured signatures to an opposite petition by harangues and placards borrowed from Lord George Gordon (Cockburn 1971/1858: 458-9).

The mobilisation and counter-mobilisation of Edinburgh's citizens repeated itself, with many variations, throughout Britain. Within Great Britain, the popular mobilisation against Emancipation generally outweighed the mobilisation for the cause. The great strength of the movement outside of Great Britain — in Ireland — nevertheless augmented its impact within the country. The success of the Catholic Association in forwarding Emancipation set a model and a precedent for the roles of the Political Unions and the National Union of the Working Classes in the Reform campaign of 1830 to 1832. The coupling of Emancipation with legislation dissolving the Catholic Association and the raising of the Irish county franchise from two to ten pounds dramatises the fear of organised mass action that the new associational activity had raised in the British Establishment.

Correlates of Association

Instead of expatiating on the rise of association, however, I want to call attention to some of the correlates of that change in British politics. For not only the issues and organisational bases of collective action, but also its very forms, altered significantly between the age of Wilkes or

Gordon and the age of Reform. Note the difference between the anti-Catholicism of 1780 and that of 1829: those who retained the aims and outlook of Gordon's followers nevertheless adopted the new means. That is the point. Like the supporters of Emancipation, its opponents associated, met, deliberated, resolved, petitioned and delegated, broadcasting the news of those actions to all interested parties. Occasionally they marched and displayed signs of their affiliations and demands. Rarely did they attack Catholics, their possessions, or their supposed protectors. Much changed between 1780 and 1828.

This essay will describe some of the crucial changes, but will fall far short of explaining them. For the moment, it is enough to specify just what has to be explained. For none of the standard formulas — not the strains of industrialisation, not the transition to order, nor even the development of class politics — captures the alterations in the prevailing forms of collective action. The strains of industrialisation, in the usual sense of those words, have nothing to do with the matter. The idea of a transition to order does convey the fact that new ways of acting, more familiar to twentieth-century observers than the ways they displaced, became prominent; but the words 'transition to order' exaggerate the nineteenth century's calm. Class politics did emerge on a national scale, but that emergence itself neither describes nor explains the shifts in the character of collective action. To put it crudely, from the 1770s to the 1830s Britain's collective-action repertoire underwent two fundamental changes: first, parochial and patronised forms gave way to national and autonomous forms; second, the creation of a national social movement became an established way to accomplish a set of political ends.

By 'parochial and patronised' forms of collective action I mean those ways of pooling effort on behalf of shared interests that depended for their effectiveness on the parties' common membership in a particular community, and that involved some sort of claim on local authorities; the claims ranged from the simple authorisation to assemble on ceremonial occasions to the demand that a dignitary communicate a community's grievances to powerful figures elsewhere. In different ways, food riots, attacks on moral offenders, election brawls, and demands of workers on their masters exemplify the parochial and patronised forms. The 'national and autonomous' forms of collective action, in contrast, invoke widely-applicable rights and identities, and rely on the participants acting at their own initiative. The public meeting, the strike, the petition march and the demonstration generally belong to this type. Need I say that the two types are caricatures, drawn to emphasise differences which are more subtle and complex in the actual historical experience?

Defining the National Social Movement

Within the trend toward national and autonomous collective action, let us single out the creation of the national social movement. Before talking about the *national* social movement, however, let us pause for a definition of social movements in general. Unfortunately, sociologists and historians have clouded the study of an important phenomenon by employing nebulous definitions, definitions which run as though the social movement were a group, a cluster of groups, or at least something rather groupish. They have also mistaken the historically-specific features of movements which have occurred in Western countries since 1800 for universal features of the phenomenon. By 'social movement', I mean a sustained series of interactions between powerholders and persons successfully claiming to speak on behalf of a constituency lacking formal representation, in the course of which those persons make publicly-visible demands for changes in the distribution or exercise of power, and back those demands with public demonstrations of support. A *national* social movement, then, pits such challengers against the people who run a national state.

Like all such definitions, this one poses practical choices: setting some minimum number of interactions; arriving at tests of the 'success' of claims to speak for a constituency; deciding how little formal representation is a lack of it; defining thresholds for the visibility of demands and the demonstration of support for them, and so on. But the definition excludes a variety of phenomena — religious innovations, crusades, local rebellions, and others — to which the term social movement has often been loosely applied. In this narrower sense, both the concept of social movement and the sort of interaction the concept fits best are products of the nineteenth-century growth of popular electoral politics on a national scale. In any case, the definition does not single out groups, but interactions.

No groups? Let me be clear on that point. Groups are crucial to social movements, as armies are crucial to wars and parties to electoral campaigns. At one point or another in the history of every social movement, the organisers of the challenge in question claim to speak for at least one important group which has an interest in the challenge's outcome. The organisers may well recruit participants and supporters from the group whose interest they claim to represent. The activists with respect to any particular challenge commonly originate in well-defined groups, and often form new groups in the process of making the challenge. At the very centre of the nineteenth-century transformation which made the social movement a standard way of doing political business, came a great broadening of the conditions under which new groups could form and mount challenges to the authorities, and old groups could bring challenges into the public arena.

A particular kind of group — the deliberately-formed association — played a crucial part in creating and sustaining the national social movement. Since then, both authorities and social-movement participants have invested a good deal of effort in sustaining a mystification: the idea of a social movement as a coherent, determined group. As leaders and participants themselves are usually aware, the day-to-day life of social movements involves patching together temporary coalitions, finding the issues and programmes that will bring together the most effective set of people for a particular action, suppressing outward signs of disunity, and regrouping from one action to the next. Nevertheless, the mystification serves important purposes on both sides: making it easier for movement leaders to reinforce the determination of their followers and to claim the support of constituents who never visibly subscribe to their programmes and may actually reject them; enabling authorities to choose between discrediting the challenge on the grounds that the group in question is insignificant or illegitimate and creating a place in the polity for its presumed representatives. But the social movement itself consists of a sustained challenge.

We need a ponderous definition, then, in order to avoid calling any group that makes demands a social movement. Although sustained challenges to local authorities reached far back in time, and although one might make a case for earlier rebellions and religious conflicts as social movements, before the nineteenth-century social movements in this strong sense of the term were very rare in the Western world. It was very unusual for persons who claimed successfully to speak on behalf of a constituency lacking formal representation to raise a sustained challenge to national authorities, to make publicly-visible demands for changes in the distribution or exercise of power, and to back those demands with public demonstrations of support. Revolutionary ruptures were the great and significant exceptions: the Protestant Reformation and the English Revolution produced many of the features of nineteenth- and twentieth-century social movements, but in terms of the forms of collective action, those ruptures were temporary; they did not normalise the social movement as a means of political business. In the nineteenth century, the social movement did become a normal feature of national politics in many Western countries, including Britain.

During the earlier decades of the eighteenth century, no challenge we can properly describe as a social movement occurred in Britain. Food riots, industrial disputes, resistance to taxation, invasions of enclosed fields, shootouts between hunters and gamekeepers, and other varieties of conflict proliferated, but none of them clustered into social movements. In the struggles around John Wilkes and George Gordon, elements of the sustained challenge — but not the full set — appeared for the first time. It took decades more for the idea and the reality to solidify. Thomas Paine and the London Radicals helped create the idea and the reality. Francis Burdett, William Cobbett, and Henry Hunt served as influential organisers and innovators. Daniel O'Connell's campaign for Catholic Emancipation marked an important step in the social movement's creation. By the start of the 1830s, by the time of the campaigns for Catholic Emancipation and Reform, all features of the social movement were visible in British politics. There were the claims, sometimes contested, to speak for an unrepresented constituency. There were the demands for change, the sustained interactions with the authorities, the public demonstrations of the numbers and determination behind the cause. The struggles of the 1830s locked these elements into place within the established routines of British politics. From that point to the present, they have changed relatively little.

Over the period from the 1760s to the 1830s, then, the British created the social movement as a distinctive form of collective action. Like the electoral campaign or the circulation of petitions, it became a recognised (if less frequent and more widely feared) way of making a political point. The ground-breaking effort of the British became a model for citizens of other countries. Today, parliamentary democracies throughout the world share the social movement as a political routine. To what extent different countries created the routine independently, one by one, and to what extent the British model spread by imitation or deliberate instruction is hard to say, and will eventually be crucial to establish. But one thing we can say now: the British were clearly precocious.

A set of ideological changes accompanied the shift from parochial and patronised to national and autonomous forms of collective action, including the creation of the social movement. The older forms of action incorporated a strong set of assumptions about the bases of political life. The assumptions included these:

1. that citizens grouped into more or less corporate bodies, such as guilds, communities, and religious sects, which exercised collective rights;
2. that the law protected such collective rights;
3. that local authorities had an obligation to enforce and respect the law;
4. that the chosen representatives of such corporate bodies had the right and obligation to make public presentations of their demands and grievances;
5. that authorities had an obligation to consider those demands and grievances, and to act on them when they were just;
6. that outside this framework, no one who had not been convoked by established authorities had a clear right to assemble, to state demands and grievances, or to act collectively.

During the eighteenth century, the extension of the theory and practice of capitalist property relations (of possessive individualism, in C.B. Macpherson's phrase) was undermining the premises of such a corporate system; the rapidly growing number of landless wage-labourers, for example, subverted the assumption that they were essentially servants, dependents of farms or shops whose masters represented them, and whose collective interest was their own. The demand for popular sovereignty which became more insistent in the era of the American Revolution likewise threatened a fundamental alteration of the system. The call for an anti-parliament to represent popular interests, which became a recurrent radical theme in the 1770s (Parssinen 1973), deftly stated the challenge. If ordinary citizens could assemble at their own initiative, identify themselves as a political interest, refuse to comply with corrupt authorities, and sometimes even create autonomous organisations and instruments of government, the corporate structure fell beam by beam. But in the meantime the available forms of collective action assumed the structure's existence.

Changing Repertoires

Those forms of collective action comprised a repertoire, in something like the theatrical sense of the word: a limited number of well-known performances repeated with relatively minor variations, and chosen with an eye to the audience and the occasion. The petition march, the illumination, the conversion of solemn ceremonies into displays of opinion, the orderly sacking of houses and looms were among the well-established eighteenth-century performances which have long since disappeared from the British repertoire. They were standard ways of doing collective business, just as strikes, demonstrations, rallies, and deliberative assemblies have become standard ways of doing collective business today. Like improvisational players, people who share an interest choose among the available performances, matching the right element of the repertoire to immediate ends and opportunities.

We must, however, improve on the theatrical metaphor in several ways. First, although the number of well-defined alternative performances in the repertoire at any given point is quite limited, the elements of the repertoire change as a function of experience, organisation, and opportunity. Secondly, interaction with spectators, authorities, rivals, allies, and objects of the action plays a crucial part in the sequence and outcome of the action. Thirdly, much more is commonly at stake than the self-esteem of the performers and the applause of the audience; people use the repertoires of collective action to defend and advance their vital interests.

Let us recall some features of the eighteenth-century British repertoire which set it off from the repertoires which began to prevail in the nineteenth century. First, there was a tendency for aggrieved people to converge on the residences of wrongdoers and on the sites of wrongdoing rather than on the seats of power (sometimes, to be sure, the two coincided). Secondly, the extensive use of authorised public ceremonies and celebrations for the acting out of complaints and demands. Thirdly, the rare appearance of people organised voluntarily around a special interest, as compared with whole communities and constituted corporate groups. Fourthly, the recurrent use of street theatre, visual imagery, effigies, symbolic objects and other dramatic devices to state the participants' claims and complaints. Fifthly, the frequent borrowing — in parody or in earnest — of the authorities' normal forms of action; the borrowing often amounted to the crowd's almost literally taking the law into its own hands. Sixthly and finally, an approach to authorities in terms of 'aggressive supplication', offering compliance with the authorities if they did their duty, and direct action against them, or in their stead, if the authorities failed to play their proper role. Between the 1760s and the 1830s, all these once-standard features of British collective action became exceptional. A new repertoire replaced the old.

The flurry of activities around John Wilkes did not fit this paradigm exactly. For its time, it had some extraordinary features; the novelty of form, indeed, helps explain the consternation Wilkes and company caused right-minded citizens. Although Wilkes's supporters, for example, provided plenty of street theatre, they also showed signs of defining themselves as a special interest, and organised some actions (notably their great petition marches) which resembled modern demonstrations in their orientation to the seats of public power and their ostentatious display of numbers and determination. To our eyes, Wilkes was a curious organiser: playing the role of a popular hero and speaking words circulated to appeal to the populace, but maintaining a genteel distance from his public. In the perspective of the eighteenth century, nevertheless, he and his entourage were great innovators. They played a significant part, as I see it, in the creation of new forms of collective action which became standard elements of the nineteenth- and twentieth-century repertoire. In deliberately maintaining the claim to speak for the disfranchised, in making dramatic public displays of their following's numbers and commitment, and in offering a sustained challenge to the existing structure of power, they were welding together the essential pieces of the social movement as a distinctive form of political action.

Wilkes and friends did not do the job alone. As we have seen, Lord George Gordon added to the repertoire at the end of the 1770s by coupling a wide-reaching Protestant Association to the sorts of marches and quasi-demonstrations made familiar by Wilkes. Aside from his channelling of popular anti-Catholicism, however, Gordon's innovations were much less important than Wilkes's; they consisted of extending the social base of the special-interest association, and joining the association's activities to the public display of symbols, numbers, and determination on behalf of the cause. The silk-weavers of London's Spitalfields district likewise devised ways of demonstrating their numbers and determination to Parliament. American revolutionaries provided models and incentives for British innovation in the 1770s, as did French revolutionaries in the 1790s. The chapels, schools and associations of Protestant Dissenters seem to have contributed, as did the clubs of London Radicals. Restless popular organisers such as Paine, Burdett, Cobbett, Hunt, Carlile and Place poured their ingenuity into the creation of new challenges to old ways. In the age of Spa Fields and Peterloo, dramatic confrontations of challengers with the authorities made the new demands, actors and forms of action visible to other potential challengers. The continuous interaction of those challengers with authorities, rivals and allies, finally produced a record of successes and failures which further shaped the creation, adoption, alteration, and abandonment of particular forms.

Lineaments of Contention

To trace the alteration of the British collective-action repertoire and the creation of the social movement as an established mode of action, we would have to move through the political history separating Wilkes and Gordon from Reform: the struggles over the American Revolution and the French Revolution, the days of Spa Fields, Luddism and Peterloo, the failed Reform campaigns of the 1820s, and more. Let us, however, take on a much less ambitious pair of tasks: to review evidence indicating that change in the everyday forms of collective action did, indeed, occur, and secondly to clarify just what has to be explained.

We can gain some illumination from catalogues of events occurring in the London area during 1768 and 1769, and in all of Great Britain, including the London area, from 1828 through 1831. 1768 and 1769 were, as we have seen, peak years for Wilkite activity. 1828 and 1829 brought important national struggles over the repeal of the Test and Corporation Acts (which imposed legal restrictions — often circumvented, but nonetheless cumbersome — on the participation of Dissenters in British public life) and the enactment of Catholic Emancipation, as well as battles to broaden the base of parish government, to hold off the tightening of regulations concerning Friendly Societies, and to promote a number of other causes. In 1829 and 1830 Britain experienced an intensification of industrial conflict, and the widespread rural conflicts in the south east which are known collectively as the Swing Rebellion. 1830 and 1831 saw the acceleration of the campaign for parliamentary reform, and unprecedented displays of popular support for the campaign. If the evidence for 1832 were now available, it would take us up to the enactment of Reform, and into its political aftermath. Alas, it takes time to sort the evidence; for the moment we must settle for stopping with 1831.

The events in the catalogue concern 'contentious gatherings' — occasions on which a number of people gathered publicly, and collectively stated demands, grievances, or other claims which somehow bore on the interests of other people. (For more precision and greater detail, see the appendix to this chapter.) Contentious gatherings do not cover the full range of collective action, by any means, but they do include many of its more visible and powerful forms. They encompass almost any occasion for which an observer might use the terms disturbance, riot, protest, demonstration, rebellion, disorder, affray, brawl, or delegation, plus a great many more. As compared to the events that John Stevenson calls 'disturbances', for example, contentious gatherings take in a wider range of electoral rallies, mass meetings, turnouts, processions, public ceremonies in the course of which people voice claims, and similar events.

In order to get a sense of the range of events involved, let us examine a list including every tenth event we have identified during the last four months of 1828:

September 1828
In Picadilly, Manchester, some people were injured during an 'affray' between Irishmen and coach drivers.

When constables broke up a bull-baiting session in Birmingham, someone threw stones at the constables.

A public dinner was held in Inverness to honour the Honourable Charles Grant.

When coach drivers blocked the street in Lincoln's Inn Fields, London, a crowd assembled and a fight began as people tried to force their way through the coaches.

October 1828
In Newton, Cumberland, after Mr Green's daughter died, people suspected the parents of killing their child; a crowd gathered around the Greens' house, broke the windows and door, and threatened Mr Green's life.

November 1828
The Friends of Civil and Religious Liberty gave a dinner at the London Tavern for Mr Sheil, following his pro-Catholic appearance at the largely anti-Catholic mass meeting on Penenden Heath, near Maidstone, Kent.

A meeting of the British Catholic Association, in Freemasons' Hall, London, petitioned Parliament in favour of Catholic claims.

A group of organisers in Leeds held a public meeting to establish an association based on Protestant principles, to resist all constitutional concessions to Roman Catholics.

At a meeting of the lace trade in Nottingham, the participants resolved to confine the operation of lace machines to eight hours a day.

Colombian bondholders held a meeting at the London Tavern to consider a document signed by the vice-consul of Colombia.

December 1828
A pro-Catholic group in Leeds held a meeting in favour of Catholic Emancipation and tolerance.

A public dinner was held in Windsor to welcome the King.

Prisoners in the County Gaol, in Leicester, attempted to escape, and injured their guards in the attempt.

The inhabitants of St Paul's Covent Garden met in the parish vestry room and prepared a petition for the passage of the overseas accounts.

A contested election of Common Councilmen and other Ward officers took place at Fishmongers' Hall, Bridge Ward, London.

Local people held a meeting in Queensborough, Kent, to discuss the distressing absence of work in the fisheries, and to propose solutions to the authorities.

Hunters attacked a game-keeper in Dunham Massey, Cheshire.

Some of these events would qualify as 'disturbances' by almost any standard. Many, however, would not. The brawls, for example, have no obvious relationship to national politics. The meetings at which people made demands, pledged support, or stated their opposition to persons or policies would disappear from most catalogues of conflicts and disorders. Yet they clearly form part of the British routine of collective action in the late 1820s. In fact, they comprise a majority of our 'contentious gatherings'. In the first case, one might wonder why occasions as trivial as a battle between coachmen and an irate crowd should appear in a study of political change. In the second case, one might wonder how anything so routine as a meeting at which people pass resolutions can be relevant to political change. In both cases, the answer is the same: only by examining the range of means people actually used to act on their interests can we single out which ones were politically significant, and which ones were changing.

The work is still in progress. As a result, the evidence reported here varies considerably in completeness, firmness and refinement. By leaping from the 1760s to the 1820s, it eliminates any description of the process by which the forms of contention changed between those dates, and therefore makes it difficult to verify any explanation of that process. Cumulatively, nevertheless, the evidence provides a warrant for thinking that Britain's collective-action repertoire underwent major alterations between the 1760s and the 1830s; that the eighteenth-century parochial and patronised forms of collective action did, indeed, give way to the nineteenth- and twentieth-century national and autonomous forms; that deliberately-formed associations became more and more prominent vehicles for the conveyance of grievances and demands; that the joining of a special-purpose association to a popular base, or at least to the appearance of a popular base, became a standard way of doing political business; that, increasingly, sustained challenges to the existing structure or use of power took the form of representations by leaders and delegates of named associations, accompanied by displays of popular support for those representations; that these processes all accelerated at the end of the 1830s; that, in short, the British were creating the social movement.

Table 2.1 catalogues contentious gatherings for Middlesex alone in 1768, 1769, 1828, 1829, 1830, and 1831. It groups the events according to a crude set of categories which give a sense of the main alternative forms of collective action, but which correspond only very roughly to the actual repertoires of the two time periods. The counts suggest a quickening of the tempo of contention in Middlesex from the 1760s to the 1820s: from 104 and 63 events in the two eighteenth-century years to some 235 in the average nineteenth-century year. That suggestion, however, could reflect no more than the greater fullness of the nineteenth-century sources; pending further investigation, let us not give it much weight.

The changing mixture of reported events, on the other hand, is much less open to doubt. In 1768 and 1769, routine meetings played a relatively small part in London's contention: 6.7 per cent of the total in 1768, 31.2 per cent in the following year. (The increase in 1769

Table 2.1: Per Cent Distribution of Contentious Gatherings in Middlesex During Selected Years from 1768 to 1831

Type of Gathering	1768	1769	1828	1829	1830	1831
meeting	6.7	31.8	77.5	68.3	64.3	86.5
strike, turnout	9.6	1.6	0.5	0.5	0.0	0.4
parade, rally, or demonstration	0.0	0.0	6.9	4.2	2.2	0.8
delegation	0.0	1.6	1.4	0.5	1.4	0.4
public celebration	2.9	3.2	1.4	0.9	0.7	1.3
unplanned gathering	22.2	30.2	0.0	8.4	9.0	2.1
attack on blacklegs or other enemies	28.8	20.6	0.0	0.0	0.0	0.0
poaching or smuggling	0.0	0.0	0.5	0.5	1.1	0.4
other violent confrontation	29.6	11.1	11.9	16.8	21.3	7.6
total	100.0	100.1	100.1	100.1	100.01	99.9
number of events	104	63	217	214	277	237

resulted largely from the fact that Wilkite action in the streets declined somewhat, while middle-class supporters of Wilkes and Wilkite candidates took to holding meetings on behalf of their cause.) From 1828 to 1831, public meetings averaged about three quarters of all the contentious gatherings that took place in Middlesex.

That was not the only change. Non-violent 'unplanned gatherings' such as market conflicts, street confrontations, and informal group displays of political preference were common — about a quarter of all events — in the time of Wilkes, but much rarer — under 10 per cent — from 1828 to 1831. Likewise, direct attacks on blacklegs and other miscreants occurred frequently during our eighteenth-century years, but did not occur at all (at least on a scale large enough to qualify as 'contentious gatherings') in our nineteenth-century period. The closest equivalents during those years were crowd actions against police informers and the varied forms of resistance to Robert Peel's New Police. Finally, the table gives hints first of a decline in the use of public celebrations and ceremonies as settings for the joint statement of demands, grievances and political preferences, and secondly a rise in the employment of parades, rallies and demonstrations, initiated by the participants rather than the authorities, for the same purpose. All in all, the differences between the patterns of contention in the 1760s and in the years around 1830 reveal a significant alteration of the collective-action repertoire in London, and are consistent with the increasing adoption of the apparatus of the social movement.

For the years from 1790 to 1821, John Stevenson has made a count of 'disturbances' which occurred in London; a 'disturbance', in his tally, is any event involving three or more people in damage to persons or property (Stevenson 1979: 306-7). Our closest approximation of that category for Middlesex is the combination of attacks on blacklegs or other enemies, poaching and smuggling events and 'other violent confrontations'. According to that criterion, our annual counts run as follows:

year	'violent'	'non-violent'	total
1768	62	42	104
1769	20	43	63
1828	26	191	217
1829	37	177	214
1830	62	215	277
1831	20	217	237

Stevenson identifies an average of 7 'disturbances' per year over the interval from 1790 through 1821. Clearly, our procedures identify many more 'contentious gatherings' in the years covered so far. I expect that our counts for years within Stevenson's period will also be higher, mainly because of our more thorough coverage of the sources. However, the important point in the tabulation is the relative change in 'violent' and 'non-violent' events: our enumeration shows relatively little alteration in the number of violent confrontations, but a quadrupling or quintupling of the non-violent contentious gatherings. That looks like a genuine change — and one missed by concentrating on violent protest.

Table 2.2 provides more detail on the nineteenth-century period. It compares Middlesex with the rest of Great Britain, year by year. Some of the comparisons are obvious, and thereby comforting: the generally greater frequency of confrontations between smugglers and (especially)

Table 2.2: Per Cent Distribution of Contentious Gatherings in Middlesex and Other Britain, 1828-1831

Type of Gathering	Middx	Other	Total	Middx	Other	Total	Middx	Other	Total	Middx	Other	Total
Meeting	77.5	77.8	77.6	68.3	68.4	68.3	64.3	54.3	56.6	86.5	80.9	82.5
Strike, turnout	0.5	0.0	0.2	0.5	0.5	0.5	0.0	0.7	0.5	0.4	1.5	1.2
Parade, rally or demonstration	6.9	6.9	6.9	4.2	2.6	3.1	2.2	3.7	3.3	0.8	2.3	1.9
Delegation	1.4	0.5	0.8	0.5	0.2	0.3	1.4	0.0	0.3	0.4	0.0	0.1
Public celebration	1.4	0.0	0.5	0.9	1.2	1.1	0.7	0.6	0.6	1.3	0.0	0.6
Unplanned gathering	0.0	0.8	1.0	8.4	5.4	6.4	9.0	8.2	8.4	2.1	5.8	4.8
Attack on blacklegs or other enemies	0.0	0.0	0.0	0.0	0.5	0.3	0.0	0.0	0.0	0.0	0.8	0.6
Poaching or Smuggling	0.5	5.8	3.9	0.5	4.2	3.0	1.1	1.3	1.3	0.4	0.6	0.6
Other violent Confrontation	10.1	6.3	8.7	16.8	17.1	17.0	21.3	31.0	28.9	7.6	7.6	7.6
Total	100.1	100.1	99.6	100.1	100.1	100.0	100.0	99.9	99.9	99.9	99.5	100.1
Number of events	217	378	595	214	427	641	277	897	1174	237	618	855

poachers with authorities outside of Middlesex, the greater frequency
of delegations (since the seats of government were at hand) in
Middlesex are the most obvious. The rise of 'other violent
confrontations' in 1829 and again in 1830 represents, first, the
increasing pace of industrial conflict and, then, the machine-breaking
and coercion of farmers which happened during the Swing rebellion,
late in the second year. The nearly 1,200 contentious gatherings of
1830 included hundreds of Swing events.

Two subtle, but no less significant, findings lurk in the table. The
first is negative: on the whole, meetings at which people stated claims
publicly and collectively by passing resolutions, issuing petitions, or
otherwise declaring their intentions were no more frequent,
proportionately speaking, in Middlesex than in the rest of Great Britain.
Furthermore, an informal supplementary tabulation shows that the lack
of difference does not result from my lumping of London's immediate
surroundings with the rest of Britain. If we define the London area as
Middlesex, Surrey, Sussex and Kent, the percentage of all contentious
gatherings that were meetings of some kind looks like this:

Year	London Area	Rest of Britain	Total
1828	78.1	77.3	77.7
1829	69.9	67.1	68.3
1830	56.6	56.7	56.6
1831	88.4	78.7	82.5

While over the full four years the London region did have a slightly
higher proportion of contentious gatherings that were meetings than
did the rest of the country, the difference was only substantial during
the Reform mobilisation of 1831. That state of affairs almost certainly
registers a significant change from the eighteenth century; at that time,
if we can trust the fragmentary information now available, meetings
were even less common ways to conduct collective business in the
provinces than in London. If we eliminate regularly-convened meetings
of vestries, municipal councils and similar assemblies, the eighteenth-
century difference between London and the rest of Britain looks very
large.

The second finding singles out the rest of Great Britain rather than
Middlesex; as measured by the sheer number of contentious gatherings,
the level of contention in London was fairly constant: 217, 214, 277
and 237 events in the four nineteenth-century years under examination.

When the national level rose, the rest of Britain made the difference. Although 1830, with its Swing conflicts, marked the high point of the four years, the frequency of events was generally rising in the rest of Britain, while staying more or less constant in Middlesex. When the debate over Catholic Emancipation heated up in 1829, the increase in public displays of opposition and support took place mainly outside of London; in the provinces, nearly half of 1829's contentious gatherings somehow concerned Catholic Emancipation, while in Middlesex the proportion was about a quarter. Indeed, events concerning Catholic Emancipation followed the rhythm of parliamentary debate, accelerating when Parliament was in session and especially when Parliament was deliberating on the bill. That interaction brought a considerable swelling of anti-Catholic activity in 1829, as the prospects for passage became brighter, and the threat to Protestant ascendancy therefore more serious.

Again, the doubling of contentious gatherings outside of Middlesex from 1829 to 1830 corresponds to what a knowledge of Swing's geography — concentrated in London's hinterland, but absent from the city's immediate vicinity — would lead us to expect (see Charlesworth 1979). In this case, the nearly 300 'other violent confrontations' which occurred outside of London in the course of the Swing events made the largest difference, and the high level of activity outside of London in 1831 fits the great importance of centres such as Birmingham and Bristol in the campaign for Reform. Altogether, the findings for 1828 to 1831 portray a country in which both contention and its forms were nationalising rapidly.

In order to get a sense of the flow of action within contentious gatherings, we have recorded each phase of each event in accordance with an elementary scheme: actor/object of action/action. The record of the action appears twice: as a direct quotation from our source, and as a verb. Where possible, we record the verb employed in the text; where the text contains no relevant verb, we write a paraphrase and mark it as such. In either case, the machine-readable record contains words, not coded summaries. The actions we record include any the text reports as occurring before the contentious gathering, properly speaking, began (e.g., an announcement that a meeting will occur) or after it ended (e.g., Parliament's hearing of a petition issued by a meeting). Although the actions within the gathering are easily separable from those outside it, in the tabulations which follow I have combined the two.

For Britain as a whole, Table 2.3 lists every verb which, in any

Table 2.3: Per Cent Distribution of Action-Verbs Appearing Frequently, 1828-1831

Verb	1828	1829	Jan-June 1830	Jul-Dec 1830	1831
ADDRESS	0.4	1.2	0.5	1.7	2.9
ADJOURN	0.8	1.0	1.3	0.6	0.9
ANNOUNCE	1.5	0.4	0.0	0.2	0.2
APPLAUD	0.5	0.6	0.8	0.9	1.4
ARREST	0.4	1.0	0.7	3.2	0.3
ARRIVE	1.3	1.4	0.5	1.1	0.8
ASSEMBLE	1.9	2.9	5.8	4.9	2.2
ATTACK	1.3	1.0	0.6	1.1	0.5
BREAK	0.1	0.0	0.1	2.0	0.3
CHAIR	0.2	0.5	1.0	1.6	4.8
CHEER	2.6	3.2	0.7	3.2	5.4
DEMAND	0.2	0.3	0.3	3.4	0.2
DESTROY	0.0	0.5	0.0	1.8	0.0
DISPERSE	0.4	1.0	0.4	0.9	0.4
END	12.9	11.0	16.4	12.3	12.0
ENTER	1.2	1.1	0.1	0.3	0.4
GATHER	0.0	0.9	1.1	5.1	2.8
GIVE	0.0	0.0	0.0	1.0	0.3
HEAR	2.7	0.2	0.0	0.0	0.0
HEAR PETITION	5.7	5.2	9.2	2.3	3.4
MEET	13.3	10.1	11.7	5.4	10.4
OPPOSE	0.9	2.7	0.9	0.8	0.3
PETITION	9.6	6.5	13.1	3.8	6.8
PROCEED	0.6	1.1	0.6	1.5	0.7
REQUISITION	0.0	0.6	2.2	0.6	2.7
RESOLVE	3.1	2.6	3.3	2.1	6.8
SEPARATE	1.4	0.9	0.9	0.8	1.3
SUPPORT	0.6	0.8	0.4	1.0	0.6
THANK	2.7	2.9	2.8	1.9	4.9
TRY	0.0	0.4	0.2	2.4	0.1
OTHER	33.7	38.0	24.5	32.1	25.9
TOTAL	100.0	100.0	100.0	100.0	100.0
Number of Actions	3224	4075	1405	5990	5968
Actions/Event	5.4	6.4	5.0	6.7	7.0

interval from 1828 to 1831, represented at least one per cent of all the action-verbs used. (In this case, I have combined paraphrases and verbs taken directly from the sources; the proportions coming directly from the sources vary from a mere 0.1 per cent for END, our convention for closing an event whose exact termination the available accounts do not describe, to virtually 100 per cent for ASSEMBLE, BREAK, DESTROY, ENTER, REQUISITION, SEPARATE, and THANK.) The table breaks 1830 into two intervals, in order to bring out the special character of the Swing events in the later months of that year.

Throughout the five intervals, the most frequent actions clearly belong to regular meetings. The sequence MEET, RESOLVE, THANK, SEPARATE describes a typical gathering in any interval. In the case of 1828, for example, we can group together all verbs with roughly equivalent meanings; in this grouping. MEET includes that word plus MET, MEETS, and other such variants, while DELIBERATE+ includes a wider range: ADD TO, ADDRESS, ADOPT, AMEND, APPOINT, ARGUE, BRING BEFORE, and so on. For that year, the most frequent sequences we find are:

MEET, PETITION, END, HEAR PETITION (27.2 per cent of all
 events)
MEET, PETITION, END, DELIBERATE+ (11.7 per cent)
ASSEMBLE, PETITION, END, HEAR PETITION (2.7 per cent)
ASSEMBLE, PETITION, END, DELIBERATE+ (2.0 per cent)

These four sequences of action-verbs account for 43.6 per cent of 1828's 217 events. They describe the standard process by which a local group assembled to petition Parliament — in 1828, most often about the repeal of the Test and Corporation Acts or in opposition to the Friendly Society Bill — and Parliament later heard the petition.

The list also includes actions shared by orderly meetings, street demonstrations, and responses to the appearance of popular or unpopular figures: APPLAUD, ASSEMBLE, CHEER, OPPOSE, SUPPORT. There are also verbs which appear infrequently in routine meetings, but often enough outside them: ARREST, ATTACK, BREAK, DEMAND, DESTROY, GATHER. Some verbs, finally, concentrate in the local conflicts of Swing; BREAK, DEMAND, DESTROY, GIVE (the response of some farmers when the local agricultural workers demanded a cash contribution), and TRY (the response of many magistrates when faced with rebellious farm labourers) are the most emphatic examples. Outside of Swing, the routines of meeting, debating, resolving, petitioning and deciding on some further course of public action dominate the forms of contention.

An important trend, however, appears in Table 2.3. On the whole, the meetings of 1828 and 1829 were more sedate and contained than those of the later years. As the years move on toward 1832, verbs such as ANNOUNCE and HEAR decline in importance, while verbs bespeaking more deliberate displays of opinion and determination gain. The rise of ADDRESS, APPLAUD, CHEER, REQUISITION and, perhaps, CHAIR show us the increasing use of the public meeting as a dramatisation of the numbers and determination of a cause's supporters. By the time of 1831's Reform campaign, political organisers were regularly hiring a hall, finding well-known and effective speakers, printing up handbills, marching supporters to and from the hall, deliberately stimulating the attention of the press and the public, making great displays of demands, grievances and affiliations, providing plenty of opportunities for enthusiastic participation, and drawing audiences of thousands. John Belchem calls the tactics involved the 'politics of the mass platform', and dates their appearance on the national scene to Henry Hunt's innovations in the Spa Fields meetings of 1816-17 (Belchem 1978: 742-3). From 1828 to 1832, we see mass-platform politics reappearing at a scale larger than ever before.

The recurrent radical meetings at Southwark's Rotunda illustrate the new techniques. The radical Richard Carlile leased the theatre building on Blackfriars Road in May of 1830, and immediately converted it to a meeting-place. At first both the reformist Metropolitan Political Union and the Radical Reform Association used the low-priced hall, but as the National Union of the Working Classes amalgamated the survivors of the declining RRA with a number of other ultra-radical fragments, the Rotunda became increasingly identified with working-class radicalism. There London's workers heard Carlile, Cobbett, Lovett and the other great radicals of the day.

In that connection, it is fascinating to see Francis Place, late in 1831, acting much like a twentieth-century movement organiser: trying to build a broad alliance and to contain the demands of Lovett and other working-class leaders for a radical programme, trying to fix the elections to the National Political Union's council by hand-picking working-class candidates and systematically excluding the men he calls 'Rotundists' (British Library, Add. MSS. 27791, pp.71-2). Although Place had not formally joined the National Political Union, and had at first avoided taking any office in it, he had busied himself behind the scenes with its creation. Then he faced the standard problem of the social-movement organiser: how to build a coalition large enough to be effective without compromising the ends he wanted the movement to serve. As Graham Wallas analysed the difficulty:

> If the National Political Union was to claim any authority, it must, according to the political ideas of the time, be formed at a public meeting, and all who presented themselves must be allowed to join. At the preliminary 'committee' meetings resolutions moved by the Rotundists and their sympathisers in favour of universal suffrage and annual parliaments had been with difficulty defeated, and it seemed likely that amendments in that sense would be carried at the public meeting advertised for Monday, October 31, at the Crown and Anchor in the Strand (Wallas 1898: 280-281).

In fact, some twenty thousand people showed up for a meeting scheduled to take place in a room measuring 12 by 25 feet. It had to be moved to Lincoln's Inn Fields. There, as Place feared, a strong sentiment in favour of radical democracy prevailed. The meeting voted an amendment requiring that half the Union's council be working men. After momentary discouragement, Place undertook the difficult search for bona fide working men who were not, in essence, Rotundists. This sort of manoeuvering has a familiar air; twentieth-century social-movement organisers continually find themselves in similar tight spots, and similarly work out of the public view in order to make the movement's public activity effective. As Wilkes and Gordon helped create the forms of the social movement's public activity, Francis Place and his contemporaries helped establish the private — or at least less public — means of manipulating those forms to a desired effect. The British were installing the apparatus of the social movement.

What is more, it sometimes worked: the social movement became a means of exerting effective pressure on the holders of power. Whatever considerations of tactics and policy influenced Wellington, Grey and the king during the struggles over Reform, the repeated displays of popular determination persuaded the authorities that they could delay no longer. Consider the entry in Greville's memories for 1 April 1832:

> At the Dss. de Dino's ball the night before last I had a very curious conversation with Melbourne about it all. He said that 'he really believed there was no strong feeling in the country for the measure.'

We talked of the violence of the Tories, and their notion that they could get rid of the whole thing. I said the notion was absurd *now*, but that I fully agreed with him about the general feeling. 'Why, then', said he, 'might it not be thrown out?' – a consummation I really believe he would rejoice at, if it could be done. I said because there was a great part which would not let it, which would agitate again, and that the country wished ardently to have it settled; that if it could be disposed of for good and all, it would be a good thing indeed, but that this was now become impossible (Greville 1938: 277).

If Melbourne was not yet persuaded, Greville and a great many other members of the ruling class were. The threat of recurrent 'agitation' had become an effective way of exacting concessions on behalf of the unrepresented. The pebbles kicked loose by Wilkes and Gordon had become an avalanche.

Yet the avalanche had a direction and an organisational base. From the 1760s to the 1830s, the British built up a combination of associations, constituencies, demands and political entrepreneurs with public displays of support and determination; they made that combination a regular feature of national politics; they created the national social movement. From the perspective of authorities, the organisers of social movements continued to be 'agitators', their work agitation. Henceforth, nevertheless, moderates and radicals alike used the new form of collective action. The national social movement – the sustained challenge to national authorities in the name of an unrepresented constituency, coupled with public displays of support and determination – became a standard device of British politics.

Does all this analysis come down to the old notion that British pragmatism won out, and politics became more orderly as the nineteenth century wore on? Certainly the crowds of the 1830s less regularly initiated attacks on the persons and possessions of presumed wrongdoers than had their counterparts of the 1760s and 1770s. Most likely it is true, as demographic historian P.E.H. Hair has suggested, that British per capita deaths from collective violence other than war declined noticeably after 1780 (Hair 1971: 22). Surely our twentieth-century eyes detect the order within the forms of the newer repertoire more readily than in the mobbing, Rough Music or window breaking of the later eighteenth century. Yet the shift toward meetings, marches, rallies, demonstrations, strikes and social movements did not, by any means, eliminate violence, indignation, or revolutionary determination from Chartism or industrial conflict. It changed the choices, the risks and the likely outcomes of demands for change. In the course of their struggles, the British were creating new ways of struggling. One of their most important creations was the social movement.

Conclusion

As I warned earlier, the scattered and preliminary evidence in this chapter does not clinch that conclusion, much less provide a convincing explanation of the great change. A simple juxtaposition of the 1760s with the 1830s elides most of the process. To trace the full development of the social movement as a means of political action in Britain requires an examination of the British response to the American Revolution and the French Revolution, of the successive forms of radicalism, of Spa Fields, Peterloo, and the failed Reform campaigns of the 1820s.

Even within the period from 1828 to 1831, I have not spelled out how the success of the campaigns for Test and Corporation repeal and (especially) Catholic Emancipation opened the way to the widespread use of social-movement forms during the campaign for Reform. After all, 'Catholic Emancipation was the battering ram that broke down the old unreformed system' (Cannon 1973: 191). That was true, I think, not only for the usually alleged reasons: because the issue split the Tories, opened the way to a Whig government, and sanctified the principle of reform. The Irish and British campaigns for Catholic Emancipation also provided a model for the creation of effective mass-based associations, and established a precedent for their action on the national political scene. In a back-handed way, Parliament recognised the likelihood of such effects when it coupled the passage of Emancipation with the increase of property qualifications for suffrage in Ireland and with the dissolution of the Catholic Association itself. Moreover, some of the personnel of the campaign for Emancipation carried their memories and expertise right into the struggle for Reform; the joining of Henry Hunt and Daniel O'Connell in the founding of London's Metropolitan Political Union illustrates the continuity from one movement to the next. But this essay has done no more than suggest how all that happened.

Nor have I translated the individual verbs and crude categories of events into the complex, flexible sequences which constituted the genuine repertoires of the time. Some pieces of the eighteenth-century repertoire, such as the punishment of an effigy to convey disapproval of its original, or the riding of a blackleg through town on a donkey, continued to serve in the 1830s. To throw together the decorous assemblies of London coffee-houses and the turbulent gatherings at the Rotunda in the same bland category of 'meeting' misses the variation by class, political tendency and tactical situation that marked all the newer varieties of collective action. Yet the evidence already in hand makes it clear enough that the forms of conflict which had prevailed in the days of Wilkes and Gordon were, by 1832, on their way to oblivion. In fact, the struggles of the eighteenth century's later decades, for all their antique coloration, were helping to create the new repertoire that would displace the old.

Appendix: Sources and Methods

The material in this paper comes from two overlapping investigations, both still very much in progress. My collaborators and I are inventorying contentious gatherings which occurred in the London area (Middlesex, Surrey, Kent and Sussex) in twenty years spread over the period from 1758 to 1834, and in all counties of Great Britain (England, Scotland and Wales) from 1828 to 1834. The 'contentious gathering' is an arbitrary unit designed to give us the means of scanning historical processes systematically. It is an occasion on which a number of people (10 or more, in the cases at hand) gather in a publicly-accessible place and visibly make claims which would, if realised, affect the interests of persons outside the group. The 'claims' range from a direct attack on a person or an object to the laying out of a programme to a statement of support or opposition directed at a candidate or public official. The events inventoried consist of all those mentioned in the *London Chronicle*, the *Times* of London (once it began publishing in 1785), the *Annual Register* and *Gentleman's Magazine* for the years before 1828, and the *Times*, the *Morning Chronicle*, *Gentleman's*, the *Annual Register*, Hansard's *Parliamentary Debates*, *Mirror of Parliament* and *Votes and Proceedings* of Parliament from 1828 to 1834. (Once an event has entered the catalogue, we feel free to draw additional descriptive material from other periodicals, from the correspondence of the Secretaries of State, from the papers of the Home Office, from published collections of documents and from historians' treatments of the subject.) These sources yield one or two hundred contentious gatherings for the London area in the average eighteenth-century year, and some thousand events per year in Great Britain as a whole during the 1820s and 1830s; the actual totals, as the tabulations in this paper indicate, vary drastically from one year to another.

We are creating machine-readable descriptions of these contentious gatherings — descriptions which retain much of the detail and actual language of the sources. The descriptions include characterisations of (a) the event as a whole, (b) each place in which some of the event's action occurred, (c) each formation — each individual or set of persons ever acting in a distinctive fashion — taking part in the gathering, or serving as the object of a claim, (d) each phase of the action, a new phase beginning each time any formation's relationship to the action, or to the claims being made, changed visibly; the phases include relevant actions occurring before the event as such began and after it ended, well-labelled and easily separable from actions internal to the event; the tabulations of action-verbs in this paper include both internal and external actions; (e) each source consulted for information on the event, (f) comments concerning difficulties encountered in describing the event, relevant background information, and links to other events. The machine-readable files thus make it easy to recapture and regroup much of the detail with which we began.

The National Endowment for the Humanities supports the work on London 1758-1834, the National Science Foundation the work on Great Britain 1828-1834. I am grateful to Keith Clarke, Nancy Horn, and R.A. Schweitzer for assistance with the data, to Dawn Hendricks and Phil Soergel for help with bibliography.

References

Arnstein, Walter L. (1973), 'The Survival of the Victorian Aristocracy', in Frederick Cople Jaher (ed.), *The Rich, the Well Born, and the Powerful*, University of Illinois Press, Urbana

Belchem, John (1978), 'Henry Hunt and the evolution of the mass platform', *English Historical Review, 93*, 739-73

——— (1981), 'Republicanism, popular constitutionalism and the radical platform in early nineteenth-century England', *Social History, 6*, 1-32

Black, Eugene C. (1963), *The Association, British Extraparliamentary Political Organization, 1769-1793*, Harvard University Press, Cambridge Mass.

Bohstedt, John (1970), 'Riots in England, with Special Reference to Devonshire', unpublished PhD thesis in history, Harvard University

Brewer, John (1976), *Party Ideology and Popular Politics at the Accession of George III*, Cambridge University Press, Cambridge

——— (1980), 'The Wilkites and the Law, 1763-74: a study of radical notions of governance', in John Brewer and John Styles (eds.), *An Ungovernable*

People. The English and their Law in the Seventeenth and Eighteenth Centuries, Rutgers University Press, New Brunswick, NJ

Brock, Michael (1974), *The Great Reform Act,* Humanities Press, New York

Brown, Brian R. (1979), 'Lancashire Chartism and the Mass Strike of 1842: The Political Economy of Working Class Contention', CRSO (Center for Research on Social Organization, University of Michigan) Working Paper 203

Brundage, Anthony (1978), *The Making of the New Poor Law. The politics of inquiry, enactment and implementation, 1832-39,* Hutchinson, London

Cannon, John (1973), *Parliamentary Reform, 1640-1832,* Cambridge University Press, Cambridge

Charlesworth, Andrew (1979), *Social Protest in a Rural Society,* Historical Geography Research Series No. 1, Historical Geography Research Group, Cambridge

Clarke, John (1977), *The Price of Progress. Cobbett's England, 1780-1835,* Granada Publishing, London

Cockburn, Henry (1971), *Memorials of His Time,* James Thin, Edinburgh. (Reprinting of book originally published in 1856)

Cowherd, Raymond G. (1956), *The Politics of English Dissent. The Religious Aspects of Liberal and Humanitarian Reform Movements from 1815 to 1848,* New York University Press, New York

Darvall, T.O. (1934), *Popular Disturbances and Public Order in Regency England,* Oxford University Press, Oxford.

Dickinson, H.T. (1976), 'Party, principle and public opinion in eighteenth-century politics', *History, 61,* 231-7

Dunhabin. J.P.D. (1974). *Rural Discontent in Nineteenth-Century Britain,* Holmes & Meier, New York

Flick, Carlos (1978), *The Birmingham Political Union and the Movements for Reform in Britain, 1830-1839,* Archon Books, Hamden, Conn.

Foster, John (1974), *Class Struggle and the Industrial Revolution. Early Industrial Capitalism in Three English Towns,* Weidenfeld & Nicolson, London

Fraser, Derek (1970), 'The Agitation for Parliamentary Reform', in J.T. Ward (ed.), *Popular Movements, c.1830-1850,* Macmillan, London

Gash, Norman (1971), *Politics in the Age of Peel. A Study in the Technique of Parliamentary Representation, 1830-1850,* Norton, New York. (First published by Longman in 1953)

—— (1979), *Aristocracy and People. Britain, 1815-1865,* Harvard University Press, Cambridge, Mass.

Greville, C.C.E. (1938), (Lytton Strachey and Roger Fulford, eds.), *The Greville Memoirs, 1814-1860,* vol. II, Macmillan, London

Hair, P.E.H. (1971), 'Deaths from Violence in Britain: A Tentative Secular Survey', *Population Studies, 25,* 5-24

Hamburger, Joseph (1963), *James Mill and the Art of Revolution,* Yale University Press, New Haven

Hay, Douglas *et al.* (1975), *Albion's Fatal Tree. Crime and Society in Eighteenth-Century England,* Pantheon, New York

Hayter, Anthony (1978), *The Army and the Crowd in Mid-Georgian England,* Rowman & Littlefield, Totowa, N.J.

Hill, Christopher (1966), *The Century of Revolution, 1603-1714,* W.W. Norton, New York

Hobsbawm, E.J. and George Rudé (1969), *Captain Swing,* Lawrence & Wishart, London

Hollis, Patricia (1973), *Class and Conflict in Nineteenth-Century England, 1815-1850,* Routledge & Kegan Paul, London

Jones, David (1973), *Before Rebecca. Popular Protests in Wales, 1793-1835,* Allen Lane, London

Macdonagh, Oliver (1977), *Early Victorian Government, 1830-1870*, Holmes & Meier, New York

Macpherson, C.B. (1962), *The Political Theory of Possessive Individualism. Hobbes to Locke*, Clarendon Press, Oxford

Main, J.M. (1965-7), 'Radical Westminster, 1807-1820', *Historical Studies, Australia and New Zealand, 12*, 186-204

Marshall, Dorothy (1968), *Dr. Johnson's London*, Wiley, New York

Marvel, Howard P. (1977), 'Factory regulation: A reinterpretation of early English experience', *Journal of Law and Economics, 20*, 379-402

Mather, F.C. (1959), *Public Order in the Age of the Chartists*, Manchester University Press, Manchester

Moore, D.C. (1961), 'The other face of Reform', *Victorian Studies, 5*, 7-34

——— (1966), 'Concession or cure: The sociological premises of the First Reform Act', *Historical Journal, 9*, 39-59

Moorhouse, H.F. (1973), 'The Political Incorporation of the British Working Class: An Interpretation', *Sociology, 7*, 341-59

Munger, Frank (1977), 'Popular Protest and its Suppression in Early Nineteenth Century Lancashire: A Study of Historical Models of Protest and Repression', unpublished PhD thesis in sociology, University of Michigan.

Musson, A.E. (1971), *British Trade Unions, 1800-1875*, Macmillan, London

Parssinen, T.M. (1972), 'The revolutionary party in London, 1816-20', *Bulletin of the Institute of Historical Research, 45*, 265-82

——— (1973), 'Association, convention and anti-parliament in British radical politics 1771-1848', *English Historical Review, 88*, 504-33

Peacock, A.J. (1965), *Bread or Blood. The Agrarian Riots in East Anglia: 1816*, Gollancz, London

Perkin, Harold (1969), *The Origins of Modern English Society, 1780-1880*, Routledge & Kegan Paul, London

Powell, G. Bingham (1973), 'Incremental Democratization: The British Reform Act of 1832', in Gabriel A. Almond, Scott C. Flanagan and Robert J. Mundt (eds.), *Crisis, Choice and Change, Historical Studies of Political Development*, Little, Brown, Boston

Rose, Richard (1964), *Politics in England*, Little, Brown, Boston

Rowe, D.J. (ed.) (1970), *London Radicalism, 1830-1843. A Selection from the Papers of Francis Place*, W. & J. Mackay, Chatham, Kent

Rudé, George (1962), *Wilkes and Liberty*, Clarendon Press, Oxford

——— (1971a), *Hanoverian London, 1714-1808*, Secker & Warburg, London

——— (1971b), *Paris and London in the Eighteenth Century. Studies in Popular Protest*, Viking, New York

Schweitzer, R.A. (1980), 'British Catholic Emancipation mobilization: Prototype of Reform?' Working Paper 220, Center for Research on Social Organization, University of Michigan

Schweitzer, R.A. (1980), Charles Tilly and John Boyd 'The Texture of British Contention in 1828 and 1829', CRSO Working Paper 211

Sennett, Richard (1977), *The Fall of Public Man*, Knopf, New York

Shelton, Walter J. (1973), *English Hunger and Industrial Disorders. A Study of Social Conflict during the First Decade of George III's Reign*, Macmillan, London

Sheppard, Francis (1971), *London, 1808-1870. The Infernal Wen*, Secker & Warburg, London

Smith, W.A. (1965), 'Anglo-Colonial Society and the Mob, 1740-1775', unpublished PhD thesis in history, Claremont Graduate School and University Center

Stevenson, John (1974), 'Food Riots in England, 1792-1818', in John Stevenson and Roland Quinault (eds.), *Popular Protest and Public Order, Six Studies in*

British History, 1790-1920, George Allen & Unwin, London.
———— (1977a), 'Introduction' to John Stevenson (ed.), *London in the Age of Reform*, Blackwell, Oxford
———— (1977b), 'Social Control and the Prevention of Riots in England, 1789-1829', in A.P. Donajgrodzki (ed.), *Social Control in Nineteenth Century Britain*, Croom Helm, London
———— (1979), *Popular Disturbances in England, 1700-1870*, Longman, London
Taylor, Charles Lewis (1966), 'Toward an Explanation of the Rise of Political Activity among English Working Men, 1790-1850', unpublished paper presented to the American Political Science Association
Thomas, Keith (1978), 'The United Kingdom', in Raymond Grew (ed.), *Crises of Political Development in Europe and the United States*, Princeton University Press, Princeton
Thomis, Malcolm I. and Peter Holt (1977), *Threats of Revolution in Britain, 1789-1848*, Macmillan, London
Thompson, E.P. (1963), *The Making of the English Working Class*, Gollancz, London
———— (1971) 'The Moral Economy of the English Crowd in the Eighteenth Century', *Past and Present, 50*, 76-136
———— (1972), 'Rough Music: Le Charivari anglais', *Annales; Economies, Sociétiés, Civilisations, 27*, 285-312
Tilly, Charles and R.A. Schweitzer (1980), 'Enumerating and Coding Contentious Gatherings in Nineteenth-Century Britain', CRSO Working Paper 210
Vester, Michael (1970), *Die Entstehung des Proletariats als Lernprozess. Die Entstehung antikapitalistischer Theorie und Praxis in England 1792-1848*, Europäische Verlaganstalt, Frankfurt a/Main
Wallas, Graham (1898), *The Life of Francis Place, 1771-1854*, Longmans Green, London
Ward, J.T. (1962), *The Factory Movement, 1830-1850*, Macmillan, New York

3 STRIKES AND THE URBAN HIERARCHY IN ENGLISH INDUSTRIAL TOWNS, 1842-1901

Lynn Hollen Lees

Although most strikes take place in cities and towns, the links between urban environments and the forms and incidence of industrial conflict are largely unexplored. Those historians and sociologists who have connected the scale and structure of urban settings with industrial disputes offer contradictory interpretations and ones that are rarely sensitive enough to differences over time and space. The most common argument has been to link city size directly to the strength of industrial protest. Friedrich Engels, writing of England in the 1840s, thought that big cities were the sites of most intense social conflict, and he saw a direct relation between the scale of workplace or community and the potentially greatest labour militancy.[1] Similar arguments have been common among European authors since at least 1850. Dismayed by events such as revolutions in Paris, Chartist demonstrations in London and Birmingham, and the uprisings of 1848 in Berlin and Vienna, analysts of political strife often saw the big city as the setting for the greatest conflict.[2] More recently, Charles Tilly and Edward Shorter have come to similar conclusions based upon a massive study of strikes in France between 1832 and 1968. They assert that 'the big city appears a place of militancy and solidarity. It is certain that the sheer intensity of conflict in the big city was higher than in small communities'.[3] A contrary argument, however, has also been widely used. Seeking to explain the high level of strikes by miners in many places and times, Gaston Rimlinger assigns responsibility to their small, closely knit communities. For him, relative isolation and homogeneity breed labour consciousness and a high propensity to strike.[4]

The connection between strikes and the urban environment is particularly important because of the wide significance often attributed to strikes. For many analysts, they stem from fundamental oppositions in the attitudes and aims of workers and their employers, and they signal tension over issues much broader than wage claims. Engels, of course, saw strikes as early engagements in the coming social war, and many observers of the 1842 plug strikes branded them as insurrections.[5] Although current explanations for the incidence of strikes differ

52

widely, twentieth-century analysts of strikes regularly link work stoppages to discontents involving the distribution of economic and political power. Kenneth Knowles argues for example in his study of British strikes that wage claims are 'symbolic of wider grievances', and he identifies a series of underlying causes for strikes that range from protest against bad social conditions and the character of industrial work to a more generalised reaction against the distribution of power and authority in society.[6] Charles Tilly and Edward Shorter call strikes 'power struggles' and depict them as 'instruments of working-class political action'.[7] Moreover, James Cronin asserts that strikes became around 1850 'the dominant form of social protest in industrial society'.[8]

However extensive a claim one wishes to make for the wider political significance of strikes, it is clear that they are an important form of conflict in the nineteenth and twentieth centuries. Relatively high levels of strike activity signal both the existence of deep seated conflicts, and the presence of a self-conscious group of workers able to act collectively and to organise themselves in opposition either to employers or to the state. Differences in strike rates among cities of different sizes should reflect differences in the nature of local labour consciousness and organisation, as well as dissimilar ways of enacting and resolving disputes between capital and labour.

It is well-established that strike rates differ among industries and regions in Britain. Both Knowles and Cronin have noted the relatively high propensity to strike by miners and textile workers and by the populations of Wales, Lancashire and Yorkshire. In contrast, the clothing trades have a relatively tame record of strike behaviour, and the counties of the Midlands and the east are the sites of relatively few labour disputes.[9] Clearly, there is a complex set of local and industrial determinants that affects the willingness of workers and employers to let problems escalate into strikes and lockouts, but the urban dimension is not absent from the influences upon the forms and incidence of industrial conflict. If we look at the labour stoppages that took place between 1889 and 1891 in two counties of regularly high and two of regularly low strike activity in an industry of similar technology and organisation — the building trades — it is evident that within regions, settlements of different sizes had widely varying strike rates. (See Table 3.1) In particular, building workers in towns with between 20,000 and 100,000 people struck several times more frequently than either building workers in the large cities or those in small towns. Moreover, a larger proportion of the local population in medium-sized settlements went out on strike. Regional centres such as Manchester, Leeds, Sheffield, or Nottingham had neither the largest nor the most frequent work stoppages.

Table 3.1: Strikes by Building Workers in Urban and Rural Areas of Lancashire, Yorkshire, Leicestershire, and Nottinghamshire, 1899-1901

Strike Rates	Size of Settlement				
	300,000+	100,000-300,000	20,000-100,000	2,000-20,000	under 2,000
No. Strikes	16	13	48	9	1
Strikes/100,000 pop.	9.3	8.5	25.5	5.3	.8
No. Strikes	1626	2198	4793	264	80
Strikers/100,000 pop.	94.8	143.9	254.7	2.6	7

How can such differences in strike rates be explained? Historians of the English city have done little systematic research on the relationship between the size of an urban population and the propensity of local workers to engage in conflict with employers or to participate in political activities of a wider sort.[10] Learning more about the ways in which an urban environment affects industrial relations requires comparisons and a close look at urban, as well as industrial structures. The few historians who have dealt with such topics have compared relatively few places and have focused upon social structure rather than either size of the organisation of the town. Donald Read, for example, who notes in his book on the English provinces that 'Birmingham and Sheffield were cities of political union: Manchester and Leeds were cities of social cleavage', bases his argument upon what he sees as the different consequences of production in small workshops and in large factories.[11] John Foster's comparisons of Oldham, Northampton, and South Shields in the 1830's and 1840's also centre upon social structural differences and the nature of work. Class conflict and a radical workers' movement arose, he argues, where the organisation of industry hindered collaboration with the bourgeoisie and facilitated the social solidarity of a widely defined occupational group.[12] Foster's argument linked social structure to social and political behaviour using the cases of three medium-sized manufacturing towns. Yet however intriguing the results of his comparisons are, they do not yield widely generalisable results, since they offer little basis upon which to judge the typicality of the cities examined. Other cotton spinning towns had histories of conflict dissimilar to that of Oldham in the 1830s and 1840s, but Foster's arguments do not permit the drawing of distinctions. Another strategy for studying towns and their labour histories is needed.

By widening his focus from town to region, Patrick Joyce is able to offer a much more balanced picture of the links between workplace and the community, between industrial and social relations. He argues that in the textile towns of Lancashire and Yorkshire, 'The factory was at the centre of political life.'[13] Although his work does not devote any systematic attention to strikes, the connections he traces among the organisation of work and a town's political and cultural activities show how deeply intertwined were urban and labour processes in certain environments. Although in the biggest cities, the power of factory owners and of the factory itself was adulterated by the presence of diverse groups and other types of employment, in smaller, more homogeneous places, an elite of owners had power that stretched outside the workplace and reinforced an atmosphere of deference toward them and their political opinions. Recent work in labour history therefore suggests that the size and organisation of cities and towns affect labour relations in systematic ways but has only begun to explore the nature of such linkage.

However illuminating the detailed study of individual communities and disputes, it is no substitute for analysis of large numbers of strikes and their settings. By charting the distribution of strikes among settlements of different sizes and by examining the local patterns by which strikes are diffused, I propose to show some of the ways in which the urban organisation of manufacturing areas affects relative degrees and styles of industrial conflict. The areas within individual counties where local culture was relatively homogeneous and where large numbers of settlements had similar industrial bases offer a good setting for such a study because the distorting effects of cultural and technological differences are dampened. In the remainder of this chapter, I will explore the relationship between city size and industrial conflict by using strike data for the year 1842 and for the period between 1889 and 1901 for Lancashire, Yorkshire, Leicestershire and Nottinghamshire. The years surveyed include two major strike waves, when the frequency of strikes rose to several times their normal level. These were the plug plot disturbances of 1842 and the extensive labour disputes of 1889 to 1891 associated with the spread of 'new unionism'. The territory covered is dominated by various types of textile and clothing manufacturing, although the location within these four counties of two major ports (Hull and Liverpool) and centres of coal mining and metal production should be remembered. The counties chosen differed markedly in their propensity to strike. Lancashire and Yorkshire were areas of the most intense strike activity in England from the late nineteenth century to the Second World War, while in the East Midlands, relatively few labour stoppages took place.[14] My sample includes, therefore, places and times of both high and low strike activity.

I will argue that in these industrial areas, medium- and small-sized towns had a pattern of much more frequent and relatively larger strikes than towns having more than 100,000 people and that in the most complex cities — the regional capitals and county towns — conflicts between capital and labour were more often mediated and directed by specialised institutions into forms that did not involve work stoppages. Whatever regional and industrial factors shaped strike behaviour, these operated along with important influences arising from the urban structure of the setting. In addition, conflict often diffused regionally through the urban hierarchy from higher order central places to simpler, smaller ones.

Let us look first at the disturbances of July and August, 1842, which as they spread across England, Wales and Scotland, almost became a general strike.[15] Begun by miners in north and south Staffordshire protesting against low wages and truck payments, the strikes reached the Scottish coalfields, Shropshire, Tyneside and the cotton-manufacturing areas of Cheshire and Lancashire by early August. After stopping work at their own mines or factories, bands of striking workers tramped from village to village and town to town to gather new adherents. Aided by local people, they brought the strike to the West Riding and East Midlands by mid-August. The path by which the strike advanced in Cheshire, Lancashire, and Yorkshire shows the ways in which the cities of the textile region became involved. The plug strikes occurred in an already disturbed and mobilised district. From the winter of 1841 and the spring of 1842, massive unemployment combined with short-time working and wage reductions had led to widespread demonstrations and short strikes in both large and small towns at a time when Chartists and anti-Corn Law Leaguers were actively bidding for popular support in the manufacturing districts. Within a week of the beginning of the miners' agitation, meetings of workers took place in Ashton and Stalybridge over the issue of resisting wage reductions and, secondarily, of confirming support for the Charter. While little went on in Manchester, several thousand Stalybridge people marched around the town on 8 August stopping the mills there and then went on to Dukinfield, Ashton, Denton, Hyde, and finally Oldham. On the following day, a crowd of several thousand from Ashton, Hyde and Stalybridge converged on Manchester to turn out the workers there. Met by magistrates, cavalry and police, most retreated home after a massive demonstration. Meanwhile, small groups of Manchester operatives began their own strike. On 9, 10 and 11 August, large crowds marched around Manchester and Salford stopping work at the factories and occasionally clashing with police and throwing stones. Thereafter, Manchester became the central place where delegates from various trades and from towns to the north and east of the city met to direct the strike and to discuss the Charter. The city served as a planning headquarters, although Manchester workers were less involved in the strikes than those from smaller towns. While the strike spread in Manchester, workers in Ashton, Oldham and Hyde sent delegates to neighbouring settlements to turn out the mills. Oldham workers joined the movement on 9 August and within a day or two, groups of people claimed to be in the thousands, marched from Ashton, Hyde and Oldham and stopped the factories in Stockport, Macclesfield and Rochdale. Day by day, the wave of strikes spread to the north and west as far as Colne, Blackburn and Preston. The labour force of many mills turned out immediately when approached by wandering workers. A local meeting at which strikers generally asked for a return to the wage levels of 1840 and a ten hour day and regularly praised or adopted the Charter then followed.[16]

The proselytising impulse continued through the middle of August as Bolton workers marched on Wigan, Rochdalers visited Bacup and Todmorden, and crowds from Haslingden converged on Accrington. Resistance to the strike surfaced briefly in Bolton, Blackburn and Preston, partly as a result of clashes between the military and workers from other towns and partly from the fights of strikers with labourers at still functioning mills. Riots and arrests took place in the larger cities, primarily in Manchester, Stockport, Burnley, Bolton, Preston and Blackburn. Yet the strike worked its way out peacefully in most places, even when objections to the stoppage by employers or local workers led to the removal of boiler plugs.[17]

The pattern of development of the plug strikes was similar in Yorkshire and Leicestershire. The strikes began in medium-sized towns, then spread to the largest city and to the villages and small towns. The plug strikes in Yorkshire began in Halifax on 13 August, triggered by the arrival of Lancashire turnouts from across the Pennines. About 3,000 Saddleworth workers also marched on Huddersfield and stopped the mills. On the next day, crowds met in Bradford and Todmorden to support the Charter and then marched to Halifax where they clashed with both cavalry and special constables, eventually retreating in some disorder. Crowds assembled in Bradford on 15 August, vowing not to work again until the Charter was enacted. In the next few days, plugs were drawn at mills in and around Greetland, Elland and Brighouse and throughout the Huddersfield district. Riots took place in Salter Hebble and were followed by the exodus of crowds into the surrounding towns to spread the strike. The movement reached Leeds only on 17 August, when a band of strikers from Bradford reached the town after visiting a host of villages to the west of the city. Later on 17 August, Leeds workers pulled the plugs of several flax mill boilers and got into small fights with the military at several places throughout the town, but the city was quiet on 18 August, and work soon resumed.[18]

In the East Midlands, the plug strikes were a comparatively mild affair. Begun in Leicestershire by workers at the Snibston and Whitwick collieries who struck because of wage reductions and the example of Staffordshire miners, the strike soon spread to Leicester (where about 1000 glove hands stopped work) and then was taken up in Shepshed and Loughborough. The few Leicester mill workers refused to strike, but the town was the site for several days of parades and Chartist meetings. Events in Loughborough and Shepshed were more turbulent. There the combination of rallies, Chartist songs and slogans, and stone throwing triggered small clashes with the military.[19]

The plug strikes got little support in Nottinghamshire. Several meetings took place in the Nottingham market place and on nearby hills between 19 August and 23 August. Although deputations visited factories in the town to encourage strikes, little seems to have resulted, and magistrates easily dispersed the small street crowds with cavalry units. The final episode in the county took place on 23 August when over a thousand people from small towns near Nottingham converged on the city; 300 were promptly arrested by the military, who met them at Mapperley Hill.[20]

Several general points can be made about the incidence of this complex series of events. The important role played by medium-sized and small towns should be stressed. Miners from small settlements in Staffordshire initiated the strike wave. Then Stalybridge, Ashton and Hyde residents propagated the strikes in southern Lancashire and Cheshire, while in Yorkshire, the Halifax and Dewsbury populations were particularly active. Workers in towns having between 10,000 and 25,000 people acted as the leaders of the movement in the textile regions. The strikes were essentially imported into Manchester and

Leeds several days after the movement had begun elsewhere, and residents of the largest cities played little part in spreading the strikes. In Leicestershire, miners began the strikes, which got only a limited response in the county town. Moreover, the size of the crowds reported in the medium- and small-sized towns such as Ashton, Hyde, Heywood and Chorley, as well as the ease with which total work stoppages were effected in the small industrial towns, make it likely that participation in the strikes was higher in places below the top ranks of the urban hierarchy. Certainly in Leicestershire, the colliery population and the knitters of Shepshed and Loughborough were more involved in the strikes than Leicester workers.

To be sure, regional capitals and county towns played a role in the strike wave. Manchester, Leicester and Nottingham functioned as central places through which and to which information was transmitted; delegates from these towns travelled regularly to the surrounding districts. The Manchester conference of trade delegates is the most obvious example of this use of a regional capital as a central meeting place.

The smallest urban places, towns with under 5,000 residents such as Elland or Brighouse in Yorkshire and Lees or Mossley in Lancashire, were drawn into the protest movement by crowds from medium-sized towns such as Ashton or Halifax. While ready to strike, their workers were less active in spreading the movement than groups from towns higher on the local urban hierarchy. Both the largest and the smallest settlements seem in general to have been less militant than the populations of cities having between 10,000 and 25,000 people. This same group of towns, places such as Oldham, Ashton, Burnley, Bury and Stockport, were both centres for diffusion of the strikes and areas where all sorts of collective activities by workers were relatively frequent in 1842. Brian Brown argues that the towns from which strikes spread had the most highly mobilised workers throughout 1842. They had, on the average, populations twice as active in the Chartist movement and in other collective activities as residents of other Lancashire parishes.[21]

A similar relationship between medium-sized towns and participation in the Chartist movement has been noted by Asa Briggs. He argues that the big cities and regional capitals, such as Birmingham and Manchester, were 'less active' than smaller places in the neighbouring textile and metal-working areas. In his opinion, 'Leeds was quieter than Halifax.'[22] There were more attempts at political co-operation in the largest towns, as well as a wider variety of reform groups to attract and deflect attention from the Chartists who found their main strength in new, expanding, single industry towns and centres of collapsing industry. And it was the small settlements in the East Midlands which threatened the most public conflict. Military commanders and magistrates in the 1840s, while regularly called into Leicester and Nottingham to patrol the streets, generally found the population quiet and well behaved, despite the active Chartist movements in these places. They judged that the people of the small industrial towns and villages were much more menacing. Shepshed workers were 'always fruitful in mischief' wrote the Duke of Rutland to the Home Office in August of 1842, as he described his efforts to keep the peace in the county.[23]

Let us look now at the incidence of strikes in the 1890s when the publications of the Board of Trade began to list all work stoppages taking place in the United Kingdom.[24] All of the strikes (N = 1624) reported to the Labour Correspondent during the years 1889 to 1891 and 1899 to 1901 for the counties of Lancashire, Yorkshire, Leicestershire and Nottinghamshire have been divided into five groups according to the population in 1891 or 1901 of the borough, urban district or civil parish in which they took place. (See Table 3.2.) By dividing the total number of strikes in each category by the total population in 1891 or 1901 of all settlements of that size in Lancashire, in Yorkshire, and in the East Midlands, I have calculated a strike rate for each type of settlement. (See Table 3.3.)

During the 1890s, small- and medium-sized towns, those having between 2,000 and 20,000 and 20,000 and 100,000 people, generally had higher strike rates than either the largest cities (over 300,000) or even those with more than 100,000 people. Although strikes were predominantly urban phenomena, the biggest towns were not the most strike prone. While in any given year, Leeds, Sheffield or Manchester had a larger absolute number of strikes than Accrington, Barnsley or Huddersfield, the population of the medium and small northern textile towns in the late nineteenth century had a greater propensity to strike. In the East Midlands, where all workers struck less frequently than in Lancashire and Yorkshire and where there were no medium-sized cities according to my definitions, workers in the county towns and small towns struck at approximately the same low rate. Greater size brought no increase in militancy. Also note in Table 3.2 the low occurrence of strikes in rural areas. Inhabitants of industrial villages throughout the north of England and the East Midlands were willing to use the strike as a weapon in their conflicts with employers but did so less frequently than urban workers.

What differences are there in the size of strikes in large, medium and small towns? If big city strikes regularly involved many more

Table 3.2: Strikes per 100,000 Population in Urban and Rural Areas, 1899-1891, 1899-1901

County	300,000+	City Population 100,000–300,000	20,000–100,000	2,000–20,000	under 2,000
Lancashire N = 847	9.1	26.2	26.7	33.1	8.9
Yorkshire N = 676	20.2	20.0	35.9	21.1	4.3
Leicestershire & Nottinghamshire N = 101	–	13.1	–	13.2	9.3
TOTAL	13.6	21.0	30.6	24.8	7.8

Table 3.3: Number of Strikers per 100,000 Population in Urban and Rural Areas

County	300,000+	City Population 100,000–300,000	20,000–100,000	2,000–20,000	under 2,000
Lancashire					
1889-1891	3300	2712	3051	5002	2546
1899-1901	345	830	1450	1089	1347
Yorkshire					
1889-1891	2551	4338	5608	2656	250
1899-1901	465	593	1947	810	274
Leicestershire & Nottinghamshire					
1889-1891	–	1221	–	6937	1418
1899-1901	–	578	–	518	906

workers than those in small towns, my argument about comparative levels of militancy collapses. Here the evidence is less clear, but a general pattern emerges in my figures of larger strikes at the middle levels of the urban hierarchy. This tendency was strongest in years of low to average strike activity, represented here by 1899 to 1901. A larger number of workers participated generally in strikes in towns of between 2,000 and 20,000 and 20,000 to 100,000 people than in the county towns and regional capitals. Cities of between 100,000 and 300,000 population show a mixed pattern, but in years of low strike activity, they too had smaller strikes than places lower on the urban hierarchy. During strike waves, the average number of strikers per strike rose markedly in settlements of every size, but except in one case, the largest cities did not have the largest strikes. The one real exception to the relationship I have outlined between strike sizes and city populations is the rate for Lancashire cities of over 300,000 people in 1889 to 1891. This figure is almost exclusively a reflection of one strike involving 20,000 workers, that took place on the Liverpool and Birkenhead docks in 1890. Unlike textile and clothing operatives, dockers could mount enormous strikes during a period of intense mobilisation. Only miners demonstrated a similar ability in the 1890s. Strike sizes clearly vary according to the industry involved, but they also vary with the size of the community in which they take place. In England, the big cities were *not* for the most part the settings for the largest strikes. Their populations were less willing and able to strike than residents of towns with fewer than 100,000 people.

How can the relationship I have outlined between city size and levels of conflict be explained? I will offer a structural argument based upon the nature of authority, politics and labour relations at several levels of the English urban hierarchy during the nineteenth century. Whatever a town's industrial base or social structure, there were systematic differences in organisation according to city size that affected patterns of labour relations, collective behaviour, and political consciousness. To be sure, these differences changed between the 1840s and the 1890s, but in both periods the institutional structure and administration of large and small towns varied considerably in ways that affected local conflicts of many sorts.

During the 1830s and 1840s, the structure of authority in regional capitals, county towns and most industrial cities with populations of more than 40,000 was qualitatively different from that of their smaller neighbours. This resulted from the limited spread during the early years of Victoria's reign of both municipal incorporation and city police forces. The Municipal Corporation Act granted borough status to 178 towns, giving their residents extensive political rights. Householders who paid their rates and met a year's residency requirement could vote in the yearly elections for local officials. While few citizens met the property requirements which limited candidacies for alderman and town councillor, the nature of the borough franchise, the large number of minor offices, and the general right to attend vestry meetings brought the opportunity for political participation to a wide section of the male population. In addition, the right of larger towns to elect members of Parliament brought election campaigns and polling which attracted widespread attention in many boroughs.[25] Derek Fraser, speaking of incorporated towns, has remarked that 'political passion was a persistent although not continuous feature' of local administration and elections during Victoria's reign.[26] Opportunities for either political activity or political fervour were markedly less in the non-incorporated towns administered by parochial or township authorities, court leets, Boards of Guardians, and perhaps simply an improvement commission.

In Lancashire, Yorkshire and the East Midlands, incorporated status was largely reserved in the 1830s for the county towns, regional capitals and major ports (Leeds, York, Hull, Manchester, Liverpool, Preston, Leicester and Nottingham) and a few other places (Wigan, Bolton and Newark). In the 1840s only seven other cities in these regions were incorporated, most having over 40,000 people.[27] In northern manufacturing areas, the status of municipal borough was almost exclusively limited to towns at the top levels of the urban hierarchy during the mid-nineteenth century.

Just as the boroughs had a distinctive administrative structure that produced a more active political life during the first half of the nineteenth century, the structures of authority in incorporated towns differentiated them from other urban places. The Municipal Corporations Act gave boroughs the right to administer justice in a local civil and criminal court and also to appoint and to supervise a police force. As a result, the incorporated towns had several resident magistrates, and in the north of England and the East Midlands, boroughs with more than 40,000 residents had a local police by 1850.[28] Yet few of the medium-sized towns, which were the most militant places during the plug strikes, had either a group of resident magistrates or police by 1842. Instead, the administration of justice and decisions concerning riots and rioters often fell to outsiders, chiefly landowners and gentry, who were neither the employers nor the elected representatives of the population they controlled.[29] Moreover, during the 1840s, the magistrates had to rely chiefly on the yeomanry and the army. There were no rural police in the West Riding in the 1840s; Leicestershire and Nottingham's rural forces were quite small at this time, and in Lancashire in 1842, about 500 constables were divided among sixteen different areas outside of Manchester. Liverpool and Manchester each had over 300 constables, but forces in the four other towns that had established new police units were tiny. Fewer than ten men were so employed in the late 1830s by the boroughs of Lancaster, Preston and Wigan. Although the Bolton constabulary was larger, it was first organised in 1842.[30] As a result, the patrolling of the streets and the control of crowds in non-incorporated towns was carried out by outsiders who were generally disliked and probably less tolerant of an urban crowd than a local police force would have been. Certainly in Leicester during the strikes of the 1830s and 1840s and the Chartist agitation, the familiarity of city officials with the framework knitters, and workers' recognition of them and usually their authority, meant that demonstrations and conflicts were carried out peacefully. Moreover, strikes were regularly averted by the intervention of town officials who mediated in an informal way disputes between the knitters and their employers.

The differences outlined between the incorporated and non-incorporated towns diminished after 1850. In any case, thirteen more cities in Lancashire, Yorkshire and the East Midlands received borough status between 1850 and 1880; by 1890, most towns of more than 20,000 people in these counties were incorporated, and smaller settlements had more complex forms of government to absorb political energies as well as better police protection.[31] While the political life of large towns remained more sophisticated and more active than that of small towns, the difference in this regard was less marked in 1890 than in 1840. Other institutional structures emerged, however, by the end of the 1890s to perpetuate differences between towns of various sizes.

Relations between workers and their employers in the later nineteenth century were mediated by a series of organisations which influenced the procedures of collective bargaining and the use of the strike. These associations — trades unions, trade councils, employers' organisations and boards of conciliation — were widespread in the north and Midlands. Yet they were both stronger and better represented at the top ranks than at the bottom of the urban hierarchy. Their incidence and diffusion illustrate the leading role played in labour relations by citizens of the largest towns.

Unionisation in the hosiery, lace, cotton and various branches of the clothing trades began in the county towns and regional capitals of the Midlands and Lancashire. Organisations among framework knitters and lace workers in the period 1800 to 1859 originated, for the most part, in Leicester and Nottingham, and most of their members resided in the county towns, despite the wide scattering of hosiery production throughout the East Midlands. Each county tended to have its own organisations which used the central town as a meeting place. Leicester and Nottingham price lists were the standards either to be adhered to or to be undercut for competitive advantage, and city workers regularly attempted to enforce their lists outside the town. The marketing and entrepreneurial roles of Leicester and Nottingham employers were paralleled by the attempted leadership of the hosiery labour force by workers from the county towns.[32]

In the cotton industry, the first trade societies appeared in Manchester, Stockport and Oldham in the early 1790s. The Manchester union became the centre for a county-wide federation in 1810, in part by underwriting and organising a major strike to bring county wage rates up to the Manchester level. Manchester spinners also led the movement for a general union in 1826 and initiated the National Association for the Protection of Labour in 1830. Early unions among the power loom weavers centred on the towns just below Manchester in the Lancashire urban hierarchy, in Oldham and in Preston, while Bolton workers assumed the leadership of the Lancashire Spinners Federation in the early 1840s.[33]

During the second half of the century, the primary role played by big city workers in organising their fellows continued. The three main branches of the machine-made lace trade formed separate craft societies in 1851 centred on Nottingham: they amalgamated in 1874. By the 1860s they claimed the membership of virtually all Nottingham males employed in the industry, but they admitted that the union was weak everywhere else. Almost all unions for female lace workers and those in allied crafts existed only in the county town. Nottingham unionists regularly tried to organise branches in places such as Long Eaton, Bulwell and Beeston, but these lodges when created were weak and regularly collapsed. Some were established as late as 1900.[34]

Midland hosiery unions were similarly centred on Leicester and on Nottingham. The Amalgamated Hosiery Union, organised in 1885, had its strongest branches in the county towns, despite the regular exodus of firms to country districts during the last quarter of the nineteenth century. In Leicestershire, hosiery unions in towns such as Hinckley, Loughborough and Earl Shilton came comparatively late, and members had to strike vigorously and repeatedly in the early 1890s to gain recognition by employers who earlier had broken several unions by firing members.[35]

Lancashire cotton unions continued in the middle and later nineteenth century to be centred on the largest cities. Manchester workers formed a general union of power loom weavers in 1840, and Blackburn weavers organised branches of their unions in neighbouring towns during the 1850s. An early spinners' amalgamation, the Association of Operative Cotton Spinners, Twiners, and Self-Acting Minders was based in Bolton; its most powerful members were the Manchester, Oldham and Bolton societies. Although this organisation collapsed in the late 1840s, it was succeeded by a new spinners' amalgamated union, which drew its main strength from Bolton and Oldham. Moreover, the Oldham union took the lead in labour affairs in its district and eventually broke away from the amalgamation to form a separate district federation in 1880. Similarly, several of the amalgamated unions in the woollen industry were centred on the bigger towns like Huddersfield and Bradford. Both the centrality of the larger cities and the greater size and wealth of their unions made their organisations the natural leaders in efforts to co-ordinate local societies.[36] But whatever the explanation, workers in the bigger cities were instrumental in creating a regional labour consciousness and in spreading the impulse to organise.

The largest towns were also the places where co-operation among workers in different industries was most advanced. Trades Councils, city-wide organisations of union officials who acted as a local pressure group for labour interests, appeared first at the top ranks of the English urban hierarchy and spread to other large and then medium-sized towns. The earliest such group was organised in Liverpool in 1848; it was followed in the late 1850s and early 1860s by similar associations in London, Leeds, Manchester, Nottingham, Edinburgh, Glasgow and Sheffield. Shortly thereafter, workers in a variety of northern and Midland towns — Birmingham and Oldham among them — also organised local councils. During the 1870s and 1880s, trades councils were to be found almost exclusively in the larger incorporated towns, but by the 1890s, towns with fewer than 50,000 people such as Ashton or Dewsbury, had acquired similar groups. The councils, while having little money or power, provided organising energy for the entry of workers into local politics and for extending trade union standards. Most engaged in successful campaigns in the 1890s to get city authorities to adopt fair wages clauses in all town contracts, and their regular efforts to elect unionists to city councils, Boards of Guardians, and school boards produced a scattering of working-class officials in the boroughs. They also acted as organisers of the unskilled in towns as disparate as Barnsley, Derby, Sheffield, Walsall and Halifax. Moreover, in a period when national negotiating machinery for labour disputes was in its infancy, the councils sponsored town boards of conciliation. By the early 1890s, city arbitration boards, generally jointly organised by trades councils and chambers of commerce, had appeared in Leeds, Bradford, Halifax, Leicester, Dudley, Derby and Wolverhampton.[37]

Activities of the Bolton trades council during the 1870s and 1880s illustrate the kinds of small successes that even a new group with a limited membership could have. Strikes were regularly reported to the council, which sometimes intervened to offer compromises or to organise boycotts and blacklists of offending firms. The council's complaints of Factory Act violations and willingness to pay for an independent union investigator helped to produce the appointment of two working-class inspectors in 1880. They organised public meetings of protest on sweated labour and cleverly raised complaints at election time about employers who were running for local office; not surprisingly, grievances were speedily rectified. Their secretary was elected to the Bolton School Board in 1880.[38]

The organisation of city workers into unions and trades councils was paralleled by the banding together of urban employers into Chambers of Commerce and specialised trade associations. In the second half of the nineteenth century, the former organisations were widespread in the incorporated towns, while employers' groups in the textile and clothing trades appeared in the large cities that served as marketing centres and major sites of production. Manchester employers organised a commercial society as early as 1794, while the master spinners there acted collectively during many labour disputes of the early nineteenth century. Blackburn and Preston employers had formal associations by the early 1850s, and the Oldham master spinners banded together by the early 1860s. Employers' federations in cotton textiles were substantially enlarged by the establishment in 1891 of the Federation of Master Cotton Spinners. In contrast, employers in the wool trade remained unorganised except in individual chambers of commerce.[39] Leicester hosiers used the Chamber of Commerce as their organisation during much of the nineteenth century. In addition, employers in the mining, building, tailoring and metallurgical industries were widely organised into local federations.[40]

Workers and employers groups during the last quarter of the nineteenth century spread the impulse to arbitrate and to mediate conflicts. By 1892, 64 trade boards had been created by industries and by localities to resolve industrial disputes. These efforts were concentrated at the upper ranks of the urban hierarchy. The staple trades of Leicester and Nottingham had working boards of conciliation during much of the period from 1860 to the early 1890s, while Leeds, Bradford and Halifax had city organisations to mediate strikes. There were also boards of conciliation in the boot and shoe, mining and building trades in several northern and Midland towns.[41] Throughout the cotton industry, standing committees of employers' associations and unions were called in to reconcile all serious strikes and to intervene when local problems could not be resolved. Yet this machinery operated only where mill owners had joined the employers' groups, and both the masters and workers were organised extensively and effectively at the top of the urban hierarchy. Most of the disputes that broke out during the late 1880s and 1890s allegedly arose in firms without the negotiating machinery developed by unions and employers' groups.[42]

The working procedures and dominant spirit of these boards of conciliation were reflected in the comments of witnesses before the 1892 Royal Commission on Labour, people who either were members of the boards or regularly dealt with them. Preston workers with a grievance were said to complain automatically to an officer of the Cotton Operatives Society. He then met with the secretary of the employers' federation to end the grievance. Nine cases in ten were said to be resolved by joint discussions. In Oldham, employers were sent letters notifying them of complaints and, later, would be visited by a union deputation. The employers' association could be brought in as well if all else failed. Union officials claimed that they and the owners met in a conciliatory spirit. A Bury employer, Mr Noble, described the master spinners' attitude to the unions, stressing the 'closer connection and feeling' that had come into existence by 1892. He thought that employers could discuss issues more intelligently with union leaders than with their men, and that more frequent association with union officials brought better understanding. He added: 'If the employers would cultivate a closer relationship with the officials of the associations, it would be the means of preventing many strikes.'[43] While the importance of unions, union officials, trades councils and employers' federations to the ordinary worker and employer may be disputed, these groups and their leaders were clearly in charge of the negotiating machinery in a variety of industries in the 1890s, and they put a great deal of energy into avoiding strikes.

It is also important to note that in the cities, many leading employers and unionists had a variety of complex political interests to absorb time and energy. Middle-class employers entered and sometimes stood for Parliament. For union officials, placing their own men in city government was a matter of great importance, especially during the 1880s and 1890s. In consequence, parties to all sides in labour disputes were forced to conciliate each other, both to gain votes and to prove their respectability. The intensification of conflict was a strategy only rarely adopted even by the most militant workers. The early working-class Socialists on West Riding trades councils and in affiliated clubs of the Independent Labour Party quickly became involved in the contests for urban office and had to keep a variety of political and industrial interests in balance.

Two rather different relationships emerge therefore between urban structures and levels of industrial conflict in England in the nineteenth century. Strikes were more frequent and strikers more numerous among the populations of medium-sized towns than of small towns or rural areas. In the regional and county capitals and in the largest manufacturing cities, there were by 1840 complex political and industrial organisations, which engaged workers' attention but dampened their propensity to strike. Both the labour consciousness and the political engagement of workers could reach sophisticated levels in such places, but these attitudes did not lead to any great willingness to interrupt work. Militancy took other forms. Towns and un-incorporated settlements fostered a dissimilar pattern of labour relationships. There, workers had fewer independent outlets for political energies than in cities, and they were less likely to be organised and to have established bargaining procedures. As a result, labour disputes more readily led to strikes and to small-scale explosions of conflict. Not only deference but defiance marked the contacts of worker and employer in small and medium-sized factory towns.

The second dynamic influencing labour conflict concerns the spread of information and of organisation. Waves of change reached outward from major urban centres and proceeded down a region's urban hierarchy. This dynamic affected labour politics as well as technology and economic affairs. Workers in the biggest cities played leading roles in regional labour movements. Particularly in the East Midlands, much of the stimulus for radical or socialist activity came from citizens of the county town. The impetus for extending workers' political awareness and reference group beyond a town boundary often came from contacts with people from higher-order urban places. The urban hierarchy was the path along which labour consciousness was diffused. Greater militancy and self awareness did not necessarily produce more strikes, however. The institutions that channelled conflicts and mediated between workers and employers spread most rapidly in the largest towns and were less advanced in smaller places. The quality of labour relations was different in large and in small settlements because the structure of cities helped to channel industrial conflicts into more subtle forms.

Notes

1. Friedrich Engels, *The Condition of the Working Class in England*, W.O. Henderson and W.H. Chaloner (eds.) (Oxford, 1958), p.31.
2. See, for example, Wilhelm Heinrich Riehl, *Land und Leute* (Tübingen, 1854).
3. Edward Shorter and Charles Tilly, *Strikes in France, 1830-1968* (Cambridge, 1974), p.275.
4. Gaston V. Rimlinger, 'International Differences in the Strike Propensity of Coal Miners: Experience in Four Countries', *Industrial and Labor Relations Review*, XII (1959), pp.393-4.
5. Engels, *The Condition of the Working Class*, p.254.
6. K.G.J.C. Knowles, *Strikes – A Study in Industrial Conflict* (Oxford, 1952), pp.212-19.
7. Shorter and Tilly, *Strikes in France*, p.343.
8. James E. Cronin, 'Theories of Strikes: Why Can't They Explain the British Experience?', *Journal of Social History*, vol. 12, no. 2, (Winter, 1978), p.194.
9. Knowles, *Strikes*, pp.162-3, 197, 203; James E. Cronin, *Industrial Conflict in Modern Britain* (London, 1979).
10. Charles Tilly and R.A. Schweitzer are well launched into a study of public events in Britain which involved at least ten people making a claim against others between 1828 and 1834. They will eventually chart strikes, as well as riots, public meetings and demonstrations. Charles Tilly and R.A. Schweitzer, 'Enumeration and Coding Contentious Gatherings in Nineteenth-Century Britain', Center for Research on Social Organization, Working Paper no. 210 (Ann Arbor, 1980).
11. Donald Reed, *The English Provinces, 1760-1960: A Study in Influence* (London, 1964), p.35.
12. John Foster, *Class Struggle and the Industrial Revolution: Early Industrial Capitalism in Three English Towns* (London, 1974), p.121.
13. Patrick Joyce, *Work, Society and Politics: The Culture of the Factory in Later Victorian England* (Brighton, 1980), p.232.
14. Knowles, *Strikes*, p.197.
15. F.C. Mather, 'The General Strike of 1842: A Study in Leadership, Organization and the Threat of Revolution during the Plug Plot Disturbance',

in R. Quinault and J. Stevenson (eds.), *Popular Protest and Public Order: Six Studies in British History, 1790-1820* (London, 1974), p.116.

16. A.G. Rose, 'The Plug Riots of 1842 in Lancashire and Cheshire', *Transactions of the Lancashire and Cheshire Antiquarian Society*, vol. LXVII (1957), pp.88-96, 106; Mather, 'The General Strike of 1842', pp.124-7; Home Office, 45/265, 268, 269.

17. Rose, pp.100-7; Home Office, 45/249.

18. Frank Peel, *The Risings of the Luddites, Chartists, and Plug Drawers*, 4th edn. (London, 1968), pp.330-42; Home Office 45/264.

19. Home Office, 45/250.

20. Home Office, 45/254.

21. Brian R. Brown, 'Lancashire Chartism and the Mass Strike of 1842: The Political Economy of Working Class Contention', Center for Research on Social Organization, Working Papers no. 203 (Ann Arbor, 1979), p.38.

22. Asa Briggs (ed.), *Chartist Studies* (London, 1959), p.3.

23. Home Office, 45/250.

24. Labour Correspondent of the Board of Trade, 'Report on Strikes and Lockouts', *Parliamentary Papers* 1890, LXVIII, 480-533; *Parliamentary Papers* 1890-1891, LXXVIII, 743-804; *Parliamentary Papers* 1894, LXXXIII, pt. 1, 594-660; *The Labour Gazette*, 'Monthly Lists of Trade Disputes', 1899-1902.

25. J.R. Somers Vine, *English Municipal Institutions, their Growth and Development from 1835 to 1879 statistically illustrated* (London, 1879), pp.11, 14-15.

26. Derek Fraser, *Urban Politics in Victorian England: The Structure of Politics in Victorian England* (Leicester, 1976), p.10.

27. Vine, *English Municipal Institutions*, pp.52-59, 60-62.

28. 'Abstract of a Return . . . of several cities and boroughs of Great Britain, their population respectively, the number of police, etc., *Parliamentary Papers* 1854 (C. 345), LIII, 509.

29. R. Quinault, 'The Warwickshire County Magistracy and Public Order, c.1830-1870', in Quinault and Stevenson, *Popular Protest and Public Order*, pp.187-92.

30. 'Abstract of a Return showing the Number of the Constabulary Force in each County or Division of a County in England and Wales', *Parliamentary Papers* 1847, XLVII, 632-9; E.C. Midwinter, *Social Administration in Lancashire, 1830-1860* (Manchester, 1969), p.141.

31. Vine, *English Municipal Institutions*, pp.60-2; *The Census of England and Wales for 1891, Parliamentary Papers* 1893-1894 (C. 6948), CIV, pp.160-75.

32. Richard Gurnham, *Two Hundred Years: The Hosiery Unions, 1776-1976* (Leicester, 1976), pp.6-16; Norman H. Cuthbert, *The Lace Makers' Society: a Study of Trade Unionism in the British Lace Industry, 1760-1960* (Nottingham, 1960), pp.10-19.

33. H.A. Turner, *Trade Union Growth, Structure and Policy: A Comparative Study of the Cotton Unions* (London, 1962), pp.62-3, 66-7, 387-8.

34. Cuthbert, *The Lace Makers' Society*, pp.31-2, 48, 54.

35. Gurnham, *Two Hundred Years*, pp.26-8, 32-3, 50-6; Royal Commission on Labour, Minutes of Evidence, Group C. vol. 1, *Parliamentary Papers* 1892 (C. 6708-III) XXXIV, p.63.

36. Turner, *Trade Union Growth*, pp.115-17, 122, 129-32, 144-6; Royal Commission on Labour, Minutes of Evidence, Group C, vol. 1, p.18.

37. Webb Trade Union Collection, Series E., A IV, British Library of Political and Economic Science.

38. Ibid. A IV, 41-49

39. Turner, *Trade Union Growth*, pp.384, 388-9, 391.

40. Labour Correspondent of the Board of Trade, 'Report on the Strikes

and Lockouts of 1894', *Parliamentary Papers* 1895, XCII, p.46.
    41. Ibid., p.260.
    42. Royal Commission on Labour, Minutes of Evidence, Group C, vol. II, *Parliamentary Papers* 1892 (C. 6795-III), XXXVI – part III, pp.51-7.
    43. Ibid., p.54.

4 1910-1914 RECONSIDERED

Joe White

Over the past 70 years interpretations of the 'Labour Unrest' of 1910-14 in Britain have come full circle. Contemporaries, who themselves coined the phrase, had no doubts that they were living through an unprecedented upsurge by working people, the likes of which had not been seen in living memory. Their assessment received literary expression in George Dangerfield's *The Strange Death of Liberal England.* [1] Dangerfield brought to bear a *sui generis* mix of Marxism and Freudianism, and in a powerful and sustained narrative wove together the themes of a Syndicalist-inspired workers' revolt, Tory revolt and women's revolt which all were aimed against the decencies of a tragically outmoded liberalism and Liberal Party. The fact that the book appeared in 1935 when Ramsay MacDonald was the 'socialist' prime minister in a thinly-disguised Conservative government and European liberalism and the British Liberal Party were in palpable decay lent added plausibility to his overarching thesis that the years 1910-14 were the seedbed for much of the intervening quarter century.

By the 1950s and 60s the historiographical mood had altered considerably. While not denying that there was *something* to be explained, both E.H. Phelps Brown and Henry Pelling attempted to minimise the ferment and to deny outright that British society before the war was on the verge of a general crisis. [2] Emphases varied. Phelps Brown saw the militancy of workers as mainly confined to unskilled workers, coalminers and railwaymen, all of whose chief grievance was stagnating real wages. Pelling was equally satisfied with a one-cause answer: a high level of employment. According to him, Syndicalists were thin on the ground and were unsuccessful in their aims in both the short and long run. Further, there were no links between the three 'revolts'. Just as the 1930s appear to have shaped Dangerfield's perspectives, one cannot help thinking that the advent and consolidation of the welfare state and the very moderate (but in electoral terms not unsuccessful) Labour Party and official trade union leadership influenced the later accounts. That is, since the post-World War II society that came into being seemed so utterly removed from the turbulence of 1910-14, it therefore could not have been all that important, or indeed, all that turbulent to begin with.

The last decade or so has seen a quickening pace of scholarship, with a renewed emphasis on the extent of the unrest and its structural determinants. There has been a re-appreciation of syndicalism as well, though, as befits a polycentristic age, interpretations have been varied and do not always point to the same conclusions. Peter Stearns, for example, quietly pleads *nolo contendere* to the charge of downplaying the influence of politics and ideology in working-class industrial life.[3] He sees 'protest' — whose definition he does not elaborate — between the years 1890-1914 as failing to come to grips with what was really bothering many working people, namely, deteriorating and dehumanising working conditions associated with the loss of on-the-job autonomy. He attributes this failure to move frontally on the most important grievance of all to deep divisions within the working class and to the related possibility that for a sizeable minority of workers the massive changes that were taking place in work were perceived and experienced as beneficial, at least in the short and medium run. But there was an element of tragedy, as he sees it, because an historic opportunity was missed, and because the problem of work and its discontents was to return with a vengeance in the late 1960s.

If, for Stearns, syndicalism was neither here nor there, Bob Holton argues the case for syndicalism's relevance and influence in Britain between 1900 and 1914, and is able to do so by making a distinction between 'the activity of committed supporters aligned with syndicalist organisations,' which he admits was limited, and 'aggressive direct action which spontaneously challenged the authority of employers and state,' which was quite widespread. Richard Price apparently agrees. In *Masters, Unions and Men*, he portrays syndicalism as the ideological correlate of a workers' offensive against official trade union leaderships irrevocably integrated into an industrial relations system and all that it implied: economism, social control and discipline, adding up to a structural divorce between systemic imperatives and the workers' historic and contemporaneous quest for autonomy. The struggle for job autonomy, in Price's account, militantly reasserted itself between 1910 and 1914, most notably in the building trades, but elsewhere as well. Where Stearns sees a missed opportunity, Price sees clear-headed and bold confrontation.[5]

Of the two broad interpretations — which can be called the minimising and the maximising view — we take our stand with the latter. If the recent research has established anything, it has established that in the years before World War I the challenge of workers indeed represented a threat to the industrial *status quo*. In other words this chapter is not intended as a continuation of an old polemic. What it is about is the shape and fit of the pieces. What aspects of the political economy of the pre-World War I years set the stage for the unrest? How is the massive wave of strikes best grouped and analysed? What theory best explains the stance of the trade unions toward their overt opponents and toward their own members? To what extent, and in what ways, and for what reasons did the state enter the conflict? Finally, since politics and ideologies do count (or else one would be hard put to explain why people have so much trouble kicking the habit of thinking and acting in these terms) we ask, why Syndicalism and not something else? In short, the aim is not to tell (or retell) a story, but to fashion and begin to assemble the elements needed for a new synthesis.

It is well known that workers' consciousness and behaviour cannot be 'read off' from general economic conditions. On the other hand, it must be insisted that neither workers nor anyone else inhabit a historic universe in which anything and everything is possible at any given period in time. Hence political economy must form the basic framework for analysis, for only within such a framework can the interplay of social relations, economic and technological forces and the institutions and processes of political and class power be properly analysed and described.

Economic historians are agreed that the British economy in the late nineteenth and early twentieth centuries was marked by a reduced rate of economic growth, productivity increases so low as to be virtually stagnant, a marked reluctance to invest in new technologies and new industries (which reluctance feeds back into the lacklustre productivity performance), and, finally, inflation, which while mild compared with the post-Second World War experience, none the less exerted considerable downward pressure upon the course of real wages. Subjectively, the check given to the rise of real income must have been felt all the more strongly since the second half of the nineteenth century as a whole was one of broad improvement for most working people.[6]

To be sure there are important exceptions and qualifications. So real and profound had been Britain's industrial hegemony in the third quarter of the nineteenth century that sheer momentum and the lead built up, if nothing else, enabled many sectors of the economy to compete successfully and even to modernise technologically. In cotton textiles, for example, four looms per weaver for plain cloth was standard for Lancashire, whereas two looms per weaver was still the norm on the Continent.[7] Production and use within the economy of steel and steam power expanded significantly. The introduction and spread of electric power were also considerable.[8] Moreover, as E.J. Hobsbawm showed years ago, trade union power could and did act as a spur to increase productivity, as happened in the gas industry, where the winning of the eight-hour day forced the companies (who because of their position as a natural monopoly were under few pressures to change) to modernise their works. The same also happened in Leeds following the Corporation workers' strike of 1913.[9] However, on balance, it is the reluctance to undertake rapid and decisive technological change that stands out. By 1900, major industries like the railways and steel manufacturing were clearly industrial dinosaurs. No amount of historiographical revisionism can easily efface the bewildered and fascinated looks of British iron and steel masters when they toured American mills. Engineering remained a congeries of unco-ordinated and often undercapitalised industries and sub-industries. In textiles, the introduction of the fully automatic Northrup loom, in very wide use in the United States, was belated and minimal. Characteristically, the first coal-cutting machine to be used in South Wales (from 1870 to 1914 the fastest growing British coalfield) was introduced only in 1914 and was manufactured in America.[10]

The overall sluggishness in productivity — and profit rates — had a direct impact on working people. In the first instance, we find reports of greater speeds, work intensity and workloads that are neatly summed up in Stearns's chapter heading, 'A Frenzied Pace'. It took several forms, depending upon the industry in question: on the railways longer trains and bigger engines manned by the same-sized crews; systematic undermanning of ships as they too grew larger; shorter turnabout times on the docks; speedup in textile mills along with longer machines; deeper and hence more dangerous mines with a new firmness and militancy shown by the employers over the wage bargain, especially for abnormal places; piece-work in engineering along with the beginnings of time and motion studies and the 'speed and feed' system; subcontracting for labour only in the building trades. In this context, if no other, it makes good sense to speak of a 'Second Industrial Revolution', and Stearns is quite right in pointing to 1890-1914 as the years in which the modern version of uninterrupted industrial work under constant discipline and supervision was consolidated.[11]

Along with the speeded up pace of work — and indeed a crucial pre-condition for its success — was the curbing and (where possible the elimination) of union power. The story has been told brilliantly by John Saville of employers' combination and propaganda efforts, the connivance with and support of the 'free labour' movement, frequent resort to the courts culminating in the Taff Vale decision of 1901.[12] Where unions were too strong to be driven off the field altogether, their role could be limited to that of bargaining agent over an increasingly circumscribed and 'economistic' range of issues. Price has shown this to be true for the building unions and for others as well.[13] By 1907, moderation and the acceptance of grievance procedures that fully protected employers' interests and prerogatives were the norm almost everywhere. A final factor that weighed heavily on working people was unemployment. In Britain between 1900 and 1910 workers experienced more unemployment not less. Here Tressell's *Ragged-Trousered Philanthropists* and the statistics of the Board of Trade Labour Department are equally reliable guides.

But having indicated the thrust and direction of both 'impersonal' forces and the employers' counter-offensive, what must be introduced here — because it is a major link in our argument — is the only partial and fitful success of the employers in attaining their own objectives. To put matters theoretically, we are dealing with the first steps in the transformation of the British economy from competitive capitalism to monopoly capitalism. Now the uniqueness of the British experience is not that the transformation failed to occur — by the end of the 1930s it was essentially complete and the British economy was demonstrably as monopolistic as any other in Western capitalism — but the belated and halting first steps and the length of time required to complete the process.

Let us consider, first, the managerial strategy of speed-up to enhance productivity and reduce labour costs per unit of output. Economic and labour historians have discovered that their best efforts — where they were made at all — were probably self-defeating. An extreme example is the cotton industry. There the machinery was lengthened and speeds increased while simultaneously the quality of raw materials supplied to operatives to work up under the new and harsher conditions was purposely allowed to deteriorate, the idea evidently being to save money at both ends. The actual result was interrupted production, as workers had to contend incessantly with yarn breakages and snarls, which in addition to making productivity lower than it could have been, caused intense pressures and anger, which were to explode during the years 1910-14.[14] A similar process seems to have been at work in the coal industry, since the owners were by this time addicted to the policy of developing mines in such a way as to get at the easiest coal first: to take the money and run, as it were. But important as technology and managerial strategies were, there was also by 1900 (at the very latest) the profoundly important matter of *class*. Thus, it is crucially important to bear in mind that, despite the best efforts of the employers' counter-offensive, the power of organised labour at both the official and workplace levels was not uniformly and universally weakened. In building, which followed its own trade cycle, rank-and-file militancy that often took the form of unofficial strikes with a view to enforcing the workers' political and moral economy, continued throughout the decade of the 1890s, though when the recession did come in the first ten years of the twentieth century, it bit deeply enough. Coal, cotton and engineering workers, while kept largely in check, were not defeated either. Here it is significant that that the South Wales miners in 1898 rejected the sliding scale method of wage determination. Secondly, for all the heterogeneity and unevenness of consciousness, even the most cautious historians agree that by the turn of the century it is not just permissible but necessary to begin speaking of the working class in the singular and of a labour movement as opposed to interest. Even in Tressell's 'Muggsborough', Frank Owen's fellow 'philanthropists' know to relax when the overseer isn't looking so as to 'get back a bit of one's own'. The working class in Britain was by no means ethnically homogeneous around 1900 and after, but what stands out here too is the essentially *integrative* capacity of the class. A notable example occurred in south Wales where Spanish miners, who often brought their own labour traditions and socialism with them, became part of the community and union with a minimum of friction and antagonism. Although more study is needed, it would appear that native/Irish antagonism in industrial Lancashire outside Liverpool declined in our period, and in Glasgow, John Wheatley was a major force in winning the Irish workers of Glasgow to socialist politics, having himself been a founder of the Catholic Socialist Society.[15] Thirdly, even in industries informed by extreme managerial discipline and deep sectional divisions, workers' power on the job could develop and flourish. Frank McKenna has shown how the notion of a 'bailiwick' is most useful in understanding how railwaymen came to create and claim their own social and industrial space on the job. This in turn is a first cousin of the craft tradition itself: engineers with their probably apocryphal but revealing chalk circle around their machine into which no agent of management dared to tread, miners with their refusal to work within the sight of management.[16]

Finally, there was politics. While the facile notion of the 'rise of labour' has quite properly been dropped from the vocabulary of labour historians, the election of 1906 all the same was a defeat for the right in Britain and a corresponding victory for the left. Later we shall look more closely at the industrial relations policies of the last Liberal government. The important point here is that, as David Martin has suggested, 'for all their inadequacies, the thirty [Labour] MPs of 1906 were closer than their rivals to the working class; they did not have to try to change their basic character in order to embody proletarian attitudes.'[17] This by no means exhausts the problem: the role of the Labour MPs during the unrest was equivocal in the extreme; and as for the Liberal government, whatever else they were, the members of the cabinet cannot be called pro-labour in any meaningful sense.

A partial summing up is in order. Discovering and 'weighing' the causes of the labour unrest, while raising all manner of technical and methodological questions, can result in a certain kind of academic 'overkill' if pressed too far. The bracing climate of international economic competition — keeping in mind that in the early 1900s exports were generating a larger proportion of the GDP than in earlier years — and the restricted size of the home market, itself reflective of the working class's overwhelming presence in the social structure, meant that the employers had little choice but to put the screws on labour if they were to remain competitive and profitable. But, as we have been arguing, before the war the employers could not apply the full programme of monopoly capital even if as a class they so desired (and there is little evidence that they did), with the result that the measures against labour which they did take probably had the minimum positive effect while at the same time causing a maximum of irritation, resentment and anger. Most important of all was the working class itself, with its growing organisations, its traditions and values. In retrospect, the question is thus not what caused the unrest, and, most emphatically, not which *one* cause, but rather what forms would it take and how powerful would it be and how would it be contained? To these questions we now turn.

The Two Unrests

The historiographical tradition in approaching 1910-14 has been to pose two questions: was the unrest broad or limited with regard to the groups of workers who made it, and secondly, was it revolutionary (or proto-revolutionary) as opposed to being ultimately containable and subject to the blandishments of reform? Except for Stearns, recent labour historians have stressed the breadth of the unrest and in doing so are on firm ground, since workers representing a very broad range of industries, crafts and skills, struck work in unprecedented numbers. However, while it is correct to emphasise the mass scale of conflict, it does not necessarily follow that strikers were homogeneous in their demands, methods and consciousness, which would in fact be rather unlikely, as the greater the numbers and trades, the greater the likelihood that the heterogeneity of the working class should be displayed. We contend that there were in fact two concurrent labour unrests during the years 1910-14. First, one may speak of the upsurge of the hitherto unorganised and unrecognised. Secondly, one may speak of the upsurge of old trade unionists. By this we do not mean strikes by members of the so-called Old Unions as opposed to post-1889 New Unions. Nor are we referring to age. Rather, we have in mind strikes waged by workers who are already members of established and recognised unions, whether 'old' or 'new'. Although there is to be found some empirical overlapping, the justification for this analytical distinction will become clear presently.

The interpretation of 1910-14 as a syndicalist uprising was never made out of whole cloth, and the main reason for its staying power is that workers by the hundreds of thousands who by all reckoning should not have been striking — because they were allegedly incapable of it — were doing so and in the process showing their collective strength and solidarity. It is this element of surprise (as regards both timing and capacity) that gave the dockers', seamen's and railwaymen's strikes of 1911, the West Midlands engineering and metalworkers' strikes of 1913 and the Dublin General Strike their dramatic and menacing appearance.

They shared certain other common characteristics. Because they were not sectional strikes whose grievances and demands were limited to specific employers, parochial matters, or individual firms within an industry, most of them spread like wildfire. Thus the railwaymen's strike began in Bristol on 5 August 1911 as a wildcat, but spread so rapidly that the railway unions had no choice but to declare an official, general (i.e., industry-wide) strike on 18 August.[18] The immediate strike demands around which the leaders of the unions were able to unite the ranks were a two-shilling rise in wages and a reduction in the working week from 60 to 54 hours. Similarly, the Black Country strikes began inauspiciously enough, with the Workers' Union initiating a movement in Birmingham, Smethwick and West Bromwich for a 23-shilling minimum wage. However, the demand for a district-wide universal minimum proved contagious. By June 1913 more than 40,000 men and women were out; and Sir George Askwith was in to negotiate a settlement.[19]

These strikes were also, by British standards, violent. Academic treatments of popular violence tend to be unrewarding exercises due to an apparently incorrigible penchant for viewing violence as a measurable 'thing' done by 'other people'. So we shall be brief and cautious. What stands out is that in addition to attacks on scabs, property was also attacked, most notably during the railwaymen's strike, but also in Hull during the dockers' strike and in several other places. It does not seem to have been the desperate, last-ditch kind of violence that is frequently seen toward the end of unsuccessful strikes and which did occur toward the end of the Cornwall clayminers' strike of 1913-14, and also in Dublin. Instead, it broke out in the early stages. David Smith has advanced the interesting argument that the Tonypandy riots of 1910, which occurred in the middle of the Cambrian Combine strike and consisted of the selective but thorough looting of shops, 'should be seen as evidence of social fracture as much as of industrial dispute,' and was part of a long process of redefinition of self and community by the mid-Rhondda working class, as the certainties of late Victorian artisan respectability were eroded.[20] The effect of the violence on public opinion is, of course, an imponderable, but it does seem to have moved Winston Churchill to view his task in the Liberal cabinet 'more in terms of law and order than industrial relations'.[21]

A final point about these strikes is that they were instances of formidable solidarity. Here, too, the railwaymen stand out. Mass direct action was the direct antithesis to the bureaucratic and utterly divisive job-classification schemes that the railway companies had developed over the years to heights hitherto unachieved in Western capitalism. In Liverpool, the 'previous history of sectarian street fighting between Catholics and Protestants' was transformed into 'resistance by working-class crowds ... based on both occupational unity and residential solidarity.'[22] The Black Country strike was notable for solidarity between men and women workers, and between semi-skilled engineering workers — often with sectional grievances of their own — and the lower-paid labourers. As Richard Hyman remarks, 'Thus the weakest sections gained large advances with the support — and perhaps even, in the short run, at the expense — of their stronger comrades'.[23]

Here a paradox emerges. These strikes were fought by men and women as though they had nothing to lose and were often led by socialists, syndicalists and revolutionaries of one stripe or another. It is doubtful, for example, that public opinion during the Black Country strikes made any overly nice distinctions between the general secretary of the Workers' Union, Charles Duncan, MP for Barrow, who was eminently moderate and patriotic, and Tom Mann, whose advice to strikers busy driving scabs out of the factories was 'to be loyal to their unions and not be too mealy-mouthed over law and order.'[24] At the same time, they were industrial struggles from start to finish, however much the firing of the Hull docks might have looked like the Paris Commune. To this extent the 'conservative' interpretation is correct and those who read history for its lessons ignore this one at their peril. The fact that the goals were the limited and 'traditional' ones of union recognition and a union wage should serve as a sharp reminder that the gap between leaders and led can either be overdrawn, or drawn in the wrong place. In the case of the Workers' Union, which was after all the union whose growth during the years of the unrest outstripped all other unions, an ideological and programmatic gap between the rank and file and the leadership simply did not exist. The same is probably true for most of the new recruits to unionism among the dockers and railwaymen as well, which explains why the success of syndicalist agitation and propaganda then was so limited. That they were industrial struggles for orthodox trade union ends also goes far to explain the ability of the Liberal government to bow to the inevitable when necessary, even when this meant putting pressure on the employers and running the risk of antagonising middle-class voters.

The strikes of the old unionists were different in several respects. They were most prominent in coal, cotton and the building trades, and, after allowance is made for craft and industrial differences, still show a remarkable similarity in terms of grievances and demands. In all three industries we find a dense pattern of small-scale, more often than not unofficial struggles, capped by three major strikes in weaving, coal and the London building industry, all of which were official and led by union bureaucrats. All three were lost.

Stearns has suggested an interpretation of small strikes which, if applied to these industries during the years 1910-14, appears to be perverse and misleading. He argues that they indicated a lack of consciousness on the part of workers, who insisted on casting their grievances in small-scale and personal terms, thereby failing to lay the axe to the root of their real discontents, which in his view was the pace, intensity and division of work itself.[25] This does not strike me as helpful. In Britain at least, these strikes were evidently waged by overwhelmingly unionised workers. This is not surprising, because the confidence and experience needed to strike over immediate and concrete grievances would seem to depend in considerable measure on prior organisation, as Tilly and Shorter have argued. Compare the behaviour of aggrieved unorganised workers, who, if unemployment levels are permissibly low, do not strike but instead quit, which at times can result in astronomical turnover rates. Moreover, there is every reason to suppose that strong organisation and high class consciousness must result in strikes of this sort by broadening the definition of what constitutes a 'legitimate' grievance in the first place and of heightening sensitivity to perishable disputes, i.e., those grievances which if not acted upon at once cannot be acted upon at all.[26]

Turning first to cotton workers, we observe that many of their strikes were aimed at the added pressure of work and reduced pay packets caused by having to work with inferior materials. Spinners and weavers, upon whom deteriorating conditions bore most heavily, were in the lead here. Piecers — assistants to the mule spinners — also struck over promotion and job security, and in this respect resembled unorganised workers, which they in fact were, attempting to form a union of their own in 1913. They are a reminder that the unrest did not run in completely separate channels. Although these earnings- and work-related disputes were endemic, eventuating in the Spinners' withdrawal in 1913 from the long-standing Brooklands Agreement conciliation scheme, they were resolvable up to a point, and no industry-wide stoppages over this particular area of grievances took place.[27]

In coal mining, where the profit/productivity squeeze was much more severe, the tendency was for both sides to raise the stakes. The result was the miners' strike of 1912, with the MFGB's demand for a nationally uniform minimum wage, and the eventual settlement in the form of legislation providing for district minima.[28] The struggle in building, which centred on the employers' ultimatum demanding the banning of all strikes, penalties against strikers, and agreement to work alongside of non-unionists, proved to be the most bitterly fought of all — a five-month long lockout by the London employers.[29] A connecting thread running through all three industries, and extending into engineering as well, was the keen desire of rank and file strikers to rid their trades of non-unionists. This was one issue in the building lockout, and the only issue in the weavers' four-week lockout of December 1911 to January 1912, while in mining scores of local strikes were fought at the pit level to drive out (or bring in) the remaining few non-unionists.

The fact that the unrest encompassed so many old unionists is of the utmost significance. First, by virtue of extending the scope of the unrest, it helped to ensure a greater likelihood of victory all round. Second, the old unionists and not the new were the real carriers of rank-and-file political and industrial militancy. To clinch this point: it was the South Wales miners who produced *The Miners' Next Step*, which remains to this day the finest statement of the case for militant rank-and-file unionism ever produced in Britain. In the Durham coalfield, we find the labour unrest being kicked off in 1910 with the strike against the newly enacted 8-hour day, which for the miners meant three-shift working and the disruption of their home life and recreational time. We also find the revolutionary propaganda of the Socialist Labour Party being spread by George Harvey of Wardley in Co. Durham who, because of it, was made checkweighman by his mates.[30] In north-east Lancashire, wildcat strikes by weavers against non-unionists were organised and led by ILP activists. In the Glasgow district, skilled engineers were disproportionately represented in the ranks of the SLP. Finally, it was the syndicalists in the London building trades who in 1914 led the only major breakaway attempt, with the formation of the Building Workers' Industrial Union.

The revolt of the old unionists opened up a gulf between the rank and file and the activists within the unions on the one hand, and the established leadership on the other. The unofficial local strikes are evidence of this tendency. More striking yet are the form and content of the settlement of the trade-wide disputes. In all three cases, the leadership reached settlements that simply did not have the support of the ranks. In the cotton lockout, the weavers' leadership capitulated — at the urging of Askwith — on the non-unionist question in return for a five per cent rise which probably would have been granted regardless of the strike. The terms of capitulation were not even put to a vote of members. The leadership of the miners could not get away with this and instead had to invent a two-thirds rule in the face of the 244,000 to 201,000 vote against their ending the strike. In the London building lockout the majorities in favour of continuing the struggle were so one-sided that the leaders who, like their compatriots in coal and cotton, were quite prepared to capitulate, had to rely instead on a strategy of attrition and were rewarded only when the Stonemasons broke ranks in June 1914. The rest followed in close succession. If still more evidence were needed, the *entire* period of 1910-14 saw the Amalgamated Society of Engineers in the throes of a bitter internal struggle: the issue once again was that of authority versus autonomy — the central leadership versus the ranks.

According to Price, the struggle between men, unions and masters lay at the heart of the labour unrest. The crisis of work and authority which it produced rocked British society. His argument is an important one and his case is tightly constructed. However, three comments are in order at this point. The first is that Price's treatment of why the building unions' leaders won in 1914 and the ranks lost leaves it unclear whether the outcome was due to contingent or to necessary structural factors. The second is that the state and its role in industrial relations plays an apparently shadowy and unimportant part once the central contradiction is located to be within the 'system of industrial relations'. Third, while it may indeed be true that 'working-class consciousness . . . attains a clarity of comprehension during these years that it had not possessed since the days of Chartism,'[31] this formulation does not tell us very much about the specific nature of that consciousness; alternatively, it can be read as a retrospective full endorsement of syndicalism, as syndicalism was far and away the most influential tendency among the building workers. These questions, beginning with the state and moving on to syndicalism and consciousness, are the subject of the remainder of this chapter.

The Unrest and the State

Systematic discussion of the British state's role in modern industrial relations must begin with the Trade Union Act of 1875. Its importance is that it established a framework of labour law unusually favourable to union growth and functioning, so much so that it has been under attack from anti-labour employers, politicians and publicists ever since, and conversely, has been jealously and at times militantly defended by the labour movement. The relative ease and complacency with which a Parliament made up almost exclusively of wealthy landowners, industrialists and professional men passed the Act of 1875 was due to three factors: first, Britain's as yet unchallenged economic supremacy; secondly the assumption that the un-unionised, and overwhelmingly low paid, majority of the working class would remain so indefinitely; and thirdly the fact that the unionised minority had themselves only partly learned what E.J. Hobsbawm has called the 'rules of the game',[32] that is, the game of organised labour using its collective muscle to best effect. As late as the end of the 1870s, the Lancashire mule spinners, to cite just one group of well-organised 'labour aristocrats', do not seem to have been all that interested in pursuing the wages question to the limit of their potential power.

The assault on unionism's legal position and bargaining power posed by the Taff Vale decision of 1901 only strengthened the determination of union leaders to restore the *status quo ante*. (Significantly, this was not the position of Sidney and Beatrice Webb, who saw no reason why a union should not be held liable in its corporate capacity for certain offences and were thus once more out of step with the mainstream of the labour movement.)[33] The Trade Disputes Act of 1906 was thus both a victory and a surprise. Moreover, its passage would have been inconceivable had it not been for the Liberal and Labour victory at the polls in 1906. But whatever pro-labour sympathies the Campbell-Bannerman government may have had (and it is easy to overestimate them), their commitment to a free-market economy and hence a minimum of state intervention into the workings of the economy and of industrial relations was far more important. Was this industrial policy based upon a realistic appraisal of the conditions and needs of British capital? It was probably not. For although Parliament could restore the legal *status quo ante* as it affected unions, what Parliament could not do was restore the political economy and balance of class forces of 1875, and indeed, that balance had shifted decisively toward labour in the intervening 30 years. We have here yet another example of Britain's retarded entry into the modern era of corporate or organised capitalism with its stress on the state subsidisation of economic growth along with firm legal and social control upon labour.

Keith Middlemas is probably correct in his assertion that the last Liberal government in general, and David Lloyd George in particular, had 'no system', and that the Labour Department of the Board of Trade was the only source of industrial relations policy.[34] Broadly speaking, the Board of Trade's goals were the encouragement of 'bona fide', moderate unionism; the encouragement and support of moderate leaders, with a view to weakening and isolating 'extremists'; and the downplaying of fears that a syndicalist-inspired revolution was imminent. The Labour Department's chief method of achieving these goals was, of course, that of conciliation, and from 1907 onward it was taking a more interventionist approach toward industrial disputes. This can be seen even in the cotton industry which, for the first time since the origins of the industrial revolution was the object of state involvement in its labour relations.

Even so, the onset of unrest undoubtedly caught the government and the Labour Department by surprise, first because industrial conflict had ebbed to very low levels in 1909 and early 1910, and secondly, because the wave of unrest would have taxed the skill and resources of any government, however well prepared it might have thought itself. Here the government was fortunate indeed in having the services of Sir George Askwith, who managed to raise the art of labour relations negotiating to new heights and to work out a surprisingly complete neo-liberal theory of industrial relations, whose central tenets have not changed to this day. The first tenet was that for industrial relations to work smoothly, both sides must be strong and organised, not only in order to come to the bargaining table from a position of credibility, but also in order for each side to police its own ranks and thus stand by agreements. The second was that industrial relations ought to be a voluntary process. Legislation should provide a framework rather than coercive sanctions. The third of his beliefs was the necessity for conciliators, like Askwith himself, to be disinterested professionals able to immerse themselves in and sort out the myriad of concrete and technical details on which so much (but by no means all) industrial conflict hinges. Finally, Askwith believed firmly in the therapeutic powers of habitual bargaining by the accredited and responsible representatives of capital and labour.[35]

To a considerable degree Askwith's methods worked. In the cotton spinning lockout of 1910, for instance, he correctly identified and fixed a procedural defect in the Brooklands Agreement: the grievance machinery could not be turned on unless one side or the other agreed to adopt the role of plaintiff. In 1911 he curtly told the employers at Hull that he was there 'to discuss claims not to put down riots'.[36] Without question Askwith's task during these years was eased considerably by the very real business prosperity and he was satisfied that the base of all the unrest was the 'economic demand, more money, in view of the increased cost of living and rising profits'. He was also, at least at the height of his successes, immensely popular with the strikers themselves. As Robert Roberts recalls from his boyhood in Salford in 1911: 'Then miraculously it was all over and the dockers had won! "Askwith!" – the name ran down the streets – "a man from London, sent by the government! He settled it! He told the bosses!"'[37]

This should warn us against accepting too one-sided a picture — as has been drawn by Pelling and Meacham — that workers were invariably hostile to all state intervention into their daily and working lives.[38] To be sure, Askwith's negotiating successes were not universal, nor indeed was he pro-labour in the sense that he believed labour possessed a historically distinctive political and moral economy of its own that *ought* to be dominant in society. For example, he consistently fudged the issue of the closed shop, for which workers struck throughout the unrest. His best effort to grapple with it was to say that it was 'not possible at the present period of industrial development' to judge the issue on its merits one way or the other.[39]

Influential and active as Askwith was, he did not monopolise the state's industrial relations practice and policy making. If only because of the scale of the unrest and the fact that the strikes did disrupt 'business as usual', it was inevitable that politicians and the cabinet should also intervene. From the literature written to date, however, no particularly clear picture emerges. Middlemas's observation that the government had a 'vested interest in promoting peace'[40] is decidedly unhelpful: except for governments of committed revolutionaries in revolutionary situations, is not this always true? Closer to the mark would be the *ad hoc* nature of it all, the cabinet *reacting* to crises, politicians with different styles, ambitions and emphases: Sydney Buxton with his low profile; Lloyd George with his outsized confidence in his negotiating skills along with his essential dislike of skilled and above all *organised* workers (as opposed to 'the poor'); Churchill with his obsession with law and order and conviction that the unrest threatened constitutional government; Asquith with his visceral anti-union animus when he told the railwaymen, 'then your blood be on your own head'. The disorientation of the cabinet is neatly epitomised in Sir Edward Grey's evidently serious suggestion that the Exchequer should subsidise the mineowners to the tune of some £250,000 in return for their acceptance of a legislated minimum wage, but as Asquith curtly pointed out, coalmining was one of the most prosperous industries in the country.[41] Yet, under the pressure of events more than anything else, a sea-change did take place. Ongoing state intervention was established beyond recall during the years of the unrest.

What are we to conclude about the state's neutrality or otherwise? As we have seen, the Labour Department and the Liberal government cannot be accused of being overly pro-labour. The most charitable formulation is that of 'englightened paternalism'.[42] Indeed, one cannot cite a single instance during 1910-13 when workers and unions came away with more as a result of government intervention than they would have been able to gain through no-holds-barred 'collective *laissez faire*', i.e., no intervention at all. But caution is needed here, because behind the dark utterances of Lloyd George, that compulsory arbitration was only a matter of time, stood the industrial relations policies of die-hard Tories and bosses: severe curtailment of picketing and the right to strike, indeed, the legal and political repression of labour. But as Bonar Law realised, it was not a tempting card to play for three reasons: first, because the Tories themselves were no more eager to deal with the unrest than were the Liberals, secondly, because a militant, anti-labour stance might alienate such trade-unionist electoral support for the Tories as existed at the time.[43] Thus, even though there was in fact a deep split within the political elite over the proper set of industrial relations policies for the state to follow, the effect for practical purposes was a 'bipartisan' policy, which in turn meant that of the Liberals. Finally, one is tempted to suppose that as far as the Tories were concerned after 1912, Ireland was a far better stick to beat the Liberals with than the unrest. In this way the various 'revolts' may well have had an impact upon one another, just as Dangerfield said. To the extent that they did, it appears that the result, if not positively beneficial to labour, at least ensured that workers were confronted by the Liberal 'lesser evil' and not the Tory greater one.

Syndicalism and Its Impact

We turn finally to what are in many ways the most difficult problems of all — the nature and extent of syndicalism, the depth of the crisis of 1910-14, if indeed it was a crisis, and the legacy of 1910-14 for the working class.

Holton makes the important point that syndicalism is a variety of 'ouvrierism' or workerism.[44] Taking the idea a step further, one may suggest that in the British context it was a spontaneous (in the Leninist sense) opposition movement that simultaneously challenged the timid, collaborationist and increasingly authoritarian, official trade union leadership on the one hand, and the equivocal stand on strikes and industrial militancy taken by the leaders of the established socialist parties — including the Independent Labour Party and the Social Democratic Federation/British Socialist Party. From this dual critique, syndicalism derived its two overarching strengths. The first was a (to this day) unrivalled statement of working-class democracy and the urgent need for working people to control their own institutions. As *The Miners' Next Step* put it,

> Sheep cannot be said to have solidarity. In obedience to a shepherd, they will go up or down, backwards or forwards as they are driven by him and his dogs. But they have no solidarity, for that means unity and loyalty. Unity and loyalty, not to an individual, or the policy of an individual, but to an interest and a policy which is understood and worked for by all.[45]

As should be clear from the argument advanced in this chapter (to say nothing of the massive outpouring of books about trade unions) the pressures upon unions toward moderation, integration and the 'management of discontent' are immense and probably permanent. However, this does not prove the validity of the 'Iron Law of Oligarchy'. On the contrary, countervailing responses, such as syndicalism, suggest an equally tough and nervy Law of Working Class Democracy.

Syndicalism's second source of strength was its commitment to mass action and the ability and willingness of individual syndicalists to lead mass struggles. In this sense British syndicalists were the direct counterparts of such socialist leaders in the early twentieth century as Rosa Luxemburg and Eugene V. Debs. That syndicalism should have fulfilled this role is traceable in part to the peculiar Marxism of the SDF and of Hyndman in particular. It must be kept firmly in mind just how stridently Hyndman opposed the use of the strike weapon. 'We are opposed to strikes altogether.' (1903) 'We ... are opposed to strikes on principle ... Political action is far safer, far better, and far less costly.' (1907) 'I have never known a successful strike.' (1912)[46] By the sharpest of contrasts:

> Syndicalists were generally much more concerned with the burning questions of the day than with the distant future ... Everybody who was willing to take part in the class struggle, regardless of his organization or his political views, was welcome ... They maintained that it would be idle to insist on theoretical distinctions at a time when the main body of workers were engaged in practical class struggles.[47]

When the explosion of 1910 burst forth, syndicalists, then, were ideally situated in political terms to give voice and direction to it. As Hinton says, 'entirely dependent on the momentum of industrial militancy, the syndicalist movement grew with meteoric speed during the great strike movement of 1910-12 . . .'[48]

However finely attuned syndicalism was to the mood of unrest, it was itself deeply flawed theoretically, and ironically the difficulty lay precisely in its approach to the unions. Tom Mann, as usual, expressed the syndicalist position pithily and forcefully when he wrote: 'The trade unions are truly representative of the men, and can be moulded by the men into exactly what the men desire.'[49] Truly representative: *there* was the rub. Because unions are by their very nature inclusive of as many workers as possible (after all, every trade union leader, from extreme right to revolutionary left regards 100 per cent organisation as the ideal, however much they might differ regarding structure, policy, ideology) the consciousness of the workers who are being 'represented' must necessarily be uneven and heterogeneous. And in the world of mature liberal industrial capitalism, with the secular decline of representative government and its steady replacement by managed politics, unions remain at least partially representative in the sense — quite different from what the syndicalists had in mind — that their officials have seen the task of leadership as providing a lowest common denominator for policy and action. Neither too far out in front nor too far behind the rank and file becomes the watchword. This is ultimately the reason also why trade unions, acting even as militant unions, cannot themselves bring about fundamental social transformation.

In the *anni mirabili* of 1910-12, all this went unnoticed, since it is an integral part of labour explosions that rank-and-file consciousness is far more homogeneous and militant than in 'normal' times. But from 1912 onwards the theoretical problems became more evident. One need not fully accept Hinton's assertion that the influence of syndicalism 'fell just as fast [as it had risen] in the year before the war' — in the London building trades it is demonstrably untrue and it seems equally difficult to make out a case for the drastic reduction in syndicalist influence in South Wales — but the fact remains that much of the syndicalist programme for the transformation of the unions was either defeated, coopted, or watered down.[50] In South Wales, the proposals for centralisation laid out in *The Miners' Next Step* were defeated by an incumbent leadership able to draw upon the rank and file's tenacious desire for the continuation of local autonomy, even though in practice it often meant union rule by 'popular bossdom'.[51] Nor were the creation of the National Union of Railwaymen and the Triple Alliance unalloyed victories for the syndicalist perspective, as in both cases it was the union officials' vision of industrial unity that won out. As Holton notes, the Triple Alliance was expressly conceived 'not as rampageous syndicalism, but as trade unionism in its right mind'.[52] Finally, at no time before 1914 did syndicalism sort out within its own ranks the crucially important question of 'boring from within' versus dual unionism. Aside from this question splitting the syndicalist movement organisationally in 1913, it must have had a considerable limiting effect upon the spread of syndicalist propaganda, as knowledgeable, class-conscious, but sceptical workers could not but have noticed that the question was answered differently depending on which syndicalist you were talking to. Nor might one overlook the fact that articulate and active members of the Socialist Labour Party like George Harvey, who advocated dual unionism, in fact continued to work within his lodge of the Durham miners. To have done otherwise would have been politically suicidal.

Syndicalism's theoretical inadequacies and their practical consequences raises the closely related question of the extent to which syndicalism's growth and influence came at the expense of political socialism. Historians have been prone to think that this is what did happen, but have not put forward much hard evidence. However, if the zero-sum assumption, i.e., that the gain of one tendency must have been the other's loss, is relaxed, it becomes possible to suggest that both tendencies might have grown together, despite the clear and theoretically irreconcilable differences separating them. To cite just one underappreciated statistic, the British Socialist Party claimed to have in early 1912 some 40,000 members and 370 branches, which of course was incomparably more than the members of all syndicalist organisations combined, though to be sure by the end of 1912 the Hyndmanite Old Guard had successfully reasserted its (anti-syndicalist) hegemony in the BSP, whose numbers by 1914 dropped to 20,000, no more than the SDF in 1908.[53] Despite its weak and confused performance in the Commons, moreover, Labour candidates appear to have gained 153 seats in local elections from 1912 to 1913.[54] This tendency for both political and industrial militancy to grow together can be seen clearly in the case of the cotton workers who in 1913 were simultaneously conducting lengthy and unofficial strikes against non-unionists (Nelson Weavers, led by young ILP activists), balloting in favour of the use of union funds to support the Labour Party (all grades) and engaging in an industrial-unionism-inspired revolt against the official leadership (Middleton Spinners).[55] The appeal that political Labourism and socialism held for many South Wales miners must also have materially aided miners' union officials like Vernon Hartshorn, whose ILP credentials were universally known, in beating back the Unofficial Reform Committee's challenges. This, again, is not surprising. Political action had by 1910-13 had a very long history in the working-class movement, and, indeed, *The Miners' Next Step* called for 'political action, both local and national, on the basis of complete independence of, and hostility to, all capitalist parties, with an avowed policy of wresting whatever advantage it can for the working class'.[56]

Our conclusion, then, is that syndicalism was — and had to be — limited in its appeal and its successes. But we would not wish simply to confirm the 'minimising' interpretation which holds that established structures and ideologies may have been temporarily shaken, but did not break. Such a conclusion would be too pat, too complacent, because in the last analysis a major crisis did exist. The two unrests strained the capacities of union officials, employers and government to contain them to the outer limit and beyond. The government was not an inch closer to 'solutions' in August 1914 than it was at the onset of the unrest; and the political elite was deeply divided over Ireland, industrial relations, votes for women and much else. Had the war not intervened, the next stage of the unrest would surely have witnessed a fresh wave of massive strikes to protect the advances won during 1910-13 in the face of recession that was on the way in the summer of 1914 and which would have been every bit as severe as the downturn of 1908-10. In this context, one must agree with Price's description of the crisis as 'the first time that the contradictions of an essentially modern system of industrial relations stood exposed'.[57]

Most important, because of the unrest's sheer breadth and power and because it did not grow out of a temporary and unique conjuncture, it imparted a permanent legacy. The lasting and strong organisation of occupation like the railwaymen and dockers was to be assured right down to the present. The years of pre-war militancy, struggle and thinking were, as Hinton has shown, the training school for the revolutionaries who were to build the first shop stewards' movements and, after the war, the Communist Party. This in turn guaranteed the existence of a left opposition within the trade union movement, varying in strength over time and between industries to be sure, but never totally absent. Finally, for rank-and-file workers themselves, 1910-13 taught and showed graphically the efficacy of direct industrial action, and surely that lesson is very much in evidence in our own time.

Notes

1. George Dangerfield, *The Strange Death of Liberal England* (London, 1935).
2. E.H. Phelps Brown, *The Growth of Industrial Relations* (London, 1959); H.M. Pelling, 'The Labour Unrest, 1911-14', in *Popular Politics and Society in Late Victorian England*, 2nd ed. (London, 1979).
3. P.N. Stearns, *Lives of Labour: Work in a Maturing Industrial Society* (London, 1975), p.335.
4. Bob Holton, *British Syndicalism 1900-1914: Myths and Realities* (London, 1976), p.20.
5. Richard Price, *Masters, Unions and Men: Work Control in Building and the Rise of Labour, 1830-1914* (Cambridge, 1980), esp. Chs. 5-7.
6. The literature is mountainous, but start with: D. Landes, *The Unbound Prometheus* (Cambridge, 1969); E.J. Hobsbawm, *Industry and Empire* (Harmondsworth, 1968); E.J. Hobsbawm, *Labouring Men: Studies in the History of Labour* (London, 1964); and Stearns, *Lives of Labour*.
7. Stearns, *Lives*, p.124.
8. James E. Cronin, *Industrial Conflict in Modern Britain* (London, 1979), pp.96-7.
9. E.J. Hobsbawm, *Labouring Men*, Ch. 9; J.E. Williams, 'The Leeds Corporation Strike in 1913', in A. Briggs and J. Saville (eds.), *Essays in Labour History, 1886-1923* (London, 1971).
10. For iron and steel, see David Brody, *Steelworkers in America: the Non-Union Era* (New York, 1960) pp.32-3; for engineering, see James Hinton, *The First Shop Stewards' Movement* (London, 1973); for textiles see A. Fowler, 'Trade Unions and Technical Change: the Automatic Loom Strike, 1908', *North West Labour History Society Bulletin, 6* (1979-80), pp.43-55; for coal see B.L. Coombes, *These Poor Hands* (London, 1939), reprinted in J. Burnett, *Useful Toil* (London, 1974), pp.111-15.
11. Stearns, *Lives*, Ch. 6 and passim.
12. J. Saville, 'Trade Unions and Free Labour: The Background to the Taff Vale Decision', in A. Briggs and J. Saville (eds.), *Essays in Labour History*, vol. 1 (London, 1960).
13. Price, *Masters, Unions and Men*, esp. Chs. 4-6.
14. Stearns, Ch. 6; J.L. White, *The Limits of Trade Union Militancy: The Lancashire Textile Workers, 1910-1914* (Westport, 1978).
15. J. Hinton, *The First Shop Stewards' Movement*, p.121n.
16. F. McKenna, 'Victorian Railwaymen', *History Workshop Journal*, 1, pp.65-9; Hinton, *The First Shop Stewards' Movement*, p.96; Carter Goodrich, *The Miner's Freedom* (New York, 1923).
17. David Martin, '"The Instruments of the People": The Parliamentary Labour Party in 1906', in D. Martin and D. Rubinstein (eds.), *Essays on the Labour Movement* (London, 1979), p.142.
18. Holton, *British Syndicalism*, pp.103-6.
19. Richard Hyman, *The Workers' Union* (Oxford, 1971), pp.51-61.
20. David Smith, 'Tonypandy 1910: Definitions of Community', *Past and Present*, no. 87, pp.162ff.
21. Roger Davidson, 'The Board of Trade and Industrial Relations, 1896-1914', *Historical Journal*, vol. 21, 1978, p.580.
22. Holton, *British Syndicalism*, p.100.
23. Hyman, *Workers' Union*, p.60.
24. Ibid., p.56.
25. Stearns, *Lives*, pp.300-2.

26. Richard Hyman, *Strikes* (London, 1972), contains a good discussion of strikes over perishable issues.

27. White, *Limits of Trade Union Militancy*, esp. Chs. 2-3, 5-8.

28. Lord Askwith, *Industrial Problems and Disputes* (London, 1920), Ch. 21; R. Page Arnot, *The Miners: Years of Struggle* (London, 1953); Holton, *British Syndicalism*, Ch. 7.

29. Price, *Masters, Unions and Men*, Ch. 7.

30. Dave Douglass, 'The Durham Pitman', in R. Samuels (ed.), *Miners, Quarrymen and Saltworkers* (London, 1977), pp.266ff.

31. Price, *Masters, Unions and Men*, p.238 and Ch.7 passim.

32. E.J. Hobsbawm, 'Custom, Wages, and Work-load', in *Labouring Men* (London, 1964), p.345.

33. S. and B. Webb, *Industrial Democracy* (London, 1903), preface to the 2nd edition.

34. K. Middlemas, *Politics in Industrial Society: The Experience of the British System since 1911* (London, 1979), p.61.

35. Askwith, *Industrial Problems and Disputes*, Chs. 13-33; R. Davidson, 'The Board of Trade and Industrial Relations'.

36. Askwith, *Industrial Problems*, p.150.

37. Robert Roberts, *The Classic Slum* (Hardmondsworth, 1973), p.96.

38. Pelling, *Popular Politics*, Ch. 1; S. Meacham, *A Life Apart: The English Working Class, 1890-1914* (London, 1977), Ch. 7.

39. Askwith, *Industrial Problems*, p.192.

40. Middlemas, *Politics*, p.57.

41. C.J. Wrigley, *David Lloyd George and the British Labour Movement* (Hassocks, nr Brighton, 1976), Ch. 3.

42. The phrase is R. Davidson's, 'The Board of Trade and Industrial Relations', p.590.

43. Wrigley, *Lloyd George*, pp.66-7.

44. Holton, *British Syndicalism*, p.19.

45. Unofficial Reform Committee, *The Miners' Next Step*, 1st edn. 1912, reprinted London, 1973, p.20.

46. Cited in Walter Kendall, *The Revolutionary Movement in Britain, 1900-1921* (London, 1969), p.28.

47. B. Pribicevic, *The Shop Stewards' Movement and Workers' Control* (Oxford, 1959), p.17, cited in Hinton, *The First Shop Stewards' Movement*, p.278.

48. Hinton, *The First Shop Stewards' Movement*, p.278.

49. Ibid., pp.280-1.

50. Ibid., p.278.

51. H. Francis and D. Smith, *The Fed: A History of the South Wales Miners in the Twentieth Century* (London, 1980), pp.14-22.

52. Holton, *British Syndicalism*, p.175.

53. W. Kendall, *Revolutionary Movement*, pp.28-51.

54. Meacham, *A Life Apart*, pp.201-2.

55. White, *Limits*, Ch. 9.

56. *Miners' Next Step*, p.23.

57. Price, *Masters, Unions and Men*, p.266. Since it was the first time, however, the reaction was extremely confused, as Standish Meecham has argued in 'The Sense of an Impending Clash: English Working-class Unrest before the First World War', *American Historical Review*, vol. 77 (1972), pp.1343-64.

5 THE WAR, THE STATE AND THE WORKPLACE: BRITISH DOCKERS DURING 1914-1918

Jonathan Schneer

World War I was a decisive factor in the history of the modern British working class. As countless historians have pointed out, it revealed in pitiless fashion the weakness of international socialist ideals among workers and the countervailing strength of nationalism. In addition, it signified British labour's 'coming of age'. That is, the war emphasised labour's indispensability to society: quite simply, it could not be won if workers ceased to support it. For the first time, the government recognised labour's importance by opening its most august councils to working-class representatives. Under Asquith, Arthur Henderson entered the Cabinet as President of the Board of Education; under Lloyd George he was admitted into the exclusive War Cabinet, and George Barnes was appointed Minister of Pensions. The Labour Party, formed only a decade and a half earlier, and the movement of which it was the parliamentary expression, had truly arrived.

Given the war's historic importance for labour, it is strange that scholars have devoted so little study to its impact upon the working class. For the most part they have looked at individuals or political parties or organisations which influenced labour.[1] Thus we have studies of the role of MacDonald, Henderson and Milner, of the ILP, BSP and the UDC, but, with the exception of Hinton's examination of the skilled engineers, and Cole's of the miners, we have no analysis of the war's impact upon working conditions. This is a significant omission not least because working conditions influence political attitudes. Any attempt to explain working-class politics during 1914-18 without reference to conditions at the workplace is necessarily incomplete.

This chapter attempts to fill part of this gap in our knowledge of the history of the British working class by focusing upon working conditions in the docks during 1914-18. It also attempts to assess the typicality or singularity of the dockers' wartime position. What generalisations, if any, about British labour during the war does a study of British dockers justify? Finally, it attempts to link working conditions at the docks with the political attitudes, in so far as they can be ascertained, of the dockers themselves. Thus it hopes to add a new dimension to our understanding of patriotic labour by tracing its connection to the working situation which the war produced.

Before the first World War, British docks were worked by casual labour. Each morning, in ports throughout the kingdom, a far greater number of men than would be hired routinely applied for work at the dock gates. This was as true in the summer of 1913, when H.A. Mess of Toynbee Hall counted 940 men of whom 431 were taken on in four separate calls at a London dock, as it had been in 1888 when Ben Tillett, later general secretary of the Dock, Wharf, Riverside and General Labourers' Union, testified before the Lords' Commission on Sweated Industries that there were 'one hundred men at least for every job that would take forty'.[2] At that time, Beatrice Potter thought the existence of this class of casual labour was 'the gravest problem of the future'.[3] Some twenty years later, W.H. Beveridge, at the Board of Trade, confirmed her prediction.[4] Agreement ended, however, with identification of the problem. For both employers and workers found reason to support the system.

The dock owners and shipowners argued, plausibly to many, that employment at the docks was dependent upon forces of nature — namely the wind and tides — which were beyond their control. Ships could only enter and leave the docks when weather permitted. This might occur at any moment. Therefore it was necessary always to have on hand enough men to load or unload a ship as it arrived or made ready to depart. But it was hardly necessary, according to the employers, to pay the men while they waited for work.

Thus the 'necessity' of casualism. Most of its consequences were as beneficial to the masters as they were disastrous to their employees. 'Call-ons' were scheduled throughout the day, so that labourers feared to leave the dock. 'Calling-on' stands were not centralised — indeed there were over 500 in the port of London — and there was virtually no communication between them.[5] A man risked missing a 'call' if he wandered from one stand to another; thus one quay would often be crowded with jobless supplicants while another needed additional men. In general, the surplus of labour which was the result of casualism meant low wages for workers and little job control. Moreover, it hampered their organisation except in periods of exceptional labour militancy.[6]

The new unionist upsurge of 1889-93 had been one such era. The years immediately preceding the first World War were another. During 1910-14, the years of 'great unrest', the dockers responded to syndicalist appeals by joining a National Transport Workers' Federation, and the massive Triple Alliance, through which they were associated with the miners and railwaymen. At the workplace itself, their successive confrontations with the employers produced the great national victory of 1911 and a prolonged, bitter, and ultimately unsuccessful struggle with the Port of London Authority in 1912. In the spring and early summer of 1914, it appeared that Thameside workers would shortly be battling against their employers again. As their general secretary, Tillett, somewhat melodramatically, though characteristically expressed himself to Lloyd George, the Chancellor of the Exchequer, 'There was nothing for it but arming our people and making a fight of it in the streets with your police and soldiers.'[7] Harry Gosling, leader of the London lightermen, and president of the NTWF, was more prosaic in his warning to the Board of Trade, but no less emphatic that 'a stoppage would take place at an early date'.[8]

The dockers' target, however, was not the casual labour system. For if it practically guaranteed that most of them would never rise above the poverty level, it also seemed to guarantee against actual starvation. It was a court of last resort for those who could find employment nowhere else. A man might work only one day, or even a fraction of a day in a week at the docks, but this was better than no work at all. Indeed, for some independent souls, these circumstances were probably more appealing than a job whose hours were rigidly defined. Moreover, any attempt to limit the casual nature of dock labour would inevitably lead to a restriction of the number of men who might apply for work. This the dockers resolutely opposed.

All attempts at reform, whether by well-intentioned outsiders, civil servants at the Board of Trade, or even trade union leaders, foundered upon the twin opposition of labour and management, and the obvious complexity of the problem as a whole. In 1914, casualism was entrenched in the life of dockland to the bafflement and despair of all would-be reformers. As Tillett put it, in a letter to Lloyd George, who had recently visited the London docks:

> This Casual-Labour problem is as great a problem as the wage system itself. I promised Cardinal Manning twenty six years ago [in 1888] that I would stick to the dockers as long as I lived, and I have been a drudge ever since . . . But there has been so little done . . . indeed I feel impotent . . . the tragedy of it all makes one almost mad. I am surprised at times that I have reason or sanity left. I feel that to

climb the hills of sorrow only lifts us to the mountains of misery —
there is ever yet more in sight.[9]

Compare this with Tillett's outlook five years later, as expressed at the
Dockers' 1919 Triennial meeting: 'Our own union has been able to
command such improvements in the conditions of labour, such
advantages in real wealth as to make me kick myself now and again to
ascertain whether I am awake.'[10]

Ironically the catastrophe of world war proved, in many respects,
beneficial to British dockers. The war strengthened certain forces in
dockland which, hitherto, had been nearly powerless; it weakened
others which once had practically dictated dockland conditions. How
this shift of power came about constitutes an important chapter in the
history of dock labour, and illuminates a key factor which influenced
working-class political attitudes during 1914-18. It is, therefore, to the
war years that we must now turn.

The British government must have been greatly relieved by the
overwhelmingly positive response of the nation to its declaration of war
on Germany in August 1914. One year before, the NTWF had passed
with only one dissentient vote a resolution demanding the general
strike 'in the event of international war being imminent'.[11] Had the
NTWF attempted to implement its resolution, which Tillett seems to
have hesitantly recommended, it would doubtless have been ignored.[12]
Throughout the country working men flocked to join the colours. By
April 1915, 23 per cent of London's dockers had enlisted.[13] Dissent
was rare, muted and ineffectual. We may, perhaps, discern an opponent
of the war in Tom Adams, secretary of the Dockers' Union London
Export Branch, who wrote to Reginald McKenna, the Home Secretary,
that his members viewed

> with regret the action taken by the Holligans [sic] and children of
> Poplar in wrecking the Shops and destroying the Flour and Bread
> belonging to Germans and Naturalize [sic] English Bakers. We deem
> it necessary that these Shops should be allowed protection as far as
> able to prevent any destruction or thieft [sic] as these Shops average
> between 30 to 40 sacks of Flour at the value of 36/- per sack which
> if not use [sic] for the proper purpose would be at the disadvantage
> of the poorer people.[14]

Perhaps the dockers of Swansea, who formed a 'Workers' Guard to number not less than 500 for the purpose of preventing any attempts of looting', were likewise expressing an uncommon attitude towards the war.[15] Malvina Walker, a docker's wife, was less oblique (and less realistic) in her call for a return to normal conditions. Recalling that German transport workers had sent £5,000 to the London dockers during the 1912 strike, she concluded that 'our duty at this time is to impress upon all that the working class do not want war.'[16] She was probably fortunate not to share the fate of Thomas Eddy, a dock labourer, who was pelted with sticks and stones by an angry crowd outside London's East India Dock, and then arrested 'for insulting the Army'.[17]

Ironically, the patriotic upsurge among dockworkers created a problem for their employers. Within a week of the declaration of war, their warehouses were stuffed to overflowing. Soon they began to complain of a labour shortage. Their doubts were confirmed in December 1915, when a Board of Trade committee estimated that there was a shortage at the docks of between 10,000 and 20,000 men. There were some 40,000 fewer dockers presently employed than in July 1914.[18] How, then, were ships to be loaded and unloaded if so many dockers had volunteered to serve their country at the front?

To be sure there were other causes of delay and port congestion. During the winter of 1914-15, heavy rain made the transportation of butter, tea, sugar and frozen meat nearly impossible.[19] In London, Bristol and Liverpool, goods were piled high on the quays, not merely owing to the increased demand for supplies by the troops, but also to the diversion of cargoes from continental ports as a result of the war. In addition, increased trade with trans-oceanic American vessels strained dock facilities designed mainly for smaller ships. Nor was it clear that men who had become accustomed to less than a full week's work would voluntarily perform one. A continuing complaint of dock employers was that their men were lazy and preferred drinking to working. Still, for the first time in living memory, and with the exception of some ports on Britain's east coast, whose trade had been diverted to London, and whose dockers were consequently short of work, there was no great reserve of dock labour upon which the employers could draw, and upon which they could rely to depress wages.

The dwindling supply of surplus labour did not concern dock and ship owners alone. As the Foreign Secretary, Sir Edward Grey, observed in a secret memorandum to Walter Runciman, president of the Board of Trade, 'Our greatest present danger in this war lies in the shortage of labour necessary to relieve merchant shipping and avoid congestion in our ports.'[20] The men in the trenches depended on the rapid delivery of ammunition and supplies from the home front. Delays could not be tolerated, whatever their cause. To prevent them the government was prepared to intervene in the affairs not merely of the dockers — which came as no surprise — but of their employers as well.

'It is very difficult to gauge what the actual effect of war under modern conditions will be upon either capital or labour', Lloyd George had written in late August 1914, 'but one thing is already perfectly obvious — it must effect a revolutionary change in the relations of the state to both'.[21] Did the Chancellor of the Exchequer mean that the war would bring the government into conflict with the inefficiencies of the casual labour system? Whatever their interpretation of Lloyd George's prophetic remarks, the dockers' leaders voluntarily agreed to an industrial truce for the duration of the war, and to the March 1915 Treasury Agreement which formalised it. Of the important unions, only the engineers stood out. And in return for labour's nearly unanimous backing, the government promised that all trade union rights would be restored when the war was won. More importantly, the government seemed to acknowledge that labour must have a voice in shaping industrial policy through representation on official committees, up to and including the Cabinet itself.

The first step directly to effect the dockers was taken in November 1915, with the establishment of the Port and Transit Executive Committee, under the chairmanship of Lord Inchape. Composed of representatives of dock labour, of several government departments, and of the largest employers as well, its task was to discover the causes of port congestion and to suggest remedies. Almost immediately it recommended that dock work be declared of national importance, and that dockers should be exempt from national service under the Derby scheme. To administer the issue of exemption certificates, it established a series of local Port Labour Committees. These consisted of equal numbers of government, labour and employers' representatives. There were, then, by early 1916, two official organisations empowered to deal with conditions in dockland, and the workers were represented on both of them.

This was really what many trade unionists (to say nothing of the Labour Party leadership) had been demanding for years. Ben Tillett, for one, was ecstatic. The war had generated a 'new relationship between the classes . . . a new spiritual sense of being . . . a closer bond of fairer, sweeter human ties of friendship'.[22] In fact, the war had not ushered in the utopian era of inter-class harmony which Tillett imagined, so much as a new balance of forces in British society. Class interests still influenced the moves of labour and capital, but the trade unions had more leverage than ever before.

Up to a point dockers took advantage of it. In May 1916, the NTWF pressed for the pooling of all dock equipment under a central authority, that is, for nationalising the means of production. 'In ordinary peace times' its spokesmen urged 'competition may have advantages, but in a crisis of war we are of the opinion that not merely men but the material and wealth resources should be conscripted for the State . . .'[23] This was too much even for Lloyd George, but the Board of Trade was willing to accept other NTWF proposals:

> There could be provided facilities for the transport of labour from one dock to another, with businesslike telephonic communications from one place of call or hiring, and the fixing of definite centres of call, which should be as central as possible, as well as covering all the departments of centres on employment.[24]

Such measures, if carried out, would have seriously impaired the workings of the casual labour system, but the necessity for efficiency at the docks during wartime, seemed to make them imperative.

The results were soon apparent. In London, by the early summer of 1916, estimates of the number of men required for the next morning's first call were posted every night. Later in the year, firms could telephone an agent, Mr Poyser, with requests for men, or with information that they had a surplus of labour that could work elsewhere. Ironically, conscription helped to make this possible. Dock labourers were exempt; but they needed to register with the Port Labour Committees to obtain certificates attesting to their status. This made it possible to list all the men who applied for work at the docks, and to limit their number. In addition, it meant that they would be directed to certain 'calling-on' stands. By November 1917, casualism was being undermined in this manner in no less than 32 ports.[25]

In the interests of efficiency the government developed another instrument which, indirectly, also weakened the casual labour system. 'What is needed' the P&TEC asserted to the war cabinet. 'is a mobile force [under military discipline] to deal with deficiencies in Civilian Labour in particular ports as and when they arise.'[26] This line of reasoning proved persuasive, and in January 1916, the 16th (Transport Workers' Battalion) York and Lancaster Regiment was formed and made available for port work. By 1918 there were numerous TWBs with over 15,000 working members. At one time or another, 24,000 men, of whom 8,000 were ex-dockers, had worked in them.[27] Since they could only be called into ports whose labour requirements could be calculated, the TWBs enabled the unions to demand the registration of dockers and the limitation of 'calling-on' stands. To the extent that this reduced the chaos in dockland hiring practices, it reduced the force of casualism as well.

Decasualisation appears to have been the crucial factor in wartime industrial relations on the docks. Aside from the continuing appeals for patriotism and a natural hatred of the enemy during wartime, which blunted class antagonism, decasualisation was primarily responsible for the relative labour peace of 1914-18; yet, paradoxically, it was also the main source of docker unrest during the war.

In other industries the demand for efficiency brought the state into conflict with labour. For example, the policy of dilution — the replacement of skilled workers who had joined the army by semi-skilled or unskilled workers — was a particular source of unrest among engineers. Their traditional craft privileges were directly threatened by the war and the government's dilution schemes that followed in its wake. As a result, they mounted perhaps the most militant working-class challenge to confront either Asquith or his successor, Lloyd George, during 1914-18.[28] The dockers' experience, however, was somewhat different. For them, dilution of labour had been a continuous process before the war. In essence that was what the casual system represented.[29] During the war, however, the dilution of labour in dockland was largely ended. As a result, uncertainty of employment practically disappeared, certain working conditions were improved and wages were increased. Hence the docks were relatively quiescent.

Of course there were other reasons for dock labour peace during 1914-18. Again, a comparison with the engineers is relevant. The war led to the invention and use of machinery which diminished the engineers' time honoured position as labour aristocrats. This too resulted in a wave of militant strikes. The policy of the Dockers' Union, however, was to accept the introduction of machinery. They had lost that particular battle during the 25 years before 1914,[30] and, in any case, World War I appears to have temporarily ended the development and introduction into dockland of new mechanical appliances.[31]

The efforts of Sir George Askwith's Office of Industrial Commissioners also helped to keep dock labour pacified during the war.

As a corollary to the Treasury Agreement of March 1915, all industrial problems were referred to legally binding courts of arbitration under Askwith's jurisdiction. It is worth noting here that Tillett had been a vocal advocate of industrial conciliation since 1888. Perhaps during 1914-18, the dockers were predisposed to accept it as a result of his longstanding agitation. Certainly the government had the strongest incentive to find in their favour, as strikes would seriously disrupt the transportation of goods to the front. The dockers, aware of their advantageous position, could even influence the selection of arbitrators: 'Men like Messrs David, Willis and Colthrop-Monroe, are types who destroy our confidence in arbitration', Ernest Bevin informed D.C. Cummings of the Chief Industrial Commissioner's Department. 'It is imperative that the arbitrator appointed shall be strictly impartial and not one whose conception of workmen is that they ought to be kept at any rate below the poverty line.'[32] Bevin's tone suggests, however, that the national effort could subsume but not eradicate tension between the classes. In fact, as the war ground on, it became more and more likely that the dockers would attempt to take advantage of the government's uncharacteristic willingness to heed their demands.

There were two main causes of disaffection among the docker rank and file during 1914-18. Like all British workers, they suffered from inflation, although it must be stressed that many dockers, who previously had been unable to obtain regular work, were unlikely, at first, to protest about lowered purchasing power when, for the first time in their lives, they were receiving steady wages. Applications for advances, relatively rare at first, grew in number starting in 1916, however, and by 1918 virtually flooded the office of Sir George Askwith's Industrial Commission. T.B. Davies, branch secretary of the Dockers' Union in Middlesbrough filed a typical submission on 27 October 1917: 'We ... have been compelled to make the present application for, in addition to the daily increase in the cost of food, all other commodities such as clothing, light, fuel, etc. have so advanced in price that an increase of 100 percent on pre-war rates of pay would not enable workmen to live up to the standard of 1914.'[33]

Despite the obvious benefits to those who remained working on the docks, the attack upon casualism threatened customs and traditions which dockers were determined to defend. Thus although dilution was not a problem for British dockers during 1914-18 the general emphasis upon efficiency proved dangerous to their interests. This was the second major source of dock labour's unhappiness during the war.

In this regard the experience of the Kings Lynn dockers may serve as an example. During the war they downed tools on at least five separate occasions, the last of which prompted an urgent telegram to Askwith from Ogden Taylor, the exasperated general manager of the dock company: 'Men definitely . . . refuse to carry out any orders [to resume work] issued by Tillett, Williams, or any other authority. Matters getting serious.'[34] Wages were only one consideration. As Mr Greenwood, the Kings Lynn Dockers' Union district organiser, explained to Tillett: 'Once we admit the right of employers to introduce altered working conditions during the war, there will be ample opportunity for them to secure advantages far outweighing the benefits accruing from high wages.' In particular, he objected to a two-hour lengthening of the working day, and to having to work at night by flickering, and therefore dangerous, torchlight.[35]

Greenwood's intransigent attitude was far from being atypical. In London, dockers objected to plans for decasualisation which failed to take their specialised skills into account. They preferred irregular payment in one dock, at one task, for one foreman, to steady but unspecialised work throughout the port. In Liverpool, in January 1915, dockers simply declined to work the longer hours which increased production of goods and the needs of the army on the Continent made necessary. Later they struck when female labour was introduced to take up the slack. In Bridgewater, in December 1917, dockers refused to work with non-union members who had accepted the speed-up which decasualisation entailed. In short, the lengthened working day and increased regimentation which the war seemed to make necessary, produced a stubborn resistance among the dockers.[36]

The Transport Workers' Battalions, which had enabled the union to systematise hiring procedures, were likewise opposed by the rank and file. At its inception Lord Derby had acknowledged that he would not regard the first TWB 'as a strike breaking battalion if it came to be used to do the work of men who were fighting their superior officials' — that is, who were conducting an unofficial walk-out.[37] If the TWBs were not used primarily to break or avert strikes, however, they nevertheless appear to have served that purpose among others. T.W. Phillips at the Board of Trade appreciated 'the stimulus given to civilian labour by the knowledge that the battalion is available if required'.[38] Lord Inchape was also pleased that the creation of the TWB. 'has made civilian labour realise that wage and other disputes will not be allowed to interfere with the flow through the ports of such traffic as must be maintained in the national interest'.[39] In addition, and again much like

the decasualisation schemes, the TWBs helped break down the dockers'
specialised skills. In order to keep them out, dockers resentfully
accepted jobs outside their usual practice which once they would have
scorned.

The bulging files of the Labour Department now contained at the
Public Record Office attest to a continuing if muted malaise in
dockland labour relations. Dockers' leaders who appreciated the power
which the war had given them, nevertheless feared to jeopardise the
national effort by calling strikes. Arbitration was safer and, given
the war emergency, almost equally effective. 'We are willing,' Tillett
assured Askwith in a typical note, 'to use our best influences in
preventing any cessation of work.'[40] During the first half of the war his
efforts, and those of the other dockers' leaders, were generally
successful. Thereafter, however, it became more difficult to avoid
serious labour trouble.

It seems inadequate to ascribe working-class unrest during 1917-18
to war weariness and the inspiration of the Russian revolution, as most
historians do.[41] Such sources of discontent were extrinsic to working
conditions in dockland which, for the most part, remained substantially
better than during the pre-war period. When these gains were
threatened, however, and as the regimentation and general speed-up
which accompanied the attack upon casualism proceeded apace, then a
militant dockers' movement began to take shape.

Perhaps the German submarine campaign represented the gravest
threat to the dockers' position. The U-boats exacerbated the
unevenness of dock work by making it impossible to predict when
convoys would arrive. In late 1917 and early 1918, as in 1913 or even
1889, men hung about the docks waiting for ships to appear. Earnings
dropped as idleness increased. In March 1918 came an equally severe
blow. The government withdrew exemption from conscription for
dockers aged 18-25, thereby undermining the enhanced status for dock
labour which the emergency situation had fostered. Robert Williams,
secretary of the NTWF, was quick to respond: 'If any strike trouble
or industrial pressure takes place as a protest against this militarism
and dragooning of transport labour, the government must accept the
responsibility.'[42]

Both the U-boat and conscription issues could be traced directly to
the war. Not surprisingly, then, increased industrial militancy was
paralleled by a political swing to the left. The union leadership, which
in 1914 was united behind the war effort had become divided. Tillett
and James Sexton, of the Liverpool dockers, remained fervent upholders

of the government, but Harry Gosling now believed that 'the democracy of all the belligerent countries' were fighting only for security. 'If this is true — and I am not going to say that it is untrue — then what an awful thing it is that we should allow this slaughter to go on.'[43] Ernest Bevin, rapidly ascending the union hierarchy, agreed.[44] Robert Williams, later a founding member of the British Communist Party, had opposed the war from the start. The Dockers' Union executive, which had been unabashedly pro-war as late as February 1917, was now explicitly against it:

> We deplore the war and will gladly cooperate with the workers of the Allied and Central Powers. We are of the opinion that the organized trade union movements of the countries concerned in this horrible war should be consulted at once on terms for a speedy settlement . . .[45]

Although the rank and file left no published record of their own political attitudes, they too had moved to the left. Otherwise, why would they have been so ready to strike, when downing tools was commonly thought to undermine the war effort?

Political disaffection and industrial militancy were a potent combination. On 30 January 1918, unions representing nearly every port worker in the country agreed that the NTWF should demand a national 8d per hour rise over pre-war rates, and negotiate on their behalf. This, as Robert Williams admitted in a letter sent to 'well over 100 firms and associations' of employers, was 'a departure from the usual practice of the Unions affiliated to the Federation'.[46]

Nor, at first, were the employers prepared to accept it. Here, though, the government stepped in. It had been warned by the dockers' representatives on the P&TEC that

> if the conference the Transport Workers had asked for were not held promptly, there was most serious risk of the men taking the matter into their own hands and stopping work in the important ports, including Liverpool, Hull, Bristol and Glasgow.[47]

The pressure which the Ministry of Labour brought to bear upon the employers proved effective, and a meeting between the NTWF and employers' representatives was scheduled for 18 June. Only one port still refused to attend — but this was London, the most important. Since 1908 all London docks had been administered by the Port of

London Authority which was under the chairmanship of Lord Devonport, the flinty victor of 1912, and a personal friend of Lloyd George. Now Devonport sought to convince the Prime Minister that the NTWF's claim to negotiate a national 8d per hour raise was 'a barefaced attempt to exploit the national situation to the detriment of the nation itself without a shred of justification'.[48] He failed. When finally the conference took place, London was represented like every other port.

The mood of the dockers at this point was extremely militant. As Williams wrote to Askwith some two months before the 18 June meeting: 'grave and growing restiveness exists among the whole of the workers in the Port [of Lond] area . . . ' and he went on to warn the Chief Industrial Commissioner of the perils which ignoring the unrest might produce: 'It is a secret which everybody knows that important officials went from this county to Russia and were unalterably assured that there was no insurrectionary possibility . . . Those officials made the saddest miscalculation of their lives.'[49] At a preliminary conference between NTWF officials and representatives of the employers, Sexton reiterated Williams's warning: 'the position is very serious . . . Liverpool are up . . .' and Bevin added: 'In the present state of the country both sides ought to prevent any agitation taking place.'[50] Indeed, even as the meeting convened, dockers in Dublin had commenced a wildcat strike which threatened to close the port. In such circumstances it is little wonder that the employers caved in, awarding the raise which the NTWF had demanded.

The NTWF's struggle for the national 8d per hour raise over pre-war rates illuminates several fundamental aspects of labour relations on the docks during 1914-18. First it shows that the government understood, even at the penultimate moment of the war, that labour's support remained crucial, more crucial even than the personal connection between Devonport and Lloyd George, that is, than the traditional connection between government and business. It suggests as well, that the dockers' leaders had clearly grasped the realignment that had taken place. They could point to the spectre of revolution in wartime, and be taken seriously. Finally, it reveals that by war's end a dramatic shift in the attitudes of dockers had taken place. They had begun by repudiating the national strike; they ended by threatening one.

The dockers' experience during World War I appears to have been typical of Britain's unskilled workers as a whole. War bonuses and across the board pay hikes seem to have kept them nearly level with the rate of inflation. Moreover, they lessened the differential between skilled and unskilled port workers since money was not awarded on a percentage basis. Membership in the major dockers' organisation, Tillett's Dock, Wharf, Riverside and General Labourers' Union, rose from about 38,000 to about 85,000 during 1914-18. Its income and expenditure rose too. The tendency toward federation was likewise strengthened. By 1918, the NTWF had secured the adherence of nearly every organised docker in Great Britain; and the Triple Alliance, to which the NTWF belonged, although it had been formed before the war, conducted the organisational and constitutional sessions during which it ratified the most formidable labour combination the country had yet seen. Surveys of British labour during the war suggest that these developments were roughly equivalent to those affecting other unskilled labourers for whom the war made possible relatively stable incomes and employment, and paradoxically, greater industrial militancy resulting in numerous confederations and amalgamations.[51]

It is more difficult to generalise about the highly skilled. The engineers suffered from the war, as has already been mentioned. So did the Nottingham lacemakers, who were hurt by the wartime preference for utilitarian fashions,[52] and the East End furniture workers, many of whom were driven to attempt learning new trades in special classes sponsored by Toynbee Hall.[53] Railwaymen, miners and some builders also appear to have suffered from longer hours, increased responsibility and inflation, all of which were consequences of the war.[54] At the same time, however, the boot and shoe operatives, steel workers, textile workers and potters enjoyed relative prosperity and steady employment during 1914-18.[55] Unlike the engineers, the highly skilled silk workers did not experience dilution.[56]

In short, and not surprisingly, the war had a different impact upon different workers. In addition, as this study of the dockers has shown, the impact of the war upon a single category of workers varied over time. If employment was regular on the docks from 1914-16, it was sporadic after the German U-boats were unleashed and the convoy system was established. If, after May 1916, exemption from conscription enhanced the status of the formerly despised dock rats, successive comb-outs and the withdrawal of exemption from dockers aged 18 to 25 in March 1918, returned them to the level of other labourers. Accordingly, dockers' attitudes towards the war varied over time as well.

We may, nevertheless, draw some tentative conclusions at least about unskilled labour in Britain during World War I, based upon the experience of that country's dockers. The war directly affected their working conditions and led simultaneously to improvements and to deterioration. Yet the former outweighed the latter, except, perhaps, during the grim last year of fighting. Basically, the war improved labour conditions and thus helped keep the workers patriotic. Industrial and political militancy surfaced mainly after the sharp deterioration of conditions which followed their unprecedented improvement during 1914-17.

The failure of internationalism in 1914 is often accounted one of history's great betrayals. It has rarely been pointed out, however, that within the parameters set by their own anti-revolutionary views and nationalist sentiments, British labour leaders remained true to one of the 2nd International's most important directives. A resolution passed at the Stuttgart conference in 1907 had exhorted the workers 'to take advantage of the conditions created by the war' should one break out despite their efforts to avert it. In an unforeseen way, British dockers did so.

Notes

I should particularly like to acknowledge the helpful comments of Julia Bush, whose own study of East London during World War I is forthcoming from Merlin Press.

1. See, for example, J.M. Winter, 'Arthur Henderson the Russian Revolution and the Reconstruction of the Labour Party', *Historical Journal*, December, 1972, pp.753-73. John Stubbs, 'Lord Milner and Patriotic Labour, 1914-18', *English Historical Review*, pp.717-54; A.J.P. Taylor, *The Troublemakers* (1958) pp.132-56, on the 'Triumph of E.D. Morel'; Walter Kendall, *The Revolutionary Movement in Britain* (1969); Marvin Swartz, *The Union of Democratic Control in British Politics during the First World War* (1971); James Hinton, *The First Shop Stewards' Movement* (1973); G.D.H. Cole, *Labour in the Coal Mining Industry 1914-21* (1923).

2. H.A. Mess, *Casual Labour at the Docks* (1915), p.34; *Parliamentary Papers*, 1888, vol, 21, p.117.

3. Beatrice Potter, 'The Docks', *Nineteenth Century*, September 1887.

4. W.H. Beveridge, *Unemployment, A Problem of Industry* (1909), p.313.

5. S.S. Bullock and E.C.P. Lascelles, *Dock Labour and Decasualization* (1924), p.20.

6. For an excellent account of British dockers before World War I see John Lovell, *Stevedores and Dockers* (1969).

7. Lloyd George Papers, c/8/6/2, House of Lords Record Office, Tillett to Lloyd George, 4 April 1914.

8. Public Record Office, LAB 2/625, Mr H. Wilson reporting on Gosling's visit to the Board of Trade, 24 June 1914.

9. Lloyd George Papers, c/8/6/1, Tillett to Lloyd George, 19 March 1914.

10. Dock, Wharf, Riverside and General Labourers' Union, *Triennial Meeting* 1919, p.10.

11. National Transport Workers Federation, *Annual General Council Meeting*, 1913, p.31.

12. On 4 August Tillett, on behalf of the Dockers' Union executive, demanded an emergency meeting of the Triple Alliance. See the *Daily Herald*, 5 August 1914.

13. Noelle Whiteside, 'The Dock Decasualization Issue, 1889-1924', unpublished PhD thesis, University of Liverpool, see Chapter 5, 'World War I and the Docks'.

14. PRO, Home Office 45/10944, Tom Adams to R. McKenna, 4 September 1914.

15. PRO, Home Office 45/10944, Ben Tillett to George Askwith, 13 August 1914.

16. *Women's Dreadnought*, 15 August 1914.

17. *East London Observer*, 8 August 1914.

18. PRO, LAB 2/1052, Report of the Port and Transit Executive Committee, December, 1915.

19. Sir Joseph Broodbank, *History of the Port of London*, vol. 2 (1921), p.458.

20. PRO, LAB 2/1052, Grey to Runciman, 17 March 1916.

21. PRO, T172/980.B, Lloyd George to Tillett, 25 August 1914.

22. Ibid., Tillett to Lloyd George, 9 September 1914.

23. PRO, LAB 2/169, 'Delegation to the Board of Trade by Dock, Wharf, Riverside and General Labourers' Union, National Transport Workers' Federation, and General Federation of Trade Unions', 23 May 1916.

24. Ibid.

25. Whiteside, 'The Dock Decasualisation Issue', p.164.

26. PRO, CAB 24/7/GT104.

27. Whiteside, 'The Dock Decasualisation Issue', p.159.

28. Hinton, *The First Shop Stewards' Movement*, pp.140-61.

29. As early as 1897 Tom Mann had blamed the dilution of dock labour by the unemployed of other industries for 'the great change' which had reduced dockers from skilled to unskilled workers. See Mann's pamphlet, *The Position of Dockers and Seamen in 1897*.

30. In 1904 Tillett wrote: 'Our own policy as the result of experience is that it is best to make the best of the bargain, and get the highest wages possible with the new machinery.' International Transport Workers' Federation Collection, no. 87, Modern Records Centre, Warwick University, Tillett to A.C. Wessells, 9 May 1904.

31. Broodbank, *Port of London*, vol. 2, p.482.

32. PRO, LAB 21/124 (n.d.).

33. PRO, LAB 2/124, T.B. Davies, Middlesbrough Branch Secretary of the DWR & GLU, to J.W. Jessop of Middlesbrough Master Stevedores Association.

34. PRO, LAB 2/125, Taylor to Askwith, 4 January 1918.

35. Ibid., Greenwood to Tillett, 2 February 1918.

36. For labour unrest in the docks see particularly PRO LAB 21/121, LAB 2/123 and LAB 2/125.

37. *The Times*, 9 April 1916.

38. PRO, LAB 2/169, Phillips to P&TEC, 17 July 1916.

39. PRO, LAB 2/169, Inchape to Asquith, 28 June 1916.

40. PRO, LAB 2/124, Tillett to George Barnes, 11 August 1917.

41. See, for example, Kendall, *The Revolutionary Movement*, pp.84-187, whose analysis on this point is typical.

42. PRO, LAB 2/1045, Williams to 'Labour Representatives on Local Committees', 30 March 1918.

43. *Weekly Herald*, 13 January 1917.

44. See Alan Bullock, *The Life and Times of Ernest Bevin*, vol. 1 (1960), pp.44-88 for Bevin's views on the war.

45. *Dockers' Record*, August 1917.

46. PRO, LAB 2/127.

47. Ibid., Tillett, Sexton and Bevin's submission to the P&TEC, 21 March 1918.

48. Ibid., Devonport to Lloyd George, 9 April 1918.

49. Ibid., Williams to Askwith, 15 April 1918.

50. Ibid., 'Minutes of Preliminary Conference', 26 March 1918.

51. See, for example, N. Robertson and K.I. Sams, *British Trade Unionism* (1972) p.4.

52. Norman Cuthbert, *The Lacemakers Society* (1960), p.89.

53. See the *Toynbee Record*, March 1915.

54. Phillip Bagwell, *The Railwaymen* (1963), p.345; R.W. Postgate, *The Builders' History*, p.430.

55. Alan Fox, *A History of the National Union of Boot and Shoe Operatives* (1958), p.368; Arthur Pugh, *Men of Steel* (1951); F. Burchill and R. Ross, *A History of the Potters Union* (1977), p.163.

56. F. Burchill and J. Sweeney, *A History of the Trade Unionism in the North Staffordshire Textile Industry* (1971), p.59.

6 COPING WITH LABOUR, 1918-1926

James E. Cronin

Labour in Britain has, for most of its organised existence, been committed to political and industrial moderation and to the pursuit of its ends through peaceful electoral advance or orderly collective bargaining. This trait has as many critics as admirers, but few would dispute that it has characterised the labour movement from the collapse of Chartism in the late 1840s right up to the present.[1] Yet, there was certainly one moment, lasting from just before the end of the First World War to the defeat of the General Strike, when that entire tradition was repudiated by large numbers of workers and activists and replaced by an aggressive labour insurgency. This chapter is an attempt to define this unprecedented militancy and to offer tentative explanations of its origins and its ultimate containment.

Contemporary opinion after the war was unanimous on several points: that the war of 1914-18 marked a sharp break with the past; that the key difference between 1914 and 1918-19 was in the relations between capital and labour; and that novel arrangements were required to integrate labour politically and industrially.[2] A meeting of the North London Manufacturers' Association on 16 July 1918 was told, for example, that 'the industrial system of this country, as we knew it in July 1914, has been suspended'; moreover, it was 'unlikely to be reestablished without modification of a far-reaching nature'. Specifically, 'no part of our pre-war industrial system is more likely to be radically changed in design and practice after the war than the relationship between employers and employed'. For their part, the employers were ready to recognise many 'errors in the past', and even to contemplate, as a group of Birmingham employers put it, 'the surrender by Capital of its supposed right to dictate to Labour the conditions under which work shall be carried on'.[3] Not all employers were so contrite, but most did share the belief of one large industrialist that 'the question uppermost in the minds of all Britain today- . . . is whether, now that the Germans are beaten, there shall be peace or war in industry'.[4]

For men of business, the problem was made more acute by the realisation that British industry was ill-equipped to compete in the

113

export markets of the post-war world. Britain's industrial retardation was visible before the war and was much discussed in the popular press.[5] Prospects after the war were even worse. F. Dudley Docker, first President of the Federation of British Industries, predicted, 'There is no doubt that competition in trade will be keener than it has ever been before. There will be a general scramble for the markets of the world and a period of bitter international competition.' The incentives to evolve 'sound and amicable relations ... between Capital and Labour' were therefore both political and crudely economic.[6] It was in the national interest to boost 'the produce of labour', and so to reform industrial relations as well.[7]

What made this problem so critical was that the means to attaining labour's co-operation in production were by no means obvious. Rather, by the end of the First World War workers were demanding higher wages, greater control at the workplace, the nationalisation of coal and other industries, and a host of social reforms connected with housing, health and employment. The difficulty was compounded by their taste for 'direct action' in implementing these goals, and their distrust of the political process and independence from labour's formal leadership. Dudley Docker again expressed the view from above:

> Perhaps the most perplexing feature of these labour troubles has been the evidence they have afforded that the rank and file of workers no longer place the reliance they formerly did in their Union leaders, but are inclined to break away from any bargain on small provocation.[8]

Lloyd George's trusted adviser Tom Jones offered a similar diagnosis, explaining in February 1919 that, 'Much of the present difficulty springs from the mutiny of the rank and file against the old established leaders and there seems to be no machinery for bringing about a quick change of leaders.' The situation was especially troubling to men like Jones and Lloyd George, who had expended considerable effort in building links to the leaders of the unions, only to learn that their labour friends were unable to deliver the allegiance of the membership. The Government's only option, according to Jones, was 'to stand by the accredited leaders ..., but,' he admitted, 'it does not get over the fact that the leaders no longer represent the more active and agitating minds in the labour movement.'[9]

'Trade union organisation was the only thing between us and anarchy,' in the view of Bonar Law, but that organisation was no longer run by its apparent leaders. As Churchill lamented in February of 1919, 'The curse of trade unionism was that *there was not enough of it*, and it was not highly enough developed to make its branch secretaries [let alone its rank and file] fall into line with the head office.'[10] The crisis within industry was in this sense a crisis of authority. The men were aggrieved and aggressive, and the old restraints of moderate trade unionism were absent. Beatrice Webb made much the same point in October 1920. 'Clearly, it was not the leaders but the mass of the men who had gone "red".'[11] But the leaders could no longer be relied upon to enforce discipline and moderation. The Government was much dismayed by the situation and by their inability to get a handle upon discontent. The Minister of Labour worried openly, 'The problem of the basis of the authority of trade union leaders has become a very real one . . .'[12]

The excess of democracy inside the labour movement was compounded by an apparent failure of the democratic process in government. The Lloyd George Coalition had won a resounding victory in the Coupon Election of November 1918, but even the victors knew that the distribution of seats was not an accurate reflection of the underlying mood of the country. The President of Harvard, Abbott Lawrence Lowell, analysed the situation after a visit to England in 1920:

> The general election was held too soon for the sentiments aroused by the war, and the popularity of the statesmen who had won it, to subside. There had not been time for opponents to gather strength, and the result was an overwhelming victory for the administration, with no opposition numerous, organised or consolidated enough to be formidable . . . [Because] the ordinary political mechanism for formulating questions on which opinion is based had disappeared . . ., public opinion became to a great extent atrophied.

In such a position, ministers inevitably 'lose the respect of both sides too completely to continue in office'. But most important, the absence of articulate opposition in Parliament provoked among the 'discontented elements in the country feelings of hopelessness about obtaining a change of policy by political means'.[13] The predictable consequences had already been noted by Basil Thomson, the alarmist but not altogether uninformed Director of Intelligence for the Home Office, in his review of 1919:

The year opened ominously, for the defeat of the pacifist and revolutionary candidates in the General Election brought into being an underground movement for Direct Action on the plea that the House of Commons had ceased to represent the country as a whole.[14]

Inevitably, what looked from on high to be an absence of order and control was experienced by those below as a major increment of freedom, strength and self-confidence. The war and post-war years witnessed an explosion of organisation among workers. Overall union membership doubled, rank-and-file movements blossomed in munitions, engineering and shipbuilding, 'vigilance committees' were active in the railways, and local democracy flourished among coalminers and throughout the labour movement.[15] An engineering worker from Sheffield remembered how the men in the shops took to the election of shop stewards in 1916: the drive 'went like wildfire. The rank and file knew they were divorced from the officials and that the officials were linked with the Government so far as the war was concerned. The rank and file wanted to express themselves and this was their medium.'[16]

Other groups — including trades councils, co-operatives and local Labour Parties — also grew as never before.[17] Perhaps the most threatening and symptomatic were the Councils of Action which sprang up during the summer of 1920 to protest government plans for intervention in Russia. Even after the prospect of intervention faded, these organs 'would not go away'. According to Middlemas, '350 of them, haphazardly set up, based largely on the still inchoate local Labour Parties and on Trades Councils permeated by shop stewards' militancy, took on a life of their own', and seemed for a while to constitute the key centres of political and industrial opposition.[18]

Such organised strength reflected heightened class feeling, and served further to stimulate the workers' sense of solidarity and antagonism. As Carter Goodrich noted of the shop stewards, who in his opinion 'exercised the greatest degree of control ever held by British workers . . .', the 'movement was both an expression of the demand for control and an incitement to further demands'.[19] Even such a moderate as J.R. Clynes grasped the augmentation of workers' power in the years after 1914: 'If the war does not change fundamentally the relations between Capital and Labour,' he said, 'it will at least tend greatly to modify in favour of Labour the basis of these relations . . . Labour,' he proceeded with a note of incomprehension, 'has been curiously elevated by the demands of war'.[20]

The elevation of labour was a dual process, involving not merely an increase in organisation but also a transformation of consciousness. With greater resources at their disposal with which to mobilise and press demands, workers' sense of self-worth grew, and their previously rather modest expectations quickly caught up with the expanding limits of their collective power. Of course, the new consciousness contained many elements inherited from the past, but its tone and depth were very different. As one author explained at the time, 'within the lower or broader stages of society there had been growing for near a century a sullen "class-consciousness" founded, for what it was worth, almost entirely on a community of economic disabilities'. By 1918, the disabilities were being matched by sources of strength and solidarity, and the sullen demeanour of labour was becoming far more aggressive and self-confident. As Robert Roberts explained of Salford workers, 'Regular work and the absence of class pressure from above had wrought in many a peculiar quality which looked uncommonly like self-respect.' As the conflict wore on into late 1917, 'Ordinary folk . . . became boldly critical of things about them and especially of those who, they believed, were making huge profits at the country's expense.'[21]

The sharpening of class allegiances and antagonisms was clear to all with eyes to see. Though it is true that the discontent manifest during the war was often expressed in sectional terms, and that the shop stewards' movement itself sprang from quite undisguised craft concerns, nevertheless by 1919-20 class sentiments *were* more polarised and solid. A Ministry of Labour official discerned in February 1920 an

> increasing tendency for the trade unionists of one shop works or small districts to act together, irrespective of their division into crafts or occupations. What is called 'class consciousness' is obliterating the distinction between those who follow different occupations in the same works.[22]

The class, as opposed to the sectional, character of the movement was strengthened both by its pronounced consumerist component and by the substantial participation of working-class women. Entire communities rose up in protest against exorbitant food prices, rent increases and actual shortages of food, housing and other necessities. There was a mushroom growth of tenants' associations, and the struggle over housing from 1915 to 1924 meant an effective end to privately-owned accommodation for the working class, even if it did not as yet guarantee the provision of an alternative.[23] In this agitation, women were especially prominent, being regularly appointed as the 'street captains' in rent strikes.[24] Moreover, in Glasgow, Coventry, Woolwich and Rosyth this community-based insurgency threatened at various moments to merge with more purely industrial action.[25] Women were also noticeably more involved in unions and strikes than ever before. Women munitions workers joined unions on a massive scale and took an increasing part in workplace struggles.[26]

The role of the government also facilitated the broadening of local and sectional grievance into class antagonisms. By intervening so drastically in economy and society, the state almost ensured that protest would be directed against it. By providing a focus for discontent outside the workplace and the neighbourhood, it facilitated a certain transcending of sectional styles of protest. The government's role was by no means an enviable one, for its bungling interference in industry simultaneously angered employers and workers. Moreover, intervention often meant an increase in the leverage of workers at the same time as it involved the co-option of businessmen and labour officials in the daily tasks of administration.[27] The outcome of this contradictory situation was thus an intensification of class conflict and class consciousness on both sides of industry, precisely the opposite of what was intended.

'Class consciousness' is, of course, an elusive quality, difficult enough to define, almost impossible to measure. Moreover, at times of mass activity such as 1919-20, consciousness becomes especially volatile, the mood and rhetoric of working people shifting rapidly with the changing fortunes of collective action. For what it is worth, however, the commentary that does exist from this period is quite unambiguous in showing an expanded sense of grievance on the part of most workers, a clear willingness to pin responsibility for problems upon capital and the state, and a very real sense that working men and women now possessed the means with which to challenge the existing distribution of power and wealth.[28] This growing sense of political capacity was surely the most striking aspect of contemporary opinion: as one young Welsh miner explained proudly, 'now we're ready to take over the job of runnin' the country'.[29] What made such sentiments truly disturbing was that they were so closely bound up with the extraordinary degree of mobilisation and organisation achieved by the end of the war.

The political ramifications of this radicalisation were necessarily profound, and represented both a threat and an opportunity to the inherited 'Labourist' traditions of the unions and of the Parliamentary Labour Party. It was, on the one hand, a major force behind the widespread adoption within the labour movement of demands for nationalisation, for a capital levy and for extended state provision of various social services, and behind the restructuring of the Labour Party and the adoption of its new 'socialist' programme of 1918.[30] Moreover, it was the networks of local activists called into existence by the exigencies of war that became the core of the new constituency Labour parties and served as the key to the party's electoral success. In this, women played a major part: commentators were particularly impressed with the practice of 'mass canvassing for women', during which the local organisers would, as the *Manchester Guardian* reported, 'send several canvassers into a street. These knock at the doors. The women, attracted by the curiosity, come out and are immediately addressed by a speaker in waiting for the purpose, and while the meeting goes on the canvassers are at work.'[31] The Labour party, allied as it was with the unions and capable of presenting itself as the logical and legitimate political vehicle for increased activism and radicalism, benefited enormously from the infusion of local supporters.[32] That this would, in the end, put limits upon the development of political consciousness can hardly be doubted, but as of 1919 and 1920 the result had been a substantial leftward shift in the political stance of the workers.[33]

Of course, the bulk of the working class were far from being committed socialists in these turbulent years, and the general situation was far from revolutionary. Most important, the governing elite never lost the capacity or will to rule, nor were they rent with divisions sharp enough to paralyse administration. And, though there was discontent within the army and among the police, in neither did it reach major proportions.[34] Indeed, the 1919 police strike, which failed so completely, served primarily as an occasion to weed out unreliable elements.[35] The forces of order were also aided by the fragmentation of the left and the consequent weakness of insurgent leadership.[36] None the less, the absence of a genuinely revolutionary potential does not diminish the severity of the post-war crisis, for it is clear from the evidence that a very large section of the population were no longer convinced of the justice or the immutability of existing institutions and were ready to opt for something vastly different. They were also — and this is perhaps the most crucial point — mobilised and engaged to an unprecedented degree. In short, there was a profound crisis of legitimacy, pervading and threatening the political and social order as it had evolved to 1918.

If one grants the reality and significance of the 1919-20 crisis, and thus elevates it to something more than the sum of the short-term dislocations and discontent generated by four years of war, then it becomes necessary to re-evaluate both its origins and the strategies adopted for its containment. Unfortunately, the historiographies concerned with the evolution of labour in the early twentieth century and with post-war stabilisation are both seriously deficient. In the main, they underestimate the novelty and significance of the insurgency of 1919-20, and so also those forces within the history of labour that produced it and those policies and political realignments that overcame it. It is appropriate, therefore, to venture briefly into the history of labour to 1918 to discover the roots of militancy, and to discuss at some length the process of containment after 1918.

At first glance, the problem of origins is simple enough, but in fact the simplicity is misleading. Contemporaries had no difficulty devising lists of grievances causing unrest. One such list came from the Home Office *Survey of Revolutionary Feeling during the Year 1919*, by Basil Thomson:[37] 'The causes which contribute to revolutionary feeling may be given,' Thomson wrote with a precision worthy of a modern sociologist, 'in the order of their importance as follows:

1. Profiteering and high prices.
2. Insufficient and bad housing accommodation.
3. Class hatred, aggravated by the foolish and dangerous ostentation of the rich, the publication of large dividends, and distrust of a "Government of profiteers".
4. Education by Labour Colleges, schools and classes and better circulation of literature on Marxian economics.
5. Influence of extremist Trade Union leaders — Mann, Cramp, Smillie, Hodges, Bromley, Hill, Williams, Turner.
6. Unemployment.
7. Labour press, particularly the "Daily Herald", "The Workers' Dreadnought", and "The Worker".
8. External influences — Russia, Ireland, Egypt, India.'

Balancing these disturbing forces were:

'1. Popularity of the Royal Family
 2. Sport'

and several lesser factors, none of which, it seemed to Thomson, were of sufficient weight to provide proper ballast for the ship of state.

Clearly, though, these were all relatively transitory grievances which can perhaps account for the anger felt by British workers, but cannot explain the extent of organisation or the profound class consciousness with which it was bound up. To explain these would seem to require an analysis of more long-term factors in the evolution of labour. These structural developments were, of course, very complicated and their impact was highly uneven. Any generalisation is therefore difficult, and subject to qualifrcation. Still, a review of the existing monographic literature suggests that in the late-nineteenth and early-twentieth centuries the structure of British society changed in ways conducive to the heightening of class awareness and allegiance and to the mobilisation of class interests in the industrial and political spheres. A variety of technical, social and economic processes conjoined to produce a working class that was, if not more internally homogeneous, at least less sharply divided within itself, and also more culturally distinct from middle and upper class society than its Victorian analogue had been.[38] These same forces simultaneously strengthened the capacity of different groups of workers to organise and press their interests in a collective fashion. The most visible consequence of these transformations was the gradual, and inevitably discontinuous, spreading of organisation beyond the relatively small stratum of (mostly) skilled workers who were unionised and politically active in mid-Victorian Britain to include increasing numbers of the less skilled.

Three distinct processes interacted to produce this reshaping of the working class. First, there was the simple expansion of the service sector, in which most workers belonged to that ambiguous, but important, category of the 'semi-skilled'. Secondly, the pattern of development within industry led to an increasing demand for semi-skilled, as opposed to either skilled or unskilled labour.[39] This was met by upgrading the latter, by increasing the numbers and decreasing the training of apprentices or, more rarely, by 'degrading' skilled workers. Thirdly, the social ecology of mid-Victorian cities slowly gave way to a more socially segregated pattern of residence during the massive urban growth that began late in the century. The effect was to create a physical space for the development of a strong and distinctive working-class culture sustained by, and itself helping to sustain, a broad array of social and political institutions that together added substantially to the resources which workers could mobilise on their own behalf.

It is impossible, of course, to relate these underlying structural changes in any direct and immediate manner to the patterns of mobilisation and militancy, for collective action depended also upon the balance of forces locally and in various industries and this was linked both to economic and political conjuncture. Nevertheless, to focus narrowly upon the conjunctural correlates of mass action would be to miss the way in which social and economic structure affected the potentialities for, and limitations upon, the self-activity of working people.

To document these long-term changes to any substantial degree would necessitate a more extensive discussion than is possible here, but one can suggest the main outlines. The growth in the ranks of the semi-skilled or unskilled is well known, and resulted from an expansion of the number of apprentices or un-apprenticed adults in trades like engineering and iron and steel; from the development of new industries that required a small number of skilled men for maintenance and much larger numbers of semi-skilled workers for production, and from the enhanced economic importance of transport, communication and service.[40] From 1890, the rate of increase of the workforce in the latter exceeded that in manufacturing industry, and added greatly to the amount of stable, semi-skilled employment. Even within manufacturing, there was a steady increase in the size of plant, the ratio of capital per worker and in industrial concentration. However retarded the modernisation of British industry, the trends were visible and important, both in new industries and even in old staple trades, like mining and cotton.[41]

In terms of labour, the main effect of such changes was to make work more regular and predictable, as well as more tightly controlled and supervised. Scientific management remained more of an ideology than a reality, but even that revealed a greater attention on the part of management to the affairs of production.[42] In some cases, this led to sharp conflicts with the skilled workers, as in engineering, but other factors combined to make such confrontations the exception. The reason is that the process of 'deskilling', as it has been called, occurred more at the level of the class or the entire population than the individual, for individual artisans were kept employed in superior grades of work, in the toolroom or in specialised production rather than displaced. This was ensured by the timing of technical change, for the diffusion of new equipment could be achieved only during periods of high demand and investment, which meant that labour shortages were also acute.[43]

The skilled were therefore challenged, and to some degree driven into opposition, but by no means defeated or eliminated.[44] The evolution of industrial structure affected the unskilled in a less ambiguous fashion. Jobs for the less skilled came to approximate more closely the norm of factory work, with greater distance between master and men, more bossing and discipline and, ordinarily, a more intensive pace of production. But the greater regularity, rationality and stability of employment afforded to the less skilled a more central place in the production process and provided the material underpinnings for organisation and resistance. It took time, naturally, for new unskilled factory hands to acquire what Hobsbawm has termed the 'habit of solidarity', and for workers in transport and government service to evolve forms of organisation appropriate to the scale and style of their employment and to the combined strength of their employers, but by 1914 the process was well advanced.[45] By that date, the semi- and unskilled had managed to knit together permanent unions and to begin the battle for better pay and conditions.[46] These efforts were pushed much further after 1914, for organisation was greatly aided by the labour shortages of the war and by the need to insure a smooth, sure flow of production. In consequence, some semi-skilled pieceworkers came to earn more than skilled time-workers. Between 1914 and 1918, the gap between the wages of skilled and unskilled workers decreased by 20 per cent in building, 33 per cent in shipbuilding, 29 per cent in engineering and 45 per cent on the railways. By the end of the war, unskilled men generally were making 70-80 per cent of the wages of skilled men.[47] There were inevitable tensions and resentments among the skilled over this equalisation, but because so much of the change seemed to have been dictated from on high, the net result was to array skilled and unskilled together against both employers and their allies in government. The fact that the levelling was so closely bound up with the general inflation of prices and money wages was especially significant, for it meant a heightening of expectations and a calling into question of the distribution of rewards throughout society, instead of a mere intensification of sectional sentiment and protest.

The impact of developments in the spatial relations of classes is more difficult to assess, but seems also to have worked in most cases to facilitate militancy. The pattern varied substantially from place to place, depending upon the nature of local transportation systems, housing and labour markets, but in general it appears that from 1890 to 1914 working-class communities acquired a degree of stability and rootedness such as to allow for the elaboration of a robust, and partially autonomous, way of life.[48] Intimately linked to this culture, or rather to these locally-based subcultures, were networks of formal and informal institutions, from adult classes to the friendships of the street and the pub. The emergence of this working-class social and cultural presence in the cities of late Victorian and Edwardian Britain has been documented by several historians, and was, of course, much discussed by contemporaries. In both instances, commentary has tended to stress the problems with this new culture — its patriarchal, hierarchical and complacent aspects being deplored by historians, its paganism, cynicism and insularity being attacked by contemporaries. Neither perspective, it can be argued, sufficiently emphasises the novelty of the development, or the implications for politics and other forms of collective action, for these increasingly solid committees represented a substantial increment to the strength of labour.[49]

The consolidation of independent working-class communities seems to have occurred throughout the country, though the precise set of processes involved varied a good deal. Communities of miners became much more stable as migration to the older fields showed, and even where growth continued, it tended to involve an increase in the density of existing settlements rather than an influx into completely new areas.[50] For older industrial centres, the process differed. Urban growth after 1870 seems to have centred in the larger towns and cities rather than in those medium-sized towns that housed so many of the mills of the first industrial revolution.[51] As cities grew, the local 'urban villages' centred on the factory and presided over by paternalistic employers, such as those in the cotton towns of Lancashire, were submerged in the larger agglomerations of working-class residences being built to house the industrial population.[52] In London, the transport revolutions around mid-century and then again in the 1880s and 1890s allowed first for the middle and lower-middle classes to vacate the centre and then, later, for a more distinctly working-class dispersal into newer 'proletarian' communities like Battersea, Islington and other areas north and south of the Thames.[53] These sections became strongholds of working-class organisation and activity and, after the reorganisation of local government in 1888, of labour and progressive political agitation and voting.[54]

In the community as well as at the workplace, therefore, the sum of social transformations seemed to further class formation and awareness. When these underlying pressures were released by a favourable short-term conjuncture, workers organised massively and militantly. This happened during the economic boom that preceded the First World War and, more importantly, during the war itself. The war was especially important, for it furthered the reshaping of the social structure that was already occurring, gave workers enormous tactical leverage, and also politicised and deepened unrest by the peculiar nature of state intervention. As one of the Commissioners on Unrest explained in 1917, 'The War has introduced a new element into questions affecting Labour, viz., the Government'.[55] Industrially, both the threat to skilled and the upgrading of less skilled labour were accentuated by dilution and the massive entry of women into the workforce. Socially, communities were made more solid by the need to cope with the disruptions of war, by the weakening of traditional sex roles, and by the prevalence of grievances related to consumption. Politically, the state's involvement in everyday life transformed hardships into grievances and made every grievance political, forcing resistance to be political as well. The government's relationship with the unions was particularly explosive, for by extracting the consent and ensuring the collaboration of union leaders in wartime industrial problems, the government opened a critical space for the elaboration of workers' organisation on the shopfloor. The result was a growth of all sorts of localised activity — shop stewards, local Labour Parties, trades councils, tenants' groups and so on — forms of collective mobilisation suited to tap the recent increase in working-class resources and the particular political needs of the war.

The increase in working-class strength in industry and in the community produced among many a sustained activism and intellectual independence that had direct and dangerous political implications. Inevitably, therefore, the containment of labour entailed a reshaping and realignment in the structure of politics. Indeed, several major institutions in British political life — the parties, the organisations of capital and labour and the state machinery itself — underwent substantial changes in the first post-war decade, the effects of which were to reconstitute the political forms through which bourgeois hegemony was exercised. The process was, of course, extremely complicated, and its progress often convoluted. It was accompanied, moreover, by splits and struggles within the 'establishment', which have led many historians to read the political history of the era in terms of factions and personalities and thus to overlook the coherence and the internal logic of the various elements in the policy of stabilisation, and the close fit between the solution achieved by Britain's rulers and the structural needs of British capitalism.

The attempts to tame labour and to re-establish political quiescence were genuinely international phenomena.[56] Just as the mass insurgency of 1919-20 swept over the whole of Europe, so the desire to put the workers back in their place also animated regimes throughout the world.[57] As such, the problem became a major factor in economic diplomacy, and the policies adopted for its solution in various countries were often similiar, at least in appearance. However, it would be a mistake to allow the international dimension of the crisis to obscure the differences between its resolution in each country, for the differences were important in themselves and in determining the further evolution of politics and social structure in different nations. More precisely, it would involve a serious misreading of the record to seek to subsume the British experience under one or another of the models that have been elaborated to account for the phenomenon in other parts of the world — models summed up in terms such as 'organised capitalism' or 'corporatism'.[58] On the other hand, it would be equally mistaken to accept what is probably the dominant view in British political history — that what happened after 1918 was simply an attempted return to the past, a re-assertion of traditional patterns of party politics and of sectional collective bargaining, produced by a 'failure of imagination', of political will and of economic theory.[59] Both arguments suffer from anachronism: the first focuses on developments evident in later years but prematurely locates them in the 1920s, while the latter view misses the novelty and short-term viability of the system developed in Britain by the mid-1920s.

What emerged by 1926 was neither 'organised capitalism', with its regular brokering between highly structured groups of workers, businessmen and an interventionist state, nor was it in any meaningful sense a re-emergence of old forms of legitimacy. Rather, it was a unique political economy characterised by the unity of several, seemingly contradictory, features. Most prominent of these were: the dominance of finance capital over industry and the state; the presence of national organisations of employers and workers engaging in industry-wide collective bargaining with modest assistance and informal encouragement from the state; a stable, class-based party system with Labour in a semi-permanent minority status; and a state machinery thoroughly dominated by the Treasury in the interests of finance and committed to maintaining a low profile in industrial matters while taking on increasing social functions. It was a sort of bastardised liberalism or, perhaps more accurately, a form of corporatism without Keynes, without the state and without the cash. The emergence of this

to provide a massive infusion of capital into industry. The Bank of England managed to emasculate the scheme, but the incident widened further the gulf separating the Coalition from the dominant institutions of British capitalism. Nor was Lloyd George notably more popular among the weaker sections of capital. Employers in general tended to overlook the benefits they might receive from government-supported investment and to remember instead his interventions in strikes, which they saw as pro-labour, and his association with the elaborate network of wartime controls imposed upon industry.[87]

For all these forces, then, the prospect offered by some continued form of coalition was less attractive than a revitalisation of the Conservative Party. The Conservative Party could also provide a mechanism for the articulation of explicitly middle-class interests. One important, but poorly documented, aspect of the post-war malaise was the disloyalty and disaffection of the middle and lower-middle classes. One symptom was the alarming increase in white-collar and civil service unionism,[88] and Lloyd George was warned more than once that, as Frederick Guest put it in January 1920, 'the greatest asset of the Labour Party . . . has been the sympathy which it has received from the middle classes . . . The middle classes see no solution except by supporting those who have already gained concessions.'[89] One suspects that the norm was not a move to the left, but a more typically middle-class reaction against the strength of labour, against taxation and social reform.[90] Whatever the balance of opinion within these middling strata, however, it is clear that they were not well-integrated into the existing party system.

Enrolling these discontented elements on the side of conservatism was necessary but difficult. The problem was that, as Morgan has argued, 'If these middle-class protesters had an ideal, it lay not in the outmoded die-hard Toryism of pre-war but rather in an up-to-date, independent Conservatism, as the voice of the salaried, rate-paying, owner-occupier.'[91] It was extremely difficult to reconcile such naked appeals to class interest with the rhetoric of the coalition headed by Lloyd George. Faced with the massive growth of the working-class electorate and the appeal of the Labour Party, the Conservative Party came to be seen as the means to obtain a popular basis for stabilisation. However, the conservatives were unable to play this role while they remained in the coalition. 'The Society of Conservative Agents', according to Middlemas, 'complained repeatedly about organizational weakness in the regions after 1919', and the party apparatus would have continued to atrophy if the coalition had been prolonged much further.[92] Moreover, after the crisis of 1919-20, Lloyd George had become tainted in the minds of working people and employers alike, and gradually the Conservatives found him more of a liability than an asset. Finally, the coalition broke apart with the Conservative decision to fight the 1922 election as an independent party.

The Conservative Party would continue to erect defences against socialism, with greater flexibility and with the weight of tradition and the powerful force of inertia behind it. It would also receive the more or less united support of the middle classes and the industrialists, who were arrayed behind the party by its adoption of the slogans of fiscal responsibility and its support, during the 1923 election, of a modest measure of protection. By 1924, the party was solid behind Baldwin who, as Cowling has said, would wear 'for the next phase of political activity . . . the mantle Lloyd George had worn in his last two years of office as leader of resistance to "Socialism".'[93]

Conservatism thus created a firm base of support for stabilisation while providing an arena in which to adjust the various competing groups within the British upper class, and to reconcile politically the split between industry and the City. The terms of the reconciliation were, of course, very favourable to the City and reflected both the general consolidation of financial power after the war and the privileged access to the state enjoyed by non-industrial capital centred in London. Well before the war, the City wielded enormous economic and political influence, and its leverage was increased still further by the massive waves of bank amalgamations that gathered pace between 1890 and 1914 and climaxed during 1917-19.[94] Indeed by 1918 the structure of British banking had assumed the highly concentrated form it has today. Manufacturing industry, however, was still distinctly small-scale and disorganised. The extent of fragmentation prompted the government to encourage the independent organisation of businessmen during the war, and so to assist in the formation of the Federation of British Industries in 1917. But the Federation remained weak, its policies diluted to a sort of lowest common denominator reflecting the disorganisation of its membership. In 1919, it was weakened still more by the secession of the National Conference of Employers' Organisations, which claimed the right to speak for industry on matters of labour policy, leaving the FBI with responsibility for trade matters only.[95]

There is some slight evidence of a temporary bridging of the gap between finance and industry just after the war, when the banks participated in the flotation of new companies during the heady boom of 1919-20.[96] Moreover, at least one bank created by the amalgamation movement, the Midland, did have extensive interests in industry. On balance, however, this speculative episode probably did more to convince bankers of the risks of industrial investment than to interest them in it permanently. By late 1920, the brief flirtation with industry was over, and the depression which overtook the staple industries thereafter only reinforced the divorce of finance from industry. Though the large banks were involved in the subsequent and extensive merger activity of the 1920s, this did not necessarily betoken any greater interest in domestic industry. Indeed, the funds provided for mergers may be considered as a substitute for more genuinely productive investment, and, as recent work has shown, mergers were seldom followed by the sort of internal reorganisation that would have facilitated increased investment and more rationalised production.[97]

Meanwhile, the traditional elements in the hierarchy of finance moved decisively to institutionalise their influence over government policy. State intervention in the economy during the war, the setting up of new ministries assuming new social functions, and uncertainties over Lloyd George and the Coalition worried the City, the Bank of England and their Treasury allies deeply.[98] They acted, therefore, to strengthen the Treasury's role in the state and to obtain the government's commitment to return to gold. Their representatives dominated the Cunliffe Committee and ensured the orthodoxy of its report. More importantly, the Treasury secured a number of administrative changes that enhanced its influence with the counsels of state. The crucial decisions were taken in 1919. Sir Warren Fisher, Permanent Secretary to the Treasury, was formally recognised as 'Head of the Civil Service' and given the major role in advising the Prime Minister on senior departmental appointments. In the same year, the Treasury forbade the practice of recruiting higher officials from outside the ranks of the Civil Service and instituted a requirement that each ministry should appoint an officer for 'finance and establishment' who was to introduce rigorous accounting procedures, oversee staffing arrangements and, one may safely assume, represent the Treasury view inside the department. The Treasury also obtained the right to name a permanent member to the increasingly powerful Cabinet Secretariat. The first of these was Frederick Leith Ross, who later recounted his perception of the job: 'One of the normal duties of the new post was to keep a special watch on all proposals for new expenditure and to make sure that the Chancellor of the Exchequer had had sufficient time to pronounce on their financial implications before they were submitted to the Cabinet for decision.' In 1924, this informal function became a formal requirement that all proposals involving public expenditure had to be submitted first to the Exchequer. By the early 1920s, therefore, the Treasury had effective control of the Cabinet agenda and could virtually guarantee that no initiatives of which it disapproved would become policy.[99]

From such positions of strength, the orthodox men of the Treasury effected the deflation of the economy from 1920 to 1925. With the fall of the Labour government in late 1924, the time had come for the final act in the restoration of fiscal responsibility, the return to gold. By 1925, the acquiescence of the Federation of British Industries was secured, and even Reginald McKenna of the Midland Bank came around, under pressure from the Treasury and the Bank of England, to its inevitability. The arguments made by the proponents of the return to the pre-war parity were both economic and political, for a modified gold standard was seen not only as necessary for the revival of world trade but also as a 'knave-proof' guarantee of social discipline and political moderation. It was viewed specifically as a device which would provide a near-automatic check on any 'irresponsible' actions which a future Labour government might be tempted to take.[100]

Over the long term, these institutional safeguards for capital would seriously hamper efforts by any party to reform and revitalise British industry. In the short run, they were probably not necessary for restraining Labour, since the party was handicapped in several additional ways. With the revival of Conservative fortunes after 1922 and the debacle of 1924, aided no doubt by the Zinoviev letter and by the incredible hostility of the press, the Labour Party was hemmed in by the limitations of its electoral strength and its consequent reliance upon Liberal support. Labour did, of course, continue to increase its share of the popular vote throughout the decade, but this should not disguise the fact that it had clearly failed by 1925 to win the battle for the allegiance of the lower middle class, and that its further inter-war growth would come from the strengthening of primarily working-class support. It would require a depression and another war to achieve a decisive breakthrough among non-working-class voters.[101]

The weakness of Labour politically was reinforced by industrial impotence. The one direct effect of the return to gold was to set the stage for the final step in the process of stabilisation, the General Strike. Its outbreak provided a rallying point for all the forces of order. Paradoxically, it served to demonstrate symbolically the strength, but also the social and political isolation, of working people.[102] With its defeat, this strong, cohesive working class would become very defensive and pessimistic, sceptical of almost all schemes for reform and resistant to virtually any change in industry.[103] Such was the price, and the legacy, of the stability achieved in the 1920s.

Notes

Earlier versions of this essay were presented at the North American Labor History Conference in Detroit in October 1980, and in seminars at the University of Bath, the Institute of Historical Research in London and King's College, Cambridge. I am grateful for comments and criticisms made in those contexts and for careful readings of previous drafts by Mary Cronin, Robert Moeller, Ronald Ross and Jonathan Schneer.

1. The most thorough critique of this tradition is Perry Anderson, 'The Origins of the Present Crisis', in P. Anderson and R. Blackburn (eds.), *Towards Socialism* (London, 1965), which was in turn brilliantly countered in E.P. Thompson's 'The Peculiarities of the English', in R. Miliband and J. Saville (eds.), *Socialist Register 1965*.

2. As David Shackleton of the Ministry of Labour put it on 21 May 1919, 'The increased industrial power of labour — and, it must be added, of employers too — has made the ordinary legislative procedure inadequate ... the supreme legislative assembly in these matters becomes merely a body for registering decisions arrived at outside itself.' Quoted in Keith Middlemas, *Politics in Industrial Society. The Experience of the British System since 1914* (London, 1979).

3. H.B. Graham, *Relations between Employers and Employed* (London 1918), 1, 3, *passim*. This was a speech given to the North London Manufacturers' Association on 16 July 1918.

4. Cited in Meyer Bloomfield, *Management and Men* (New York, 1919), p.153.

5. D. Read, *Edwardian England* (London, 1972), pp.116-22.

6. F. Dudley Docker, in S.J. Chapman (ed.), *Labour and Capital after the War* (London, 1918), pp.132-4.

7. Much to the chagrin of employers, even the most moderate of union leaders believed that the call for increased productivity was inherently anti-labour. See J.R. Clynes, in S.J. Chapman (ed.), *Labour and Capital after the War*, pp.32-3; and also W.F. Watson, *Should the Workers Increase Output?* (London, 1920).

8. See Chapman, *Labour and Capital after the War*, p.132.

9. Tom Jones, *Whitehall Diary, 1916-1925*, edited by K. Middlemas (London, 1969), p.73.

10. Law and Churchill both quoted in Middlemas, *Politics in Industrial Society*, pp.143-4.

11. *Beatrice Webb's Diaries, 1918-1924*, edited by M.I. Cole (London, 1952), p.197.

12. 'The Labour Situation. Report from the Ministry of Labour for the Week ending 14th January 1920', PRO CAB 24/96, C.P. 450, 21.

13. A.L. Lowell, *Public Opinion in War and Peace* (Cambridge, Mass., 1923), pp.253-4, 262. The *Daily Herald* made a similar point in less neutral terms in its 14 May 1919 edition: the 'reactionaries', they said, '. . . tricked themselves into power; Labour need, and should, and will resort to neither trickery nor violence in getting them out of it. But out of it they must go.'

14. Directorate of Intelligence (Home Office), 'A Survey of Revolutionary Feeling during the Year 1919', PRO CAB 24/96, C.P. 462, 5. The reliability of Thomson's estimates is not entirely clear. Bentley Gilbert has used them extensively in his *British Social Policy, 1914-1938* (London, 1970), and refers to Thomson at different points as a man 'whose political intelligence was usually excellent', (p.25) and as someone 'whose economic intelligence was usually excellent'. (p.46) Others have been more sceptical. It is clear that Thomson did occupy a position atop a network of spies and informers that made his weekly reports, and hence also his annual summaries, very detailed. One may doubt seriously, however, the value of his information on workers' own perceptions and sentiments. A particularly revealing glimpse of the post-war intelligence network, and its weaknesses, is provided by the strange case of W.F. Watson. See W.F. Watson, *Watson's Reply. A Complete Answer to the Charges of Espionage Levelled against W.F. Watson and an Exposure of the Espionage System* (London, 1920).

15. B. Pribicevic, *The Shop Stewards Movement and Workers' Control* (Oxford, 1959).

16. W. Moore, *Verbatim Report of a Discussion between Veteran Engineers in Sheffield* (London, 1953), cited in James Hinton, *The First Shop Stewards' Movement* (London, 1973), p.169.

17. On trades' councils, see A. Clinton, *The Trade Union Rank and File* (Manchester, 1977), pp.54-137; on local Labour party organisation, see R. McKibbin, *The Evolution of the Labour Party, 1910-1924* (Oxford, 1974).

18. Middlemas, *Politics in Industrial Society*, p.166. John Foster, 'British Imperialism and the Labour Aristocracy', in J. Skelley (ed.), *The General Strikes 1926* (London, 1976), pp.28, 56, suggests that the figure of 350 Councils of Action is somewhat exaggerated, although it is based on at least one contemporary estimate. His own review of the record turned up 288 such organs, still an impressive total.

19. Carter Goodrich, *The Frontier of Control* (London, 1975, reprint of 1920 edition), p.11.

20. Clynes, in Chapman, *Labour and Capital after the War*, pp.17-18.

21. W.A. Orton, *Labour in Transition* (London, 1921), p.xiv; R. Roberts, *The Classic Slum* (Harmondsworth, 1973), pp.210-11. On the general heightening of expectations just after the war, see W.G. Runciman, *Relative Deprivation and Social Justice* (London, 1966).

22. Cited in Middlemas, *Politics in Industrial Society*, p.159.

23. M. Swenarton, *Homes Fit for Heroes* (London, 1981), analyses the long-term impact of the agitation for future housing policy.

24. On this extensive movement, see David Englander, 'Landlord and Tenant in Urban Britain: The Politics of Housing Reform, 1838-1924', PhD Dissertation, Warwick University, 1979, pp.310ff.

25. There was even a theoretical recognition, albeit an inadequate one, of this residentially-based movement among the leaders of the shop stewards. Thus, J.R. Campbell and W. Gallacher, in *Direct Action* (1919), called for the organisation of local 'social committees' which, taken together with factory-based shop stewards' groups, would constitute the nuclei of workers' power in Britain. Of course, they gave theoretical and political primacy to organisation at the point of production. In general, see J.T. Murphy, *Preparing for Power* (London, 1934), pp.187-9.

26. The most comprehensive survey is Marion Kozak, 'Women Munition Workers in the First World War', PhD Dissertation, University of Hull, 1976; but see also Harold Smith, 'The Issue of "Equal Pay for Equal Work" in Great Britain, 1914-1919', *Societas —A Review of Social History*, VIII (1978), pp.39-52.

27. Middlemas, *Politics in Industrial Society*, provides substantial evidence of business involvement in the running of the industrial machine during wartime. This did not prevent employers from complaining vociferously over state intervention in general and the government's conciliatory attitude towards labour in particular. Cf. Noelle Whiteside, 'Industrial Welfare and Labour Regulation in Britain at the Time of the First World War', *International Review of Social History*, XXV, pt. 3 (1980), p.323; and G. Rubin, 'The Origins of Industrial Tribunals', *Industrial Law Journal* VI (1977), p.163, who argues that, 'For the employers, decontrol was all. Their factories effectively nationalised during the war, they were in no mood to consider anything but a return to *laissez-faire. . .*'

28. In addition to the sources cited above, see L. Macassey, *Labour Policy — False and True* (London, 1922); A. Gleason, *What the Workers Want* (London, 1920); Directorate of Intelligence, 'Survey of Revolutionary Movements in Great Britain in the Year 1920', PRO CAB 24/96, C.P. 2455; and St Philip's Education and Economics Research Society, *The Equipment of the Workers* (London, 1919).

29. Quoted in W. Williams, *Full Up and Fed Up: The Worker's Mind in Crowded Britain* (New York, 1921), p.71.

30. The relationship between radicalisation in the country and change in the Labour Party is explored in J.M. Winter, *Socialism and the Challenge of War* (London, 1974), esp. pp.234-88.

31. This report, and the general phenomenon of local organisation, are discussed in McKibbin, *The Evolution of the Labour Party*, pp.137-50.

32. One important mechanism strengthening the Labour Party's claim to be the key representative of working-class opinion and interest was the War Emergency Workers' National Committee. See R. Harrison, 'The War Emergency Workers' National Committee, 1914-1920', in A. Briggs and J. Saville (eds.), *Essays in Labour History, 1888-1923* (London, 1971), pp.211-59.

33. The argument about the limitations of 'Labourism' is made very effectively in Ralph Miliband, *Parliamentary Socialism* (London, 1972).

34. On the army, see D. Englander and J. Osborne, 'Jack, Tommy, and Henry Dubb: The Armed Forces and the Working Class', *Historical Journal*, XXI (1978).

35. V.L. Allen, *Trade Unions and the Government* (London, 1960), pp.123-4; Murphy, *Preparing for Power*, p.183.

36. W. Kendall, *The Revolutionary Movement in Britain, 1900-1921* (London, 1969), p.195, puts the matter succinctly: 'Put to the test, the maturity of the ruling elite proved far greater than that of the revolutionaries who sought its overthrow.' Whether smarter and more mature revolutionaries would have made a difference is, needless to say, highly debatable.

37. 'Survey of Revolutionary Feeling during the Year 1919', pp.4-5.

38. Obviously, it is a bit too simple to speak as if the mid-Victorian working class was divided into two, distinct and cohesive strata, one 'aristocratic', the other plebeian, for there were always intermediate groups that did not fit into either. Still, the distinction between 'rough' and 'respectable', between the skilled and organised and the unskilled and generally unorganised, was very real to contemporaries and was reflected in many aspects of politics and collective action which may, in fact, have served to heighten and reinforce the contrast. See, most recently, H.F. Moorhouse, 'The Significance of the Labour Aristocracy', *Social History*, VI, 2 (1981), pp.229-33. Also J. Cronin, 'Strikes, 1870-1914' in C.J. Wrigley (ed.), *The History of British Industrial Relations* (Brighton, 1982).

39. On the arbitrariness and ambiguity of virtually all classifications according to skill levels, see the discussion in Charles More, *Skill and the English Working Class* (London, 1980).

40. Reliable statistics on the 'rise of the semi-skilled' are very hard to come by, for the very category of 'semi-skilled' is a residual one, and it is also a rather modern creation. Indeed, it can easily be shown that no group of workers ever really considered themselves 'unskilled' and that therefore the notion of an intermediate layer between skilled and unskilled was totally foreign to their conceptions. Moreover, even the census takers, who ultimately imposed the category upon some quite recalcitrant data, had not done so early enough for us to measure its expansion directly in the period before the First World War.

Still, we do have some information about the growth of certain classes of workers who would today — perhaps anachronistically — be labelled 'semi-skilled', a selection of which appears as follows:

	Numbers of workers in			
Occupation	1881	1891	1901	1911
Cotton manufacture	156,971	176,991	173,139	210,697
Miners of coal and shale	355,363	482,525	609,402	843,681
Porters and other railway workers	37,187	65,029	88,874	106,644
Engine drivers	65,643	81,268	105,351	110,249
Metal machinists	14,828	16,773	28,219	35,916
Tramways service	2,591	6,723	17,996	41,219
Steel smelting	22,905	25,304	30,178	39.087

It is possible as well to reanalyse the census data from pre-First World War into the social class categories adopted later, e.g. in 1951, and this exercise, too, reveals a marked growth in the category of 'semi-skilled' and a stabilisation — even, after 1901, a slight but absolute decline — in the category that approximates the distinction 'unskilled'. The above data, and the recalculation on the basis of the 1951 categories, appear in J.A. Banks, 'The Social Structure of Nineteenth Century England as seen through the Census', in R. Lawton (ed.), *The Census and Social Structure* (London, 1978), pp.179-223. See also J.M. Bellamy, 'Occupational Statistics in the Nineteenth Century Censuses', in the same volume, pp.165-78.

41. See, in general, P. Stearns, 'The Unskilled and Industrialization: A Transformation of Consciousness', *Archiv für Sozialgeschichte*, XVI (1976), pp.249-82; E.H. Hunt, *British Labour History, 1815-1914* (London, 1981), pp.312-13, 331-2; and J. White, *The Limits of Trade Union Militancy* (Westport, Conn., 1978), for the cotton industry. The transformation of work in the coal mines has been surprisingly little studied, but some of the changes operative in the late nineteenth century can be glimpsed in the various essays in R. Harrison (ed.), *The Independent Collier* (London, 1978); and something of the emerging structure of the workforce in J.W.F. Rowe, *Wages in the Coal Mining Industry* (London, 1923). On the broad situation prior to 1870, see R. Samuel, 'The Workshop of the World: Steam Power and Hand Technology in mid-Victorian Britain', *History Workshop*, no. 3 (1977), pp.6-72. On the service sector, see P. Bagwell, 'The New Unionism in Britain, 1880-1914: The Service Industries: Transport', Paper presented to the Conference on the Development of Trade Unionism in Great Britain, France and Germany, 1880-1914: Tutzing, Germany, May 1981, and the literature cited there; on manufacturing and service more

broadly, see R. Hyman, 'Mass Organisation and Militancy in Britain: Contrasts and Continuities', (Tutzing, 1981).

42. E.J. Hobsbawn, 'Custom, Wages and Work-Load', in *Labouring Men* (Garden City, NY, 1963), p.406; R. Price, 'The New Unionism and the Labour Process', (Tutzing, 1981).

43. See J. Zeitlin, 'The Labour Strategies of British Engineering Employers, 1890-1914', and K. Burgess, 'New Unionism for Old? The Amalgamated Society of Engineers in Britain, 1880-1914', (Tutzing, 1981).

44. J.B. Jeffreys, *The Story of the Engineers* (London, 1946), pp.117-96; J. Melling, '"Non-Commissioned Officers": British Employees and their Supervisory Workers', *Social History*, V, 2 (1980).

45. G. Alderman, 'The Railway Companies and the Growth of Trade Unionism in the late 19th and early 20th Centuries', *Historical Journal*, XIV (1971), pp.129-52; P.S. Gupta, 'Railway Trade Unions in Britain, c.1880-1920', *Economic History Review*, XIX (1966).

46. Hobsbawm, 'General Labour Unions in Britain, 1889-1914', in *Labouring Men*, pp.211-39.

47. Calculated from K.G. Knowles and D.J. Robertson, 'Differences between the Wages of Skilled and Unskilled Workers, 1850-1950', *Bulletin of the Oxford University Institute of Statistics*, XIII (1951), pp.109-27. On the effects upon attitudes, see B. Waites, 'The Effect of the First World War on Class and Status in England', *Journal of Contemporary History*, XI (1976), pp.27-48.

48. The most general statement is S. Meacham, *A Life Apart* (London, 1977), but see also P. Thompson, *The Edwardians* (London, 1975).

49. The emphasis upon the 'integrating' and conservative implications of this development can be seen in Meacham, *A Life Apart*; in G. Stedman Jones, 'Working-Class Culture and Working-Class Politics in London, 1870-1900', *Journal of Social History*, VII (1974), pp.460-508; in P. Stearns, 'The Effort at Continuity in Working-Class Culture', *Journal of Modern History*, LIII, 4 (1980), pp.626-55; and, from a rather different point of view altogether, in F.M.L. Thompson, 'Social Control in Victorian Britain', *Economic History Review*, XXXIV (1981), pp.189-208.

50. For the general pattern, see C. Storm-Clark, 'The Miners, 1870-1970: A Test Case for Oral History', *Victorian Studies*, XV (1971); R. Gregory, *The Miners and British Politics, 1906-1914* (Oxford, 1968), pp.2-4; and J. Cronin, *Industrial Conflict in Modern Britain* (London, 1979), pp.180-3.

Obviously, there was substantial variation between coalfields in the different regions. The most distinct case was probably South Wales, where emigration continued to be substantial up to 1911. However, since it was increasingly an English migration, it was connected with a general decline in the specifically Welsh character of local society, which had previously made for a political and cultural unity overriding those tendencies towards class awareness and allegiance. So, in this instance it was the continued immigration to the coalfield rather than its slowing down that led to class formation. See Peter Stead, 'Working-class Leadership in South Wales, 1900-1920', *Welsh History Review*, VI (1973), pp.329-53; K.O. Morgan, 'The New Liberalism and the Challenge of Labour: The Welsh Experience, 1885-1929', *WHR*, VI (1973), pp.288-312; and Colin Williams, 'Language Contact and Language Change in Wales, 1901-1971: A Study in Historical Geolinguistics', *WHR*, X (1980), pp.207-38.

51. R. Lawton, 'Census Data for Urban Areas', in Lawton (ed.), *The Census and Social Structure*, pp.82-145; J. McKay, *Tramways and Trolleys: The Rise of Urban Mass Transport in Europe* (Princeton, 1975), pp.205-25; R. Dickinson, *The West European City* (London, 1961); S.D. Chapman (ed.), *The History of Working-Class Housing* (Newton Abbot, 1978); J.R. Kellett, *The Impact of the Railways on Victorian Cities* (London, 1969).

52. P. Joyce, *Work, Society, and Politics. The Culture of the Factory in Later Victorian England* (Brighton, 1980). His characterisation of class relations in mid-Victorian Britain may or may not be accurate, but Joyce's description of changes after 1880 seems very reasonable: 'Both industry and the town were by the end of the nineteenth century taking on their modern forms, forms marked by the mutual ignorance and antagonism of the classes . . .' and again, 'The changing ecology of the factory town, and the increased degree of organisation and commercialisation in popular culture combined to enlarge the scope of people's lives, and break the hold of the old communities of work, religion, and politics on their daily lives.' Cf. also R.M. Pritchard, *Housing and the Spatial Structure of the City* (Cambridge, 1976), for a more technically sophisticated study of similar processes as they occurred in Leicester.

53. H. Pollins, 'Transport Lines and Social Division', in R. Glass (ed.), *London: Aspects of Change* (London, 1964), pp.34-46; G. Stedman Jones, *Outcast London* (Cambridge, 1971).

54. C.J. Wrigley, 'Liberals and the Desire for Working-Class Representation in Battersea, 1886-1922', in K.D. Brown (ed.), *Essays in Anti-Labour History* (London, 1974), pp.126-58; A. Reid, 'Labour, Capital and the State in Britain, 1880-1920', (Tutzing, 1981).

55. Commission of Inquiry into Industrial Unrest, 'Report of the Commissioners for the North-Eastern Area', *Parliamentary Papers*, Cmd. 8662 (1917-18), vol. XV, II.

56. Cf. A. Mayer, *Politics and Diplomacy of Peacemaking, 1918-1919* (New York, 1967); C.Maier, *Recasting Bourgeois Europe* (Princeton, 1975); and, for a slightly revised perspective, Maier, 'The Two Postwar Eras and the Conditions for Stability in Twentieth Century Western Europe', *American Historical Review*, LXXXVI (1981), pp.327-52.

57. On the international dimensions of the insurgency, see J. Cronin, 'Labour Insurgency and Class Formation: Comparative Perspectives on the Crisis of 1917-1920 in Europe', *Social Science History*, IV (1980), pp.125-52; and A.S. Lindemann, *The 'Red Years': European Socialism versus Bolshevism, 1919-1921* (Berkeley, 1974).

58. The models are discussed very thoroughly in Maier, *Recasting Bourgeois Europe* and in H.A. Winkler (ed.), *Organisierter Kapitalismus* (Göttingen, 1974). The main attempt to use the corporatist model to explain British developments is Middlemas,. *Politics in Industrial Society*. The literature on corporatism has grown enormously in recent years. For brief summaries and discussions, see L. Panitch, 'Trade Unions and the Capitalist State', *New Left Review*, No. 125 (January-February, 1981), pp.21-43; and R. Price, *Masters, Unions and Men* (Cambridge, 1979), pp.282-3.

59. As, for example, in R. Lowe, 'The Erosion of State Intervention in Britain, 1917-24', *Economic History Review*, XXXI (1978), pp.270-86.

60. R.H. Desmarais, 'The British Government's Strike-Breaking Organisation and Black Friday', *Journal of Contemporary History* (1971), pp.112-27. The danger of a national transport strike had, of course, begun to trouble officials even before the war and was one major factor pushing the government towards a greater role in industrial relations. See C.J. Wrigley, *David Lloyd George and the British Labour Movement* (Hassocks, 1976).

61. As the Minister of Labour explained in 1919, '. . . it was worth while to pay the extra cost of the railwaymen's demands in order to secure their support at the present time'. Quoted in C.J. Wrigley, '1919: the Critical Year', in *The British Labour Movement in the Decade after the First World War* (Loughborough, 1979), p.10.

62. G.A. Phillips, *The General Strike* (London, 1976), contains a thorough discussion of the vagaries of the coal industry from 1918 to 1926, including the Royal Commission.

63. V.L. Allen, *Trade Unions and the Government* (London, 1960), pp.58-9; J.T. Murphy, *Compromise or Independence? An Examination of the Whitely Report* (Sheffield, 1918); W.R. Garside, 'Management and Men: Aspects of British Industrial Relations in the Inter-War Period', in B. Supple (ed.), *Essays in British Business History* (Oxford, 1977), pp.247-50; R. Lowe, 'The Failure of Consensus in Britain: The National Industrial Conference, 1919-1921', *Historical Journal*, XXI (1978).

64. P.B. Johnson, *Land Fit for Heroes* (Chicago, 1968); Englander, 'Landlord and Tenant in Urban Britain', pp.440ff.

65. S. Howson, 'The Origins of Dear Money, 1919-20', *Economic History Review*, XXVII (1974), pp.88-107.

66. Gilbert, *British Social History*, pp.51-97.

67. John Burns, '"Social Control" and the Modernisation of Social Policy', pp.121-46 and J.R. Hay, 'Employers' Attitudes to Social Policy and the Concept of "Social Control", 1900-1920', pp.107-25 in P. Thane (ed.), *The Origins of British Social Policy* (London, 1978).

68. Quoted in Williams, *Full Up and Fed Up*, p.252.

69. Arthur Beck, Member of the National Union of Manufacturers' Deputation to the Ministry of Labour re: the amendment of trade union law, 12 October, 1926. PRO LAB 10/4, 3.

70. S. Webb, 'The British Labour Movement and the Industrial Depression', *International Labour Review* II (1923), p.216.

71. James Hinton and Richard Hyman, *Trade Unions and Revolution: The Industrial Politics of the Early British Communist Party* (London, 1975) , p.18.

72. Lloyd George to Bonar Law, PRO CAB 63/29, quoted in Lowe, 'The Failure of Consensus in Britain'.

73. *Beatrice Webb's Diaries*, 1918-24, p.208.

74. Thomas, quoted in John Foster, 'British Imperialism and Labour Aristocracy', in J. Skelly (ed.), *The General Strike 1926* (London, 1976), p.36.

75. On the hesitancy with which the TUC approached the entire problem, see John Lovell, 'The TUC Special Industrial Committee, January-April, 1926', in A. Briggs and J. Saville (eds.), *Essays in Labour History 1918-1939* (London, 1977), pp.36-56.

76. See Phillips, *The General Strike*; M. Morris, *The General Strike* (London, 1976); A. Mason, 'The Government and the General Strike', *International Review of Social History*, XIV (1968).

77. Quoted in Middlemas, *Politics in Industrial Society*, p.204.

78. Mowat, *Britain between the Wars*, p.330.

79. This effect is quite evident in the report of the conference of January 1927, on the general strike. See TUC General Council, *The Mining Crisis and the National Strike, 1926. Official Reports* (London, 1927). The effectiveness of the strike is evident in the various local reports sent in to the TUC. TUC Archives, HD 5366, 'General Strike 1926: Reports from Districts'.

80. Reports on Trade Union Reactions to Proposed Trade Union Legislation from Chief Conciliation Officers, January 1927. PRO LAB 10/5.

81. R. Scally, *The Origins of the Lloyd George Coalition* (Princeton, 1975); G.D. Phillips, *The Diehards: Aristocratic Society and Politics in Edwardian England* (Cambridge, Mass., 1979); G. Searle, 'Critics of Edwardian Society: The Case of the Radical Right', in A. O'Day (ed.), *The Edwardian Age: Conflict and Stability* (London, 1979), pp.79-96.

82. See G.R. Searle, *The Quest for National Efficiency* (Oxford, 1971).

83. Lloyd George to Philip Lloyd Greame in January, 1921, quoted in Gilbert, *British Social Policy*, p.37.

84. M. Cowling, *The Impact of Labour* (Cambridge, 1971), p.44.

85. K. Morgan, *Consensus and Disunity: The Lloyd George Coalition Government, 1918-1922* (Oxford, 1979), p.280.

86. R.G. Hawtrey, *The Exchequer and the Control of Expenditure* (London, 1921), p.71.

87. Johnson, *Land Fit for Heroes*, p.470; Howson, 'The Origins of Dear Money', 96; Gilbert, *British Social Policy*, pp.46-8.

88. See F.D. Klingender, *The Condition of Clerical Labour in Britain* (London, 1935) on clerks in general; Allen, *Trade Unions and the Government*, pp.71-89 on the Civil Service; and J. Melling, 'Non-Commissioned Officers', on foremen.

89. Guest to Lloyd George, quoted in Englander, 'Landlord and Tenant in Urban Britain', p.453.

90. Such a reaction was typified, of course, by Lord Rothermere's 'Anti-Waste' movement which led to the appointment of the Geddes' Committee in 1921. See Morgan, *Consensus and Disunity*, pp.243-5.

91. Morgan, *Consensus and Disunity*, p.300. On the ultimate success of the party in capturing these loose middle-class voters, see J.A. Ramsden, *The Age of Balfour & Baldwin* (London, 1978), esp. pp.244-64.

92. Middlemas, *Politics in Industrial Society*, pp.169-73.

93. Cowling, *The Impact of Labour*, p.1.

94. W.D. Rubinstein, 'Wealth, Elites, and the Class Structure of Modern Britain', *Past & Present*, no. 76 (1977), pp.99-126; T. Balogh, *Studies in Financial Organisation* (Cambridge, 1950), pp.7-11.

95. S. Blank, 'Industry and the State: The Changing Relationship of Government and Industry', PhD Dissertation, Harvard University, 1960, Chapters 1 and 2; E. Wigham, *The Power to Manage* (London, 1973), pp.101-10.

96. Foster, 'British Imperialism and the Labour Aristocracy', pp.9-12.

97. Howson, 'The Origins of Dear Money', L. Hannah, *The Rise of the Corporate Economy* (London, 1976), pp.64-70; L. Hannah and J.A. Kay, *Concentration in Modern Industry* (London, 1977), pp.64-83.

98. On the implications of this extension of government activity, see S.J. Hurwitz, *State Intervention in Great Britain* (London, 1968); and H.R.G. Greaves, *The Civil Service in a Changing Society* (London, 1947), p.41.

99. R. Lowe, 'The Erosion of State Intervention', pp.282-3; R. Davidson and R. Lowe, 'Bureaucracy and Innovation in British Welfare Policy, 1870-1945', in W.J. Mommsen (ed.), *The Evolution of the Welfare State in Britain and Germany* (London, 1981), pp.269-95; N. Newman, 'The Role of the Treasury in the formation of British Economic Policy, 1918-1925', PhD Dissertation, University of Durham, 1972. For an interesting discussion of the consequences, see R. Crossman, 'Introduction' to W. Bagehot, *The English Constitution* (London, 1964), pp.48-51.

100. The issue is dealt with thoroughly in D.E. Moggridge, *The Return to Gold, 1925* (Cambridge, 1969), esp. pp.45-60; and D.E. Moggridge, *British Monetary Policy, 1924-1931: The Norman Conquest of $4.86* (Cambridge, 1972). See also S. Pollard (ed.), *The Gold Standard and Employment Politics between the Wars* (London, 1970). On the feeling within the elite that fiscal responsibility provided a useful antidote to socialism, see R. Skidelsky, 'Keynes and the Treasury View', in Mommsen, *The Evolution of the Welfare State*, p.169.

101. The processes by which new sections of the population were brought around to support of the Labour Party between 1935 and the election of 1945 are by no means yet clear, but some interesting hypotheses have been offered in T. Jeffery, *Mass-Observation – A Short History*, Centre for Contemporary Cultural Studies, University of Birmingham, Occasional Paper S.P. 55, 1978.

102. M. Morris, *The General Strike* (London, 1976); Klingender, *The Condition of Clerical Labour*, pp.82-3.

103. The defensive mentality of British workers after 1926 has been extensively documented and can be glimpsed in the literature on the 'traditional working class' and its culture, which tends to treat these attitudes in a rather timeless fashion. For one of the best contemporary accounts, see Jack Common, *The Freedom of the Streets* (London, 1938); for the classic retrospective analysis, see R. Hoggart, *The Uses of Literacy* (London, 1957).

7 BRITISH LABOUR AND THE COLD WAR: THE LONDON DOCK STRIKE OF 1949

Peter Weiler

Introduction

In the summer of 1949 a dispute developed between the London dockers and their employers. The dockers refused to unload several Canadian ships being struck by their crews, members of the Canadian Seamen's Union. The employers, acting through the National Dock Labour Board, the administrative agent for the port, insisted that the men had contractual obligations to unload all ships and refused to hire them unless they first worked the two Canadian vessels. The dispute shut down much of the port, forcing the Labour government to resort to the 1920 Emergency Powers Act to keep goods moving. In justification of its strike-breaking, the government charged that the dispute was a Communist conspiracy deliberately engineered to cripple the British economy. It labelled the stoppage as a classic example of Communist tactics, comparing it with the strikes in France and Italy in late 1947 and 1948.

This study will show, however, that the Communist issue was largely a smokescreen. In reality, the 1949 dispute concerned questions of political power, capitalist economic relations and social class. This chapter, therefore, will first describe the course of the strike and the official charges levelled at the time. It will then turn to the context of the dispute and the various participants in it: the Canadian Seamen's Union; the National Dock Labour Board; the Labour government; the Transport and General Workers' Union; the British Communist Party; and the unofficial movement. Finally, it will offer an interpretation of the incident very much at odds with that generally held. This chapter seeks to show that the crucial issues at stake in the London docks in 1949 were the Labour government's commitment to a revived capitalism, the corporatist role of the trade union leadership and the persistence of class antagonisms on the docks.

The Dispute

In February 1949, after a four month conciliation process, the

Communist-led Canadian Seamen's Union (CSU) failed to agree on a new contract with the Canadian East Coast Shipowners. Just over a month later, the CSU struck vessels arriving in Halifax in an attempt to strengthen their bargaining position. The shipowners reacted by signing a contract with the Seafarers' International Union (SIU), an affiliate of the American Federation of Labor (AFL) with little representation at the time in Canada. In response, the CSU extended its strike to the rest of Canada and to a number of foreign ports, including a number of English ones.[1]

In April CSU crews tried to sit in on two Canadian ships after they docked in London. Prevented by court injunction from staying on board, the crews threw up picket lines on the docks. British dockers, members of the stevedores' union (NASD), refused to cross the picket lines to unload the ships. Fearing an extension of the strike, the National Dock Labour Board (NDLB), which directed work in all British ports, allowed the dockers to 'black' the two Canadian ships while continuing to work all other vessels in the port. This situation continued unchanged for two months. But on 13 June the NDLB, responding in part to pressure from the employers, changed their position, announcing that the men would be denied other work after 20 June until they agreed to work the two Canadian ships. On 21 and 22 June the stevedores, defying their own executive, refused to work the two ships. An extended stoppage seemed to be in the offing, but was avoided temporarily because the CSU, which had been negotiating with the shipowners, arrived on 23 June at a satisfactory agreement. The agreement, however, broke down, and on 27 June the CSU called a mass meeting where its leaders alleged that they had been double-crossed by the shipowners; the men voted to support the CSU.[2]

At this point the dispute became major. The NDLB and the employers resolved not to employ any men until the two vessels were unloaded. The next day, despite the employers' resolution, dockers from the stevedores' union and the much larger Transport and General Workers' Union (TGWU) voted at a mass meeting, where representatives of the CSU and their own executives spoke, to work all but the two Canadian ships. On 30 June an unofficial 'lockout' committee formed and issued a manifesto demanding the right not to take sides in the dispute but to be allowed to work other ships. The committee, which included a number of Communists, insisted that the dockers had to respect the 'fundamental trade union principle' against blacklegging.[3] During the next week, work in the port ground to a halt as more and more dockers became involved.[4] On 7 July the Labour government sent in troops to unload ships with cargoes of food. Four days later it declared a state of emergency under the 1920 Emergency Powers Act and took over the running of the port. It extended the number of servicemen working in the port to over 12,000; eventually they managed to work all but 22 of the ships docked there.

In spite of unanimous opposition from their own union leadership, from the government, and from the press, the men remained firm throughout July, repeatedly ignoring both government and trade union claims that the whole affair was a demarcation dispute played up by the Communists and emotional appeals for loyalty. Faced with the successful use of troops and the exhaustion of their strike funds, however, the CSU called off its dispute on 23 July. The dockers then voted to return to work at a meeting which was not attended, *The Times* noted, by 'defeated or repentent men'.[5]

Both the government and the leadership of the TGWU contended that the dispute between the CSU and the Canadian shipowners had been deliberately trumped up by the Comintern as part of a scheme to wreck the British economy. George Isaacs, the Minister of Labour, said that the Communist party aimed to 'disturb the flow of merchandise' in British ports.[6] Chuter Ede, the Home Secretary, elaborated:

> The only reason we are having to deal with the trouble in this country is that the Communists see in it a chance of fomenting unrest, injuring our trade, and so hampering our recovery and with it the whole process of Marshall Aid on which the recovery of Western Europe depends. The issue with which we are faced is not one of a legitimate industrial dispute.[7]

Arthur Deakin, General Secretary of the TGWU, agreed, arguing that the dispute was 'merely a specious attempt to give effect to that policy of international communism [to sabotage the Marshall Plan] which was decided on by the Cominform twelve months ago'.[8]

The Labour government even went so far as to charge that Communists aimed to take over the country. Chuter Ede said that they were 'faced with a challenge to the whole authority of the state'.[9] Hartley Shawcross, the Attorney General, contended that the Communists were carrying out a 'carefully coordinated plan' which aimed to 'give rise to conditions in which Communist dictatorship, controlled from Moscow, could take control'.[10] In their view, therfore, the dockers had no rational reason for supporting the CSU but were being misled. 'This Canadian dispute is being used — and you are being used — by the Communists in this country . . .' George Isaacs told them.[11]

According to the government and the trade union leadership, the 1949 London dispute represented a classic example of Communist Cold War tactics. It was, after all, indisputable that the CSU had a Communist leadership and that British Communists played a prominent role on the unofficial strike committee. The dispute did disrupt the British economy just as the pound sterling was under heavy international pressure.

Nevertheless, the dipute was not a Communist plot. Such a charge cannot explain why over 15,000 men stayed on the streets for a month in a dispute that could bring them no immediate financial benefit. As one participant later pointed out, 'We did not stand out for a month for fun . . .'[12] The Communist plot theory also ignores the dockers' longstanding discontent with their employers, with their own union, and with the Labour government. As Richard Hyman has pointed out, strikes are 'merely one point in a chain of events'.[13] In short, to understand the meaning of the 1949 dispute it is necessary to examine the chain of events that produced it, to set it in a broad historical context, and to examine the actions of all of the participants.

The Dispute: Context and Participants

The CSU versus the SIU and the AFL

Since the government and the TGWU repeatedly charged that the CSU had deliberately created this dispute as part of an international Communist plan to disrupt the Marshall Plan, it is necessary to begin by examining the Canadian origins of the issue. The CSU developed in the 1930s, successfully organising most Canadian seamen on both coasts as well as on the Great Lakes. Led in part by Communists, the union pursued a militant policy on behalf of the seamen, winning substantial improvements in wages, conditions and hours. 'Its action on the economic front', one historian of Canadian trade unionism concluded, 'has been vigorous and its accomplishments are deserving of the gratitude of the seamen.'[14]

The employers never fully accepted the CSU as a bargaining agent and strenuously resisted its demands. In 1938 the shipowners tried to displace it with another union; only strike action stopped them.[15] The war imposed a period of labour peace, but immediately afterwards the owners tried to reduce the seamen's wages and to increase their hours. The CSU prevented this by another strike, winning a substantial wage increase, the eight-hour day, and union control of the hiring of labour.[16] It won this strike in part because the American National Maritime Union refused to load Canadian ships using non-union labour, a precedent perhaps for the similar strategy followed in 1949.[17] Thereafter, the union continued to push for improvements in wages and conditions. The owners responded with red-baiting and by supporting rival company unions, notably the Canadian Lake Seamen's Union (CLSU).[18]

In May 1948 the struggle between the CSU and the shipowners sharpened. Seven Great Lakes companies refused to negotiate a new contract, seeking instead to bargain with the Seafarers' International Union (SIU). The SIU, an affiliate of the AFL, had almost no representation in Canada. In the summer of 1948 the SIU absorbed the 'company dominated' CLSU in a 'deal' engineered by Frank Hall, the anti-Communist leader of the railwaymen's union. The *New York Times* reported that the 'SIU came into Eastern Canada with the evident intention of driving the CSU out of the seamen's field'.[19] The CSU responded to these tactics with a strike that was strongly supported by the Canadian Trades and Labour Congress (CTLC). At its 1948 convention the CTLC denounced the SIU as a 'dual union'. 'The companies', it said, 'created a company union which they use as a union-busting and strike-breaking agency and which serves them as the means of recruiting strike-breakers from the gutters of the big cities and the underworld.'[20] The CTLC gave its 'full support' to the CSU and suspended the railwaymen's union because the actions of Frank Hall 'violated both the letter and the spirit' of the CTLC constitution.[21] In the event, the CSU won a resounding victory.

The SIU's attempt to displace the CSU can be fully understood only as a move in the world of international trade union diplomacy. The late 1930s and the years of the Second World War witnessed the growth of Communist influence in trade union movements in most countries in Western Europe and North America. This trend reached a climax in 1945 with the creation of the World Federation of Trade Unions (WFTU), the first trade union international to include both Communist and non-Communist trade unions. The leaders of the AFL, strong supporters of American capitalism and militant anti-Communists, did everything possible to oppose these developments. They worked behind the scenes to sabotage the WFTU. Acting in concert with the American State Department, they split the French and Italian trade union movements in an unsuccessful attempt to remove them from Communist control. In short, the AFL used its financial resources and diplomatic contacts to boost anti-Communist unions, however unpopular, throughout the world.[22]

In Canada, the AFL determined in 1948 to eliminate all Communists in the CTLC. That summer, Frank Hall organised a committee made up of the leaders of a number of AFL unions affiliated to the CTLC. The committee demanded the ouster of all Communists. The CTLC executive denounced Hall's action as an undemocratic campaign 'not being inspired or paid for by those friendly to organized labour'.[23] That response aroused the ire of the AFL which in February 1949 served notice on the CTLC that 'it would not compromise with Communists'. It demanded that Hall's union be reinstated and that all references to its suspension be 'expunged'.[24] Further, by threatening to order all AFL affiliates to withdraw from the CTLC, the AFL executive pressured it to adopt an anti-Communist line and to expel the CSU. In June, faced with the threat of disintegration, the CTLC caved in to AFL pressure. At its annual convention it condemned communism, urged its affiliates to ban Communists from office, and expelled the CSU. However, it still refused to admit the SIU because of 'their willingness and readiness to man the ships of the men on strike with inexperienced crews, with the full support of the struck companies, to say nothing of the questionable methods used'.[25]

Given the wide support it had enjoyed in its most recent battles with the employers, the CSU must have found it difficult to realise how quickly its own position could deteriorate, let alone to anticipate its expulsion from the CTLC. Perhaps remembering its recent successes, the CSU refused a compromise offer in its dispute with the East Coast Shipowners in February 1949. Partially the expression of overconfidence, the CSU's position was also an understandable response to deliberate provocation. The government sponsored compromise, which the shipowners accepted, reduced CSU control over hiring and pledged them to exclude 'subversive elements,' an impossible demand.[26] Moreover, the employers had already challenged the CSU to a showdown by firing CSU crews in foreign ports.[27] Signing a new contract with the SIU was the employers' final and decisive blow against the CSU which tried to recover by striking in Canada, only to find itself unsupported by the CTLC and harassed by the government. It tried, therefore, to play the card used successfully in 1946 — support from foreign dockers.

Three conclusions emerge from this story. First, the CSU's dispute was not trumped up in order to sabotage the Marshall Plan. It had a long history of militancy, bitterly opposed by the shipowners who took advantage of the changing political climate to eliminate a troublesome opponent. The owners imposed a life and death struggle on the CSU by trying to 'break their control' over the seamen.[28] Secondly, the dispute was not a simple jurisdictional one as the TGWU and the Labour government insisted. The SIU was a dual union. As late as May 1949 the CTLC *Journal* noted that 'efforts to dispel wholesale strike-breaking with government assistance by parroting that it is a jurisdictional dispute is not satisfactory to most people'.[29] Thirdly, the dispute *was* part of the Cold War, but behind it lay the long arm of the AFL, not Moscow.

The National Dock Labour Scheme

Dockwork has often been regarded as the quintessential example of the evils of casual labour. The workforce on the docks always exceeded the number of available jobs since the unemployed resorted to dockwork in hard times, swelling the already substantial core of regular dockworkers. The work itself was irregular, depending on the traffic in the port. When the port was busy, dockworkers could earn sufficient wages to support themselves. But work came only in spurts; except for very busy periods large numbers of men remained idle. The situation was tailor-made for employers who used this permanent labour surplus to keep wages low, forcing the men to compete ruthlessly for available jobs. As a result, the employers' immediate power over the men always remained visible and direct as the men were forced each morning to scramble for work. Two results followed. Dockers remained poor and they developed a strong sense of class solidarity and class hatred.[30]

Most observers agreed that the remedy for these evils lay in some scheme of decasualisation, but before the Second World War, attempts at registration, limiting the jobs to men signed up as regular dockworkers, failed. However, in 1940, because of the recognised need to direct and control the workforce and to insure its regular attendance on the job, Ernest Bevin, the Minister of Labour and former general secretary of the TGWU, was able to introduce the famous Dock Labour (Compulsory Registration) Order. This order varied slightly in different parts of the country. In London and on the east coast it created a National Dock Labour Corporation, with equal representation from the employers and the trade unions, to supervise the workforce. In return for regular attendance at the docks, the men obtained a guaranteed wage. They had to appear two times a day (eleven times each week) at an established call point and to accept any work offered to them. In return, they received 'attendance money' even if no work were available. Traditionally, dockers preferred to specialise at particular forms of work, unloading one kind of cargo as opposed to another. Now, they exchanged their freedom to accept or refuse certain jobs or even to skip work in return for job security and a minimum wage.[31]

At the end of the war the TGWU insisted that the dockers 'could never go back to the old casual conditions'.[32] The Labour government agreed, passing the Dock Workers (Regulation of Employment) Act in 1946. In essence, the act extended the wartime measure and directed the employers and the unions to draw up a new scheme. During the next year the employers sought to reclaim some of the prerogatives they believed they had lost during the war, but in the end they were overruled by several special investigators and by the Minister of Labour who introduced the Dock Workers (Regulation of Employment) Order in July 1947, the Dock Scheme.[33] Arthur Deakin hailed the scheme as 'the end of casual employment in dockland and the end of a 50 years' fight'.[34]

The Dock Scheme created a National Dock Labour Board (NDLB) on which the employers and the unions were equally represented. Continuing the procedures established during the war, all dockworkers registered with the Board and made themselves available for work eleven times a week, receiving attendance money and a minimum wage in return. However, while the scheme provided dockers with security and a minimum standard of living, it did nothing to change the nature of dockwork itself. The NDLB continued to treat the men like any other employer. Under the rules of the Scheme a man was required to 'carry out his duties in accordance with the rules of the port or place where he is working', 'to work for such periods as are reasonable in his particular case' and 'to comply with any lawful orders given him by his employer'.[35] If the man failed to accept work or disobeyed his employer, he was subject to various penalties — the loss of attendance money, suspension without pay, or dismissal. In theory, employers, who also registered with the NDLB, could be disciplined too, but since they had no cause to violate the rules of the Scheme, they never had it applied against them. In fact, the disciplinary clauses increased their power.

In spite of the improvements in their living standards created by the Scheme, the dockers' experience of work remained much as it had always been: casual. The men first appeared at a control stand in order to be chosen by a foreman. Those left over then applied to the local

NDLB which either assigned them to employers who still needed men or noted their attendance at the call.[36] Dockers' wages, therefore, still varied, depending on the amount of work available to them. They still worked for a variety of different employers and remained dependent on foremen to hire them for the best jobs. In addition, in return for job security, the men now lost the one freedom they had previously had — to skip work when they chose. In short, the Dock Scheme did not touch the dockers' fundamental subjugation, and the improvements it brought had been paid for by stronger work discipline and enhanced employers' control. In consequence, the scheme increased the dockers' discontents at the same time that the higher standard of living it created made it easier for them to defend themselves.

The Employers and the NDLB

The employers regarded the Dock Scheme as a reinforcement of their authority, not as a change in traditional work relations. In 1946, when they discussed the Scheme with the unions, their major concern was to preserve management prerogatives; in particular, they wanted hiring and firing to remain a 'management function.'[37] Once the Scheme was in operation they sought to increase productivity by introducing new machinery and speeding up the work. Over the years dockers had built up a variety of customary procedures which increased their control over the work itself, working only with specific gangs, for example, or only when a gang was fully constituted.[38] Employers challenged these customs, trying to rearrange work crews or to allocate men in new ways. The disciplinary clauses of the Scheme reinforced the employers' challenge, since refusal to accept their demand subjected the docker to loss of attendance money or to suspension. The consequence was continued labour unrest.

The day-to-day administration of the docks — the allocation of labour, maintenance of the registers, payments, discipline — fell to the NDLB under the chairmanship of Lord Ammon. Born in 1879, largely self-educated, Charles George Ammon had been one of the founders of the Union of Post Office Workers. A devout methodist and teetotaler, 'puritan in outlook' with a 'profound intolerance',[39] Ammon typified a strand in the English labour movement that in its own attitudes to work and duty found areas of accommodation with employers. 'He was a striking example of the belief that "Methodism rather than Marxism" was the driving force of the earthly Labour Party.'[40] His attitudes indicate how the NDLB and the employers perceived the dockers and dockwork; they were a factor in the dispute.

Ammon regarded the men with a mixture of arrogance, condescension and contempt. In spite of much contrary evidence, he insisted that he and the NDLB truly understood the men. 'No other body understands or is likely to understand the psychology of the dockers better than the National Dock Labour Board', he told the House of Lords.[41] In fact, his understanding was limited, filtered through the prism of his own narrow experience. Thus he wrote that, 'For a calling which has been the reservoir for the failures, the weaklings and the misfits of society over many generations quickly to mould itself into a stable, organised, disciplined body is expecting much.'[42] Such attitudes ignored the dockers' accomplishments. In fact, as we shall see, dockers had developed strong traditions of solidarity and self-control, but Ammon saw only the opposite. To him the typical docker was 'basically' as 'good a Britain as can be found' but in need of 'firm and confident leadership'.[43] In consequence, when the dispute developed, Ammon and the NDLB remained blind to the evidence before their own eyes of self-confident, self-motivated working-class activity. Faced with the united opposition of thousands of dockers, Ammon, like others on the Board, failed to revise his 'understanding' of the men, instead attributing their actions to the deceptions of 'recalcitrant elements' or 'mischief-makers'.[44] Because he could not see the men as capable of acting rationally to defend their own interests, he had to explain their actions as the result of manipulation. He never asked why the dockers chose to follow some leaders instead of others, nor did he take seriously their later demand for his dismissal as head of the NDLB.

Given Ammon's attitude to the men and their work, it is not surprising to find that he continually urged the government to take a firm stand against them. When disputes over Canadian ships first arose in May in Bristol and Avonmouth, Ammon asked the government to pursue a 'firm line' even though this involved the 'risk of a strike'.[45] The government hesitated and only acted later in the month, prompting Ammon to remark acidly to George Isaacs that 'had this same statement been made earlier the trouble would have been avoided'.[46] When the dispute spread to Liverpool, Ammon again urged the government to 'call the bluff or have the showdown whatever it may turn out to be . . . It is time some very definite and drastic steps are taken'.[47] Similarly, throughout the London dispute Ammon insisted that the government should intervene to break the strike. 'Again and again', he told the House of Lords, '. . . the Prime Minister and others concerned — were approached by myself individually and personally, by letters . . . asking that actions should be taken against the fomenters of this trouble.'[48] Later he insisted that only firm measures and added power for the NDLB would end disputes in the docks. 'Troubles . . . will not be cured . . . by any measures of appeasement.'[49]

Ammon's attitudes corresponded to those of the employers. Throughout the dispute — both in London and elsewhere — the employers pressured the NDLB to fulfil its obligations, that is, to force the dockers to load the blacked Canadian ships. In particular, they threatened legal action if the Board failed to act.[50] These threats frightened the NDLB which insisted that the government authorise it in writing to continue the policy of isolating the Canadian ships in order to relieve it of responsibility from legal action.[51]

Ammon's and the employers' demands for firm government action reflected more than a limited view of the dockers' abilities. More significantly, they indicated a concern to preserve undiluted their own authority. In spite of the 1947 Dock Scheme, the traditional component of the employer-employee relationship remained; the boss commanded and the workers obeyed. If the dockers could themselves decide whether or not to obey an order to unload a particular ship, that relationship would be fundamentally changed. Thus the entire period after 1945 was marked by an unceasing struggle for control over the workplace. Between January 1948 and June 1949, for example, there were 118 stoppages in all English ports involving disputes over pay, hours of work, extra overtime, methods of loading and unloading and the employers' power to discipline the men.[52] To the employers, therefore, it was important to force the men to unload these two ships as an assertion of their authority. Otherwise, that authority would be reduced, transferred in part to an uncontrolled body elected by the men. Hence Ammon wrote to Attlee:

> The point that is worrying me, however, is that this matter seems likely to drift on to a stage when the strike leaders, who now hold the initiative, will continue to do so and order the men back to work, setting up cries and claims of 'no victimization' and so get back to a position of 'as you were,' except the last stage will be worse than the first and in another two or three months' time we shall be faced with the trouble again.
>
> It does seem to me that while we are in this difficulty the matter should be fought to a finish. If it is not possible to declare a state of emergency, then action should be taken against some of the people who are willfully misleading the men — with particular reference to imported agitators — not only to have them deported,

but also brought to trial.[53]

Ammon feared, in other words, that the dispute would change the balance of power on the docks. Failure to force the men back would 'confirm the recalcitrant and sabotaging elements in their position'.[54] The real issue for the NDLB and the employers was not the CSU or even the Cold War, but who would rule the workplace.

It is worth noting here that the Dock Scheme itself created an institutional structure which limited and constrained the actions of all who participated in it. It reinforced at law the employers' power over the men and the NDLB's responsibility to enforce that power. When the Board initially allowed the dockers to work other ships while not working the Canadian ones it *did* act illegally. The Dock Scheme, then, limited the options available to those who administered it and doubtless influenced the way they thought about the dockers' actions and their own obligations. Had the men succeeded in isolating the ships, the Scheme itself would have been changed, because the men would have usurped a management prerogative. This, in turn, would have brought into question the legal underpinnings of capitalist economic relations in general.

The Labour Government of 1945

Britain's debilitated economic position after the Second World War formed a serious constraint on the Labour government. To pay for the war, Britain had been forced to sell a number of overseas assets. Replacement of aging plant had stagnated, leaving a desperate need for extensive new investment. Widespread bomb damage placed a severe strain on the construction industry to replace schools and homes.[55] As a result, Britain remained heavily dependent on the United States for raw materials, finished products and capital to revive industry and balance the external account. The United States took advantage of this situation, as it had during the war, to force the British to accept the American vision of a post-war economic order — a world of free trade, without imperial preferences, with sterling in its traditional role as a world currency.[56] In consequence, the economic options open to the Labour government, particularly after 1947, became increasingly restricted to traditional capitalist policies to encourage exports and discourage imports. This is not to argue that the United States forced Labour to limit or abandon its socialist goals, but rather that Britain's economic needs made it almost impossible for Labour ministers to follow a course which would have brought them into conflict with the

United States.[57]

To overcome these economic problems, the Labour government repeatedly called for increased production. Lacking new machinery, such demands meant primarily that British workers should work harder and faster. 'In the final analysis,' American intelligence reported 'the Government's plan for increased output is based as much upon an increase in individual effort as upon mechanical improvements.'[58] By mid-1947 this effort required not only a willingness to work harder, but also to accept less. Convinced that rising prices were a major cause of their economic difficulties, the government moved to restrain wages which they regarded as the primary cause of inflation.[59] But it remained an open question how far the 'self-sacrifice of the British people [could] be pushed'.[60]

In a period of full employment, traditional remedies to restrain wages did not work. *The Times* noted that 'perhaps the most important political fact in Britain today is the implacable refusal of the workers to accept unemployment as the normal method of adjustment to economic change'.[61] The government, therefore, turned to the unions for support. In February 1948 it issued a white paper which called for no wage increases without increased productivity. The leaders of the TUC accepted the demand, agreeing in effect to act as overseers of the government's policy. In March the TUC called a special conference of trade union executives who endorsed a government policy that, as *The Economist* noted, was 'inimicable to the whole tradition and outlook of the movement'.[62] This 'remarkable bargain between government, labour and capital', Samuel Beer noted, formed a 'kind of extra-governmental legislation'.[63] Exemplifying the kind of corporatist policy that both the political and economic wings of the labour movement endorsed during this period, it rested on the implicit assumption that a consensus had been created about the running of the economy, that is, that the conflict between labour and capital had been overcome. In reality, trade union leaders had abandoned their role as defenders of working-class living standards on the grounds that this served the national interest.[64]

Thus by 1948 the government and the leaders of the trade union movement had developed a qualitatively new relationship. Because this relationship involved the trade unions as 'administrators' of government policy, the government had an added stake in supporting the power of the official leadership in opposition to any rank-and-file movement. Ernest Bevin warned the cabinet when it was considering the new wages policy that 'in any informal approaches to trade union leaders on the subject of wage claims, great care must be taken to avoid undermining the authority of the leaders in their unions'.[65] The government's attitude to all disputes in this period followed from this concern. They could not recognise any autonomous working-class activity or they would undermine their own corporatist policies. 'It is the policy of this government, and I think of this house' Attlee said, 'that we should deal with the union representatives and respect their authority.'[66] In short, the government substituted the trade union leadership for the working class.

In opposing the unofficial strike in London and in other ports, the Labour government was centrally concerned to secure the position of the official trade union leadership as the only recognised spokesman of the working class. 'The men owe it to themselves, their families and their fellow trade unionists to give loyal support to their Trade Union leaders,' George Isaacs told them.[67] Hence the government concluded that failure to break the dispute in the docks would 'jeopardise all authority in the ports' and enhance the power of the 'instigators' of the strike, that is, of the unofficial movement.[68] The government acted, in other words, to preserve traditional relations of authority in the docks. 'Until the men carry out obligations into which they have entered,' George Isaacs told the House of Commons, 'we cannot have any confidence in their carrying out further instructions given to them.'[69] Indeed, the government, despite some initial hesitation, wanted a test of strength as a way to break the unofficial movement. As Chuter Ede told Deakin, the Canadian dispute gave them a perfect opportunity for dealing with 'the elements which fomented these continual strikes'.[70]

To be sure, the Labour government initially treated the dispute with a certain amount of restraint, because it underestimated the depths of the men's feelings and assumed the dispute would collapse by itself. It tried therefore not to provoke an extended stoppage.[71] But this stance changed as government leaders came to see fundamental questions of authority at stake. They also came under heavy pressure from the employers, who threatened to take legal action, and from the AFL, who threatened to organise an American boycott of British ships. The government panicked over this last threat and secretly asked the American Ambassador to reassure the AFL and SIU that it was doing all it could to end the dispute. Lewis Douglas reported to the State Department that the government was in 'some difficulty' because 'it is neither appropriate nor customary for [the] Government to be in direct communication with unions in another country. On the other hand, for obvious reasons, they do not want Seafarer's Union to think that cable has been ignored.'[72]

While the government insisted that the CSU dispute was political, it made no objections to the political action of the AFL with its threat to attack the entire British economy. Rather, it knuckled under by sending troops to Bristol to break the strike at the end of May. For the moment it left the Canadian ships in London alone because it lacked the resources to deal with more than two ports at one time.[73] Once the disputes outside of London were settled, however, the government moved to engage the unofficial movement there as well. The Minister of Labour 'most strongly' recommended that the government reverse its previous policy of having the NDLB work all but the Canadian ships, and allow them to act as they saw fit, in other words, to provoke a stoppage. 'If we miss the opportunity of the collapse of the Bristol and Avonmouth strikes it will be some time before another opportunity arises', Isaacs wrote. Attlee agreed.[74] The NDLB were informed of the government's decision; it, in turn, told the dockers that they had to work all ships or none.[75] Thus the shut down of the port of London, which the government labelled a Communist plot, was in fact *created* by the government as a test of strength with the dockers' unofficial movement, and implicitly with all unofficial movements.

In provoking the stoppage, the government were concerned about larger questions of trade union authority and implicitly about their own economic programme, but it was difficult for them to explain the real reasons for their actions. Nor could they acknowledge any validity to the docker's claims. It knew that the Dock Labour Scheme had problems, but decided not to admit that lest it encourage, as Bevin put it, 'those unsettling elements' which made up the unofficial movement.[76] It knew that the dispute was not just a Communist plot, because the police were once again unable to turn up evidence of a Communist conspiracy, as they had been unable to do in previous disputes.[77] It also knew that the CSU had a case. When a Cabinet sub-committee debated how Isaacs should address the dockers, it was pointed out that if he gave more information about the origins of the strike in Canada it might lead to a total stoppage. Isaacs himself noted at the time that the Canadian employers had been 'only too quick to call in the SIU which the CTLC still condemned'.[78] Consequently, it was decided that Isaacs should appeal to the dockers on grounds of national interest, *not* questions of trade unionism.

Not surprisingly, the dockers insisted throughout the dispute that they had been locked out. The Attorney General told the cabinet that 'in the main' the police agreed that it was a lockout,[79] but in public the government insisted that the men alone were responsible for the stoppage. It was, Isaacs told Parliament, a Communist 'manoeuvre to pretend that there is any other explanation of the position . . . This is not a lockout'.[80] The government's line thus obscured its own role in bringing about the situation which it so earnestly denounced.

The government's concern to secure the position of the established trade union leadership reflected a real distance from the men; it resembled, in one way, the employers' attitude. Specifically, it regarded the dockers with condescension. It saw the Dock Scheme as a gift to the men for which they should be grateful. Bevin wrote to Ammon that he did 'sincerely hope the men appreciate' the Scheme, 'and that they will recognise its value, give us good output and justify the cost we have incurred. . .'[81] Several times members of the government mooted ending the Scheme in order to teach the men a lesson. The Minister of Transport wrote that 'it should be made clear to the dock workers that they cannot indefinitely accept the benefits of the scheme without accepting its obligations'.[82] The Attorney General urged that the men should be stricken from the rolls if they failed to answer a call in order that 'the men might realise the serious consequences which their action was bringing on their own heads.'[83] They never seem to have considered that the men had a right to the Scheme or that they had earned its benefits by hard work.

In fact, despite such debates, the government were not prepared to end the Scheme, in part because they feared the tremendous repercussions that would follow both on the docks and in the labour movement if they did. When on its own initiative the NDLB announced on 19 July that if the dockers did not return to work the Scheme would be jeopardised, the government immediately repudiated them.[84] It was prepared to co-opt or to dominate the dockers, but not to declare open warfare.

By labelling the dispute a Communist conspiracy the government mystified it, obscuring the dockers' continuing discontent with the Scheme and with the changed role of their own union. It also hid the role of the AFL, its own concern to support particular structures of economic power, and to revive British capitalism by restraining working-class living standards. By appealing to the dockers on the grounds of national interest the government tried to harness for its own purposes the dockers traditions of solidarity, of class loyalty. 'Who is to have your support?' Isaacs asked them, 'the nation in its present-day need; or the Communists in their opportunity to cause damage and mischief'.[85] Privately, the government regarded these traditions as outmoded, an embarrassment from the past that undermined the Dock Scheme and that should have given way to a new 'spirit of cooperation', a 'spirit of loyalty to the employer'.[86] They might, of course, have attempted to preserve and use those traditions to transform England further. Instead, they sought to use them to integrate the dockers more firmly into capitalist society. By reducing the dispute to a simple black and white dichotomy, they tried to turn one of the dockers' main strengths into a weapon that could be used against them.

The TGWU

The position of the TGWU in this dispute highlights important contradictions noticeable in the British trade union movement since the Second World War if not earlier. Although from the mid-nineteenth century British trade unions generally accepted the limitations of capitalist economic structures, they remained excluded from the locus of political and economic power. During the Second World War, however, their position changed drastically as union leaders supported the war effort in exchange for the right to participate in circles of administrative power. As they became incorporated into existing or new political structures their role as trade union leaders changed. They ceased to act only as the spokesmen of the working class but now sought to mobilise its support for the policies or institutions which they helped to shape along with the government and the employers, that is, for corporatist policies like the Dock Scheme.[87]

Throughout the negotiations with the employers in 1946-7 the TGWU insisted on retaining joint control of the Dock Scheme. The employers and the Ministry of Labour made clear at that time that the union had to accept capitalist rationality as the price for its position. If there is to be joint management, one official noted, 'the union representatives in the joint management must play their part in a responsible way'.[88] The union saw its participation in management as the creation of a new economic order on the docks. In reality, joint control strengthened the employers since the Scheme made no fundamental changes in the dockers' work relations. To the men, therefore, the union now appeared as an enforcer of traditional work discipline; they resented it. The Leggett Committee concluded that 'the participation of Union officials who are members of the Board in the exercise of the Board's disciplinary powers and particularly the power of dismissal, has had the effect of damaging the standing of these officials with their Union membership'. [89]

The union's power rested on its acceptance of these institutional structures. Hence, throughout this period Arthur Deakin, General Secretary of the TGWU, insisted that the Scheme required the men to accept union leadership and to carry out orders. 'We have got a very clear and definite obligation. We either carry out our agreement or we do not . . .'[90] The union could not 'maintain' its 'position' if it did not carry out agreements, he insisted.[91] 'I believe the future of the Trade Union movement depends upon our ability to carry out agreements properly negotiated and approved by our members.'[92] Failure to carry out agreements struck at the heart of the union's power because employers and the government accepted it only in so far as it was able to provide an organised and disciplined workforce.

Correspondingly, Deakin denounced unofficial strikes in the most violent terms, in part because they undercut the nation's new institutional position, in part because they violated the basic structure of the union. Whatever he may have thought about them in private, in public he never acknowledged the slightest legitimacy to unofficial actions, although these occurred frequently during these years. 'Unofficial action has never achieved any worthwhile object and never will,' he wrote.[93] Similarly, he said the CSU dispute had been caused by 'too many people, who in the mistaken belief they can lead, are betraying the interests of the rank and file. Continuance of the dispute is a challenge to trade union authority and discipline.'[94] In this case, he argued, the unofficial leaders were Communists concerned only to fulfill the policy of 'international communism' to disrupt the Marshall Plan.[95]

Insistence on the necessity of honouring agreements involved more than the obvious and understandable acceptance of the terms of collective bargaining. It also involved a corporatist conception of the role of trade unions. Deakin told a delegate conference that 'propaganda is alright in its place but we have got beyond the period of time when our sole job is to carry on propaganda'.[96] In this case, the job included seeing that the Dock Scheme functioned smoothly and that the men worked as hard as possible. In part because of their loyalties to the Labour government and its economic policies, Deakin and the TGWU continually insisted after 1945 that the dockers had to work harder and produce more. In 1945 Deakin issued an appeal for 'work, loyalty, and team spirit'.[97] In 1946 he told the dockers that economic improvement 'depends on you'.[98] The TGWU's 1946 annual report insisted that there had to be the 'fullest measure of production'.[99]

The *TGWU Record* constantly exhorted workers to increase production.[100] After 1948, moreover, the TGWU strongly supported the government's call for wage restraint and increased productivity.

The corollary to a policy of increased production was an acceptance of the need to reduce workers' resistance to harder work and a faster pace. Deakin explained that the need for increased production required an end to all 'bottle-necks', including those made by workers.[101] The chairman of the TGWU's Biennial Delegate Conference stated that 'any restrictive practice or outmoded consideration which stands in the way of progress must go'.[102] Herbert Tracey, secretary of the TUC's publicity department, described the government's 1948 productivity campaign in words the TGWU could have endorsed.

> In a word the members of the trade unions are being told by their leaders that a union does not exist simply to get more wages, shorter working hours, and better conditions for them; it is the unions' responsibility too, they are being told, to see that industry is so efficiently organised that their labour is not wasted or misapplied with consequent loss to the community as a whole.[103]

The TUC, he explained, was arranging conferences to examine 'workshop customs and practices which, in terms of full productivity, can be set aside as having served their purpose'.[104]

The TUC stressed the same position as the TGWU. At the 1948 conference Tom Williamson moved a resolution condemning 'the disloyal activities of small factions of the Movement which are ignoring constitutional trade union practice, and thereby undermining trade union solidarity and responsibility'.[105] Such actions, he made clear undercut the newly established position of the trade union movement. 'We are', he explained, 'in the most responsible position we have ever attained.'[106] In other words, the movement's corporate position was threatened by rank-and-file action. The next year Will Lawther stressed the same theme. 'I should like it to go forth to the world from the Congress,' he told the delegates, 'that our Trade Unions have found and are using better methods of settling industrial disputes than the use of a strike weapon.'[107]

Implicit in this attitude not merely towards unofficial strike action, but towards customary procedures in the docks and the need for increased productivity, lay the assumption that the Dock Scheme had created a new consensus about the ends of industry. Deakin and other

TGWU leaders assumed that both sides of industry had an equal stake in increasing production, and therefore that no further gains could be achieved by traditional policies of reducing the share of employers' profits. In short, they assumed an end of class conflict. Because trade union officers sat on the NDLB they concluded that there was no reason for the men to continue to treat it as a class enemy. They worked therefore to integrate the dockers into the Scheme and to mobilise their support for it. 'We should say to our members in this respect that revolutionary changes will not take place merely by reason of a change of ownership. The division of the proceeds of industry will depend on the total volume of production.'[108] The rank and file, however, rejected these notions and continued to view the employers and the NDLB as a class enemy. Hence they turned away from their elected officials to unofficial leadership because their union at times seemed to have switched sides in the class war.

The Dockers, the Unofficial Movement and the Communist Party

Extensive dock disputes marked the decade after 1945. These disputes had their roots in the dockers' work relations which remained largely unchanged since the mid-nineteenth century. Most work (80 per cent) was done by the piece, the rate for which changed with each job. This proved to be an endless source of disputes. The dockers' constant resort to unofficial action formed part of this bargaining process. Because they changed jobs frequently, they could not afford to use the regular union negotiating machinery. By the time it produced a settlement, they would have moved to another job and lost their original bargaining position.[109]

Disputes over wages formed only one part of a constant struggle for control of the workplace. The employers interpreted the Dock Scheme as requiring every docker to work overtime on demand.[110] Here was another source of trouble. The dockers resented employers' attempts to change traditional forms of work.[111] They also objected to the disciplinary powers employers now had over them. We can get some sense of this ongoing struggle by sampling the causes listed for the 118 dock disputes that occurred between January 1948 and June 1949: payment of tonnage rates, method of discharge, manning scale, protest against disciplinary action, extra rates of pay, protest against abnormal storage, protest against police interrogation, rate for discharge, method of loading, paying off three men who refused to work late.[112] Clearly, the men still regarded the employers as their adversary, not, as the TGWU leadership put it, as their industrial partner.

As we have seen, during the post-war period, the official leadership of the dockers never supported strike action, in part because it loyally endorsed the Labour government's call for increased productivity and, after 1947, for a limit on wages. Under the circumstances, then, the dockers took action on their own. In addition to the hundreds of disputes lasting a few days or less, major disputes occurred in every year after 1945. These disputes were not about rates of pay, but about conditions of work, or a protest against discipline imposed on them by the Scheme, or an expression of solidarity. As the following examples demonstrate, the dockers had an unusually strong tradition of solidarity which had developed out of the conditions of casual labour and remained rooted in their tight knit community living in the neighbourhood of the docks.[113]

In 1947, for example, the London dockers struck to protest the NDLB's attempts to reduce the dock registers in Glasgow. To the Board and the government the proposed reduction was a rational attempt to remove 'ineffectives' from the Scheme. The dockers, however, believed that 'a man should never be deprived of his livelihood on the docks'.[114] The men *were* old and unable to work but could receive more money by regular attendance at the daily call then they could from a pension. In this simple issue, we see a root of unofficial action. The dockers did not respond to the claims of industrial rationality, but to the needs of their 'mates'. In 1947, this produced a 'feeling of hostility', according to the Minister of Labour, between the TGWU and the rank and file.[115]

Similarly, in 1949 the stevedores struck to protest the removal of 'ineffectives' from the Scheme in London. The leadership of the union supported the action in this case, but the Labour government saw it as an attempt to end the Dock Scheme and to disrupt the Marshall Plan, a view which had no substance whatsoever.[116] It directed the police to 'gather such material as they can' in the hopes of mounting a prosecution for 'criminal conspiracy ... of Communist origin'.[117] That attempt failed. In contrast, the Communist Party called on the men to 'stand by [the] aged dockers'.[118] Possibly the Communists had an ulterior motive, but they did respond to the dockers' felt needs. Here was an important source of their influence.

Thus one major difference between the unofficial and the official leadership lay in their attitude to the men's situation. The TGWU and the Labour government tended to regard the Dock Scheme as something that they had given to the men and for which they should be grateful. In contrast, unofficial leaders vehemently repudiated such attitudes. Bob Constable, a leader in the 1948 and 1949 strikes, disputed Ammon's claim that the Scheme was not an unemployment or pension scheme by asking. 'What does this mean to us? How is this Scheme financed? It is financed from the arms and legs of individuals.'[119] During the London dispute one leaflet of the unofficial committee noted, 'Always the cry has been — it will wreck the Scheme. The Scheme that is paid for by portworkers' blood, toil, and sweat'.[120] Such attitudes — of the value of the men and their work — had deep roots in the labour tradition as well as a continued sense of class conflict. As one Communist docker remarked at the TGWU's 1949 Biennial Delegate Conference, 'My father said to me, "lad, remember the employers will give you nothing, only that which you are able to fight for as a result of your organisation!"'[121]

The unofficial movement on the docks developed, therefore, in response to real conflicts dockers had over their work and to counteract the co-optive position of the official trade union leadership. The movement came into existence in 1945 and continued after the 1949 dispute.[122] Known originally as the Portworkers' Defence Committee, it appeared clearly only at disputes, but seems to have maintained a shadowy existence at other times. After 1949 it became more established, publishing the *Portworkers News*, which was 'fairly widely bought and read'.[123] Membership on the committee was not fixed. Although Communists re-appear on it and played an important role, the leadership varied. Thus in 1948 one government official noted that 'The organisation is a very mixed bag indeed and includes, I am told, people who are not extremists.'[124] In 1949 the Minister of Transport noted that the men 'accept fresh leadership for nearly every stoppage of work'.[125]

The Labour government and TGWU view of this movement as a conspiracy denied the obvious evidence that it existed only because the men supported it. All observers, even the government, admitted that the Portworkers' Defence Committee never caused a dispute, but always responded to the spontaneous action of the men. It came to life only after the dockers recreated it. '15,000 men could not all talk at once; it had to be that the Committee did it for them.'[126] One leader of the London dispute, who insisted he was a Catholic and non-Communist, explained that he was chosen because he had on 'previous occasions negotiated the rates of new and abnormal cargoes'. As he explained,

There will always be unofficial disputes in the dock industry for it is not always practicable for trade union officials to be always on the spot at the inception of a dispute, hence a momentary decision to stop work. On the spot spokesmen will continue to be elected for the principle of trade unionism in the dock industry is born and bred in the body and soul of every port worker, which in itself is inherited from their fathers, grandfathers, and other ancestors of many generations ago.[127]

The TGWU investigation of the 1949 strike indicates that the men decided spontaneously to come out and then chose representatives. Not surprisingly, those chosen often had been unofficial leaders before, including Communists. But, as a later Royal Commission stressed, a typical unofficial leader tended to be a 'militant trade unionist ... whose fault is that he and those who follow him refuse to recognise that times have changed'.[128] In other words, he still believed in the class war.

Democracy was an essential element in the unofficial movement. The unofficial leadership could only take the men where they already wanted to go. When they tried to urge a course of action of which the men disapproved, they got nowhere. The leader of the unofficial committee in Bristol pointed out that 'We never told the men to stop work. They had already stopped work before the Committee was formed. As the strike progressed we were howled down when there was any mention made of going back to work.'[129] Similarly, in the 1948 dispute the dockers responded to a personal appeal from Attlee to return to work. When the unofficial leaders criticised the Prime Minister, they were 'howled down'.[130] The men controlled the committee, not the reverse.

The men's choice is also evident from their periodic rejection of the official leadership. When the TGWU failed to support the men in their attempts to obtain a higher wage, or to protect some customary form of work, or to act in concert with a mate, the men would not listen to the union's appeals for loyalty. In the Bristol dispute, the men 'severed their connection with the Union' and shouted down the TGWU area representative.[131] The stevedores defied their left-leaning leadership in 1949 when it ordered a return to work. *The Times* noted that the 'union had almost completely lost control of its members'.[132] In the 1948 dispute Deakin was 'shouted down' when he tried to get the men to return to work. They began to sing 'Tell me the old, old story' to which Deakin responded, 'The only reason I am here is to get a resumption of work, and I will get it. It does not matter how long the dispute lasts, the fact remains you will go back on the proposals I have made to you.'[133] Such incidents occurred repeatedly in 1949 and throughout the period.

The evidence is thus extensive that beneath the 1949 dispute, as well as other disputes after 1945, lay the men's deep dissatisfaction with their union and its corporate position. As one docker put it, 'We go to see the boss and we find our trade union leader. We go to see our own trade union official and we find the Government. We don't know where we are.'[134] In 1950 Mass Observation surveyed the dockers and produced such responses as 'We don't run the Trade Union; its the bloody Union that runs us.' 'The Union is supposed to represent the men but they don't support the striker.'[135] This dissatisfaction was implicit in the men's response to the unofficial leaders' claims in 1949 that they were the true defenders of trade union principles. 'We are fighting,' they insisted, 'for a principle for which the Tolpuddle martyrs fought.'[136]

Communists played an important role in the unofficial movement. Although genuine trade union militants, supported by the men because of that, their party membership doubtless influenced their actions. As Jack Dash put it, 'I could no more separate my political from my trade union work than I could the trinity.'[137] Certainly by the time of the CSU dispute the British Communist Party had declared open warfare on the official Labour movement. Since 1947 it had called for the removal of the Labour government.[138] In 1948 it came out strongly against the government's wage policies, calling for a mass campaign to defeat them.[139] Wage restraint was 'not what trade unionists had voted for in 1945,' it insisted.[140] While this position reflected much rank-and-file sentiment, it also no doubt made Communist dockers more willing to support the CSU. The CSU would certainly have had a difficult time financially without the early support of British Communists.[141] Nevertheless, the CSU probably would have secured the support of the dockers had no Communists been involved in the dispute. Moreover, Communist leaders of the unofficial movement did not necessarily follow a party line so much as they responded to the initiatives of the dockers themselves. Thus in 1945 and 1946 the Communist Party tried to affiliate to the Labour Party and supported the Labour programme, including a call for increased productivity, although it remained critical of Labour foreign policy.[142] Yet, Communists participated in these years in the unofficial movement on the docks, that is, in the years before party policy changed to open opposition to the Labour Party.

Hence, while it is certainly clear that the British Communist Party followed the lead of the Soviet Union, denouncing Marshall Aid or praising the Cominform, it also expressed and responded to genuine working-class needs. As the *Daily Worker* pointed out, 'Communists have not infiltrated into the trade union movement. They joined it on the same basis as Mr Deakin.'[143] Deakin insisted that Communists were not 'true trade unionists' because their ultimate loyalties lay with their party, but the identical charge could be laid against the TGWU which throughout this period acted as an agent of the Labour Party.[144] Moreover Communists did respond to the men's situation in a way that the union often did not. It was the *Daily Worker*, for example, which supported the men's resistance to employers' attempts to speed up and change the conditions of work.[145] The *Manchester Guardian* pointed out that TUC's desire to defeat Communist influence in the unions had 'to reckon with the fact that idealism dies hard'.[146] In other words, Communist activity represented more than Cominform policy; it represented a genuine strain in the British working class.

Labour — both the Party and the TUC — never acknowledged the Communist Party as one element in the common movement, often its most militant. For understandable historical reasons, the leaders of both the Labour Party and the TUC intensely disliked the Communist Party and resisted all its efforts to draw closer. Starting in 1946, when it successfully defeated the Communist affiliation campaign, the Labour Party waged an unceasing propaganda war against communism as seeking the 'triumph of tyranny and intolerance'.[147] By late 1947 the Labour Party and the TUC were laying joint plans to crush Communist influence,[148] and the next year the TUC began a campaign to bar Communists from trade union office.

Although not political innocents, British Communists were not the subversive agents Labour made them out to be. They spoke for genuine working-class support for peace with the Soviet Union and for socialism at home. The Labour Party and the TUC adopted policies directly contradicting these desires. Indeed, Labour's total acceptance of the Cold War by 1946 was not fully admitted in public because of rank and file opposition.[149] Similarly, the wage freeze and the end of socialist planning aroused much rank-and-file opposition. Attacking the Communist Party allowed the government and the TUC to gather support for such unpopular policies by wrapping them in the Union Jack. It also allowed them to discredit the opposition in ways which mystified the real political issues at stake. Thus the American embassy reported that the TUC planned to counteract opposition to the government's economic programme 'with an anti-Communist drive inside the trade union movement, to supplement its productivity drive'.[150] Just as Communist support for the CSU represented more than a genuine belief in the issue itself, so too, TGWU, TUC and Labour Party opposition to the CSU dispute represented much more than it was made out to be. Underlying the issue of the CSU were basic political issues – the policies of the Labour government, the hopes of the rank and file, the position of the working class in a revived capitalist economy.

Conclusion

The London dock strike of 1949 was not a Communist conspiracy, although Communists participated in it and may well have been pleased to embarrass the Labour government.[151] It originated in a genuine dispute in Canada between the CSU and the shipowners who sought to eliminate a militant union when circumstances and the co-operation of the AFL allowed them to do so. British dockers supported the CSU out of genuine regard for principles of trade union solidarity. Their actions also expressed deep discontent with the Dock Scheme that had brought them material benefits but did not allay their long-standing feelings of class hostility. At the same time, the dockers' actions indicated widespread disillusion with the corporatist position of their own union and the policies of the Labour government which it sought to enforce.

The actual question of the legitimacy of CSU claims was in certain ways inconsequential to the real issues being contested in 1949. The government and the TGWU sought to harness the men to the 1947 Dock Scheme. Although the Scheme certainly improved dockers' living standards, it also re-inforced the power of the employers, including their right to control the direction and the speed of work. The men refused to accept these claims. In so doing they challenged the whole corporatist policy developed in these years by denying that there was a community of interest between the different sides of industry. Because their actions called into question the government's immediate economic policies, the power of the trade union leadership on which it depended to carry these out, and, ultimately, capitalist relations in general, the government and the employers deliberately created a showdown by locking out the men. They hoped thereby to put down the men's challenge and secure their own position.

If this analysis is correct, then the Cold War argument raised by both the Labour government and the TGWU to justify their actions can be seen as an ideological construct. Like all ideology it mystified real events, disguising the role the various actors played in the dispute. It totally obscured the action of the AFL in extending the Cold War to Canadian labour; denied the dockers' discontent with their own union and with their own government; and transformed the real issue of working-class power into an international struggle between the Soviet Union and England, making the dockers seem an unwitting pawn of the Communist Machiavelli. In reality, at the heart of the dispute lay the issue of social class — whether the dockers would accept their subordinate position at work and validate the TGWU as their spokesman; that is, whether the dockers would accept the institutional constraints of a revived British capitalism parading in terms of a new community interest. In other words, the Labour government, the TGWU and the NDLB were struggling to preserve very specific institutional and ideological structures that the dock strike challenged either directly or implicitly. They could not, however, acknowledge that corporatist policies, or working-class subordination were the issues at stake. Rather, they tried to transform the issues into the single one of basic national loyalty, chanelling the dockers' class interest in a way that would not challenge those structures. This tactic worked almost completely for the community at large, at least if the press is at all representative. In view of the later history of unrest on the docks, however, it seems to have failed badly to impress the dockers.

Notes

1. *Parliamentary Papers*, 1948-49, vol. XXIX, Cmd. 7851, 'Review of the British Docks Strikes, 1949.'

2. The review of the strike, compiled by George Isaacs, the Minister of Labour, contends that the stevedores had deliberately gone back to work just long enough to finish unloading the section of the ships that was customarily reserved to them before giving way to dockers from the TGWU. When the dispute resumed on the 27th, TGWU dockers were thus automatically involved. In fact, there seems to have been real confusion over the terms of the original agreement, particularly whether the CSU crews would be guaranteed legal immunity on returning to Canada.

3. London Portworkers Lockout Committee, Open Letter by T. Mahoney, July 1949 (TGWU files).

4. The NDLB locked out dockers in the Royal Surrey Docks, where the two Canadian ships were berthed. Other dockers then struck in sympathy.

5. *The Times* (London), 23 July 1949, p.4a.
6. *Parliamentary Debates* (Commons), 5th series, 28 June 1949, 466:982.
7. Ibid., 8 July 1949, 466:2593.
8. TUC, *Annual Report*, 1949, p.326.
9. *Parliamentary Debates* (Commons), 8 July 1949, 466:2593.
10. *The Times*, 11 July 1949, p.4d. Arthur Deakin said that they sought to create 'chaos and confusion' and perhaps even a 'coup d'etat'. (TUC, *Annual Report*, 1949, p.326.)
11. Transcript of radio broadcast, 11 June 1949. Prem 8/1081. Vincent Tewson wrote that the dockers had been 'deluded' by the Communists (Tewson to J.J. Thomasson, 23 June 1949, TUC files, 253.37.) Isaacs also told the dockers that their sense of loyalty was being exploited (*The Times*, 14 July 1949, p.4b.). See also 'How Communists Hoodwinked the Dockers', *Labour*, XII (January, 1950), pp.586-7.
12. Proceedings of the Executive Inquiry held at Bristol on 10-11 November 1949 (TGWU Files).
13. Richard Hyman, *Strikes*, paperback edition, 1977, p.107.
14. H.A. Logan, *Trade Unions in Canada* (Toronto, 1948), p.289.
15. Ibid., p.290.
16. Ibid., pp.291-2. The eight hour day applied only to the Great Lakes.
17. *Searchlight*, 23 August 1946, p.1. (*Searchlight* was the CSU journal.)
18. *New York Times* (7 April 1949, p.31) called them 'company unions'.
19. Ibid. The CTLC (*Report of Proceedings*, 1948, p.77) called the CLSU 'company dominated'.
20. CTLC, *Report of Proceedings*, 1948, pp.78, 353.
21. Ibid., pp.354, 78; See also *Trades and Labor Congress Journal*, XXVIII (September 1948), p.19. The 1947 convention also called the SIU a 'dual union'. The CTLC had developed as a Canadian twin of the AFL. Most of its members belonged to unions affiliated to the AFL and it remained under strong AFL influence, although it tolerated Communists in the movement.
22. Peter Weiler, 'The United States, International Labour, and the Cold War: The Break-Up of the World Federation of Trade Unions', *Diplomatic History*, V (Winter, 1981), pp.1-22.
23. *Trades and Labor Congress Journal*, XXVIII (September, 1948), p.19. John Crispo, *International Unionism: A Study in Canadian-American Relations* (Toronto, 1967), pp.105-6.
24. *New York Times*, 9 February 1949, p.20; *Trades and Labor Congress Journal*, XXVIII (March, 1949), p.1; London to State Department, RG59, 842.5043/2-144 Decimal Files, Department of State, National Archives. (Hereafter cited as DF, DSNA.)
25. CTLC, *Report of Proceedings*, 1949, p.22.
26. *New York Times*, 20 February 1949, V, p.8; *Searchlight*, 3 March 1949.
27. *New York Times*, 7 January 1949, p.43; 5 February 1949, p.29. The CSU organised a demonstration in London to protest the firings. This may explain their presence there before the spring dispute. George Isaacs charged (Cmd. 7851, p.8) that they had come to London as part of a plan to organise the later disturbances.
28. London to State, RG84, Box 1044, 560.2 Britain, DF, DSNA. The CSU insisted that the whole dispute had been provoked by the employers (*Searchlight*, 8 April 1949, p.2); the CSU president, Harry Davis, claimed that they had been on the verge of a settlement when the owners signed with the SIU (*Toronto Globe and Mail*, 1 April 1949, p.7).
29. *Trades and Labor Congress Journal*, XXVII (May, 1949), p.11.
30. The literature is voluminous. Michael Jackson, *Labour Relations on the Docks* (Westmead, England, 1973) has a complete bibliography.

31. Alan Bullock, *The Life and Times of Ernest Bevin*, II (London, 1967); Vernon Jensen, *Hiring of Dock Workers and Employment Practices in the Ports of New York, Liverpool, London, Rotterdam and Marseilles* (Cambridge, Mass., 1964).

32. 'Report of National Docks Delegate Conference, London, 24 August 1945', *Transport and General Workers' Record*, XXV (September, 1945), p.73 (hereafter cited as *TGWU Record*); Michael Jackson, *Labour Relations*, p.38.

33. V.L. Allen, *Trade Union Leadership* (Cambridge, Mass., 1957), pp.177-83

34. Cited by Jackson, *Labour Relations*, p.38.

35. National Dock Labour Board, *The Scheme*, Clauses 8:5a, 5b, 15.

36. Jensen, *Hiring of Dock Workers; Parliamentary Papers*, 1955-56, vol. XXVI, Cmd. 9813, 'Port Transport Industry: Report of a Committee Appointed on 27th July, 1955, to inquire into the Operation of the Dock Workers (Regulation of Employment) Scheme, 1947', p.4.

37. Jensen, *Hiring of Dock Workers*, p.199; V.L. Allen, *Trade Union Leadership*, pp.177-83. Lab 8/1358.

38. Jean Tripp McKelvey, *Dock Labor Disputes in Great Britain: A Study in the Persistence of Industrial Conflict* (Ithaca, 1953), p.53; 'Restrictive Practices in the Dock Industry,' *Trade and Harbour Authority*, April, 1952, p.393. The article also complains about the dockers' long tea breaks, their refusal to transfer immediately from one job to another, or to use new machines; see also National Dock Labour Board, *Review of the Work of the National Dock Labour Board, 1947-1949* (March, 1950), p.22.

39. Letter from T.G., *The Times*, 13 April 1960, p.15.

40. 'Obituary,' *The Times*, 4 April 1960, p.19.

41. *Parliamentary Debates* (Lords), 27 July 1949, 164:559.

42. *Daily Telegraph*, 23 August 1951, p.4.

43. Ibid. He told the House of Lords that there were 'plenty of able, intelligent, and decent fellows amongst the dockers but they are still a little apprehensive and are rather inclined to be led away by yarns and slogans', *Parliamentary Debates* (Lords), 11 March 1952, 175:638.

44. Ibid., Ammon to Isaacs, 28 April 1947, Lab 8/1356. The NDLB wrote that the susceptibility of the men to such agitators made the union 'necessarily somewhat vulnerable to the tactics of mob rule' (NDLB, *Review of the Work*, p.27).

45. Ammon's remarks were reported to the Prime Minister by a government official on 12 May 1949, Lab 10/833.

46. Ammon to Isaacs, 27 May 1949, Lab 10/833.

47. Ammon to Attlee, 7 June 1949, Ammon Papers (Hull University Library), 3/1.

48. *Parliamentary Debates* (Lords), 27 July 1949, 164:559.

49. Ibid., 11 March 1952, 175:639; the 'board', he said, 'must be master in their own house' (ibid., 16 November 1954, 189:1555).

50. S.C. Parkin to Ammon, 31 May 1949, Ammon Papers, 3/1. The NDLB believed that the policy of isolating the Canadian ships was *ultra vires*.

51. Ibid. S.C. Parkin, Memorandum, 16 May 1949, Ammon Papers, 3/1. Parkin to Hogger, 31 May 1949, Prem 8/1081.

52. Minister of Transport, 'The Dock Labour Industry and the National Dock Labour Board', 6 July 1949, CP (49) 145.

53. Ammon to Attlee, 5 July 1949, Ammon Papers, 3/1.

54. Ammon to Attlee, 7 June 1949, Ammon Papers, 3/1.

55. Arthur Marwick, *Britain in the Century of Total War* (Boston, 1968), pp.257ff.

56. Richard Gardner, *Sterling-Dollar Diplomacy* (Oxford, 1969); Lloyd Gardner, *Architects of Illusion* (Chicago, 1970), pp.113-38.

57. For the contrary view, see D.C. Watt, 'American Aid to Britain and the Problem of Socialism, 1945-51', in *Personalities and Policies* (University of Notre Dame, 1965), pp.53-80.

58. 'British Capabilities and Intentions: 1947', 'Research and Analysis Report, no.4327, 21 April 1947.

59. Panitch, *Social Democracy*, p.20.

60. R&A no.4327.

61. *The Times* (London), 4 September 1947, p.5.

62. Panitch, *Social Democracy*, pp.27, 23.

63. Samuel H. Beer, *British Politics in the Collectivist Age* (New York, 1967), pp.208, 203.

64. See Panitch, *Social Democracy*, pp.27-9.

65. C.M. 15(48) 5, 9 February 1948.

66. *Parliamentary Debates* (Commons), 24 June 1948, 452:1466.

67. Cmd. 7851, p.3. .

68. Minutes, Coordinating Committee of the Emergencies Organisation, 25 May 1949, Prem 8/1081. (A sub-committee of the Cabinet, it was responsible for maintaining services during a strike.)

69. *Parliamentary Debates* (Commons), 7 July 1949, 466:234.

70. 30 May 1949, Prem 8/1081. The government realised that the Dock Scheme had problems but agreed not to admit this or to investigate the difficulties on the grounds that this would encourage 'those unsettling elements'. (C.M. 46 (49) 6, 18 July 1949.)

71. Cmd. 7851, p.11. Prem 8/1081.

72. Lewis Douglas to State, 3 June 1949, RG84, Box 1044, 560.2 Britain, DF, DSNA.

73. Prem 8/1081, 23 May 1949. C.M. 40 (49) 4, 2 June 1949.

74. Memo, nd, (clearly, mid-June) Lab 10/832.

75. Memo, 14 June 1949, Lab 13/833.

76. C.M. 46 (49) 6, 18 July 1949.

77. C.M. 44 (49) 3, 7 July 1949. In 1948 the government made 'extensive inquiries' into the rumoured presence of a Mr Zarov, who was said to have created the strike to sabotage the Marshall Plan. It found no Mr Zarov or any Cominform influence, A.W. Peterson to F.L.T. Graham-Harrow, 2 July 1948, Prem 8/1086.

78. Isaacs made this observation to a meeting of Cabinet Ministers who were concerned with the strike, 10 June 1949, Prem 8/1081.

79. C.M. 44 (49) 3, 7 July 1949.

80. *Parliamentary Debates* (Commons), 4 July 1949, 466:1789; see also ibid., 1 July 1949, 466:1660; 4 July 1949, 466:1794.

81. Bevin to Ammon, 30 April, 1948, Ammon Papers, 4/8.

82. Memorandum, 6 July 1949, CP (49) 145.

83. Memorandum, 8 July 1949, CP (49) 148. Similar thoughts had been mooted and rejected in 1948, see Lab 13/128, C.M. 44 (48) 2, 28 June 1948.

84. *Parliamentary Debates* (Commons), 20 July 1949, 467:1377; the government feared that such action would prolong the stoppage (C.M. 47 (49) 7, 21 July 1949). The board complained that the government had taken away its 'authority' (Minutes of Meeting, Minister of Labour and NDLB, 20 July 1949. TGWU Files), and Ammon denounced the government for its stupidity. It has, he said, 'gone crazy . . . spoilt the whole show' (*Daily Telegraph*, 21 July 1949). This indiscretion cost him his position as chief whip in the House of Lords.

85. *The Times* (London), 14 July 1949, p.4b.

86. Minister of Transport, Memorandum, 6 July 1949, Communist Party (49) 145.

87. I am here following Leo Panitch, *Social Democracy & Industrial Militancy*

(Cambridge, England, 1976). In 'Trade Unions and the Capitalist State, Corporatism and its Contradictions' (*New Left Review*, no.125, January-February 1981, pp.21-43), Panitch defines corporatism as 'a political structure within advanced capitalism which integrates organised socio-economic producer groups through a system of representation and cooperative mutual interaction at the leadership level and mobilization and social control at the mass level'.

88. Mr Wile to Minister of Transport, 18 December 1946, Lab 8/1356: 'I think the present situation provides a very good test of whether we can rely in future on the unions accepting their responsibilities for seeing that the labour force in the dock industry will not be over-inflated'. See V.L. Allen, *Trade Union Leadership*, pp.177-87.

89. The Committee, chaired by Sir Frederick Leggett, Bevin's wartime aide at the Ministry of Labour, presented the first investigation of the persistent unrest in the London docks, *Parliamentary Papers*, 1950-51, vol. XVI, Cmd. 8236, 'Unofficial Stoppages in the London Docks, Report of a Committee of Inquiry', p.13. A later inquiry (*Parliamentary Papers*, 1955-56, vol. XXXI, Cmd. 9813, 'Port Transport Industry: Report of a Committee Appointed on 27th July, 1955, to inquire into the operation of the Dock Workers (Regulation of Employment) Scheme, 1947', contested this conclusion.

90. TGWU, *Biennial Delegate Conference*, 1949.

91. Ibid.

92. Arthur Deakin, 'Union Policy on Wages, Unofficial Strikes and the "Closed Shop"', *TGWU Record*, XXVI (October, 1946), p.90.

93. Arthur Deakin, 'Trade Unions vs. Communism: The Gloves are Off!' *TGWU Record* XXIX (July 1949), p.41. This always had been the position of the TGWU.

94. *Daily Telegraph*, 18 July 1949.

95. See note 93. Quite unfairly, Deakin charged that 'strong arm methods – intimidation and even violence is threatened'. In the CSU dispute the TGWU insisted that their proper role was to remain neutral. In fact, they tacitly sided with the SIU. The head of the TGWU's docks' section, Arthur Bird, circulated a letter to all docks' officers in which W.D. Henderson, an SIU official, set out the SIU case, claiming, with no truth, that it was a 'much more powerful organization than the discredited CSU' (W.D. Henderson to Bird, 4 May 1949, TGWU Files). Other circulars from TGWU headquarters stressed that the strike was an inter-union affair for which there was no reason to intervene (5 April 1949, 2 May 1949, TGWU Files).

96. Transcript, London Docks Delegate Conference, 30 August 1949, TGWU Files.

97. 'The Nation's Fight for Economic Survival: An Appeal for Work, Loyalty, and Team Spirit', *TGWU Record*, XXV (November, 1945), pp.104-5.

98. 'How to Fill the Shops with Consumer Goods', *TGWU Record*, XXV (April, 1946), pp.206-7.

99. TGWU, *Report and Balance Sheet*, December, 1946.

100. For example, A. Deakin, 'Full Speed Ahead in the Great Drive for Exports', *TGWU Record* XXV (September, 1945), pp.68-9; A. Deakin, 'The Need for Increased Productivity', *TGWU Record* (December, 1948), pp.152-3; 'Why More Production is Necessary', *TGWU Record*, XXVIII (May, 1949), p.263.

101. *TGWU Record*, XXVII (December, 1948), p.152.

102. Edward Figes, speech to the Biennial Delegate Conference, 1949.

103. 'The Productivity Campaign', *Trades and Labor Congress Journal*, XXVII (January, 1949), p.3.

104. Ibid.

105. TUC, *Annual Report*, 1948, p.336. That year the TUC told its affiliates that unions had to overcome their suspicion of scientific management. *Labour*, X

(August, 1948), p.371.

106. Ibid., Charles Dukes, the 1946 President of the TUC, made a similar plea: 'It will be fatal to our future development as a responsible and constructive force in the national life if the unity of our unions is undermined by irresponsible and headstrong minorities which try to usurp the elected and representative leadership of our Movement.' (TUC, *Annual Report*, 1946, p.3.)

107. TUC, *Annual Report*, 1949, p.75. Strikes, he argued, represented a 'sectional interest'. Such arguments did not go unchallenged. As one delegate from the USDAW said, 'This question of loyalty it seems, is being somewhat prostituted. I am going to submit to Congress that the first loyalty of every trade unionist is to his or her class. Loyalty is a class question.' (TUC, *Annual Report*, 1948, p.336.) The dockers echoed these sentiments.

108. TGWU, *Report and Balance Sheet*, 1948, p.14.

109. Cmd. 8236, p.5.

110. Ibid., p.20.

111. Ibid., p.6.

112. See note 52.

113. Cmd., 8236, p.6. Stephen Hill, *The Dockers: Class and Tradition in London* (London, 1976), p.55; Kenneth Knowles, 'The Post-War Dock Strikes', *Political Quarterly*, XXII (July-September, 1951), pp.266-90.

114. Cmd. 8236, p.21.

115. Lab. 10/735.

116. C.M. 27 (49) 2, 18 April 1949.

117. Shawcross to Attlee, 20 April 1949, Prem 8/1085. George Isaacs argued that concessions would be 'unjustified'. The strike had to be 'firmly resisted' because the docks could not carry such a 'burden'. (CP (49) 89, 12 April 1949.) The government were on the verge of sending in troops when the strike ended.

118. *Daily Worker*, 13 April 1949. They claimed the protest was also against a policy of speeding up the work.

119. TGWU, Proceedings of the Executive Inquiry, 26-7 January 1950, into the Unofficial Dock Strike, London 1949, TGWU Files.

120. London Portworkers' Lockout Committee, 'Ammon's "Showdown" Exposed,' nd TGWU Files.

121. TGWU, Biennial Delegate Conference, 11 July 1949.

122. The movement came into existence in 1945 and continued after the 1949 dispute (see Jack Dash, *Good Morning, Brother* [London, 1969], pp.53-5). While it maintained a certain continuity of membership, particularly among the Communist members, it did not have a regular existence until after 1949.

123. Cmd. 8236, p.27.

124. [illegible] to A. Stillwell, 23 June 1948, Lab 10/787.

125. CP (49) 145, 6 July 1949.

126. Ted Dickens, one of the Communist leaders of the unofficial movement. Transcript, TGWU Appeals Committee, 14 April 1950. Another movement leader commented, 'There are always difficulties arising and there will always be stoppages of one kind and another because of these complexities.'

127. Proceedings of the Executive Inquiry, 26-7 January 1950, into Unofficial Dock Strike, London 1949, TGWU Files.

128. Cmd. 9813, p.18.

129. Proceedings of the Executive Inquiry Held at Bristol on November 10-11 1949, TGWU Files.

130. J.R. Whitlock, Memorandum, 25/5/50 (sic), Lab 10/783.

131. A TGWU official reported this to the regional officer of the Industrial Relations Department of the Ministry of Labour, 20 May 1949, Lab 10/833; H.P. Priday to A. Deakin, 25 May 1949, TGWU Files.

178 *British Labour and the Cold War*

132. 9 July 1949, p.4b.

133. *Daily Telegraph*, 26 June 1948, p.2; The *Daily Worker* (26 June 1948) reported the same event more graphically: Deakin said, 'I'm going to get you back to work.' 'You're wasting your time, Arthur,' came the retort. He then told them to use the constitutional machinery of the union. Someone shouted he was a dictator to which he replied, 'I wish I was a dictator, I would soon have you back to work.'

134. Cited by Knowles, 'Post-War Dock Strikes,' p.28.

135. Cited by Leo Panitch, *Social Democracy*, p.237, n.82.

136. *Daily Worker*, 5 July 1949, p.1. 'We are fighting to maintain our traditions'; ibid., 18 July 1949. The London Port Workers Central Lockout Committee wrote that it was 'an attack on trade union principles' (leaflet, TGWU Files). The literature put out by the Lockout Committee indicates that the question of a speed-up of the work and the failure of the union to achieve the 'Dockers' Charter' — 25s per day, 40 hour week, pensions, better work conditions — played a role in the stoppage.

137. Interview, Jack Dash, 5 June 1979.

138. For example, *World News and Views*, 9 August 1947, p.367.

139. *Daily Worker*, 15 December 1948, p.3.

140. *Daily Worker*, 25 March 1948, p.1. This opposed union executives' acceptance of the wage freeze. The party called for a 'big offensive' for higher wages (*World News and Views,* 20 September 1948, p.1). 'We are out to get millions of workers moving into a head-on clash with the policy of the Labour government and the capitalists (John Mahon, quoted by the *Daily Telegraph*, 13 December 1948, p.1).

141. For example, 'The East End Opens Door to Seamen', *Daily Worker*, 13 May 1949, p.1; see also *Daily Worker*, 28 April and 9 May 1949. The CPGB clearly provided financial support for the CSU.

142. For example, John Gollan, 'Win the People for Our Policy', *World News and Views*, 23 March 1946, p.89; 'Notes of the Month', *Labour Monthly*, XXVIII (April, 1946), p.106.

143. *Daily Worker*, 17 December 1947, p.1.

144. V.L. Allen, *Trade Union Leadership*, pp.274-5. At the 1949 TUC conference Deakin said it was true that British trade union officials worked with their own government, but that they didn't take orders, 'Well, I ask you is that a crime? Is it wrong that we are doing those things in cooperation with our own colleagues, our own government, which holds the same point of view that we hold? Not at all.' (*Annual Report*, 1949, p.323.) Indeed, it was not a crime, but such co-operation was exactly his main charge against Communist members of the TGWU.

145. For example, 'Try Punishing the Employers', *Daily Worker*, 14 September 1948, p.1.

146. *Manchester Guardian*, 23 December 1947.

147. 'The Labour Party and the Communisty Party', 27 February 1946.

148. Hugh Chevins in the *Daily Telegraph*, 23 December 1947.

149. As late as 1947 the delegates to the TUC's annual conference howled down the representative of the AFL for attacking the Soviet Union.

150. 841.5043/11-2648, DF, DSNA.

151. In concluding thus, we obviously take issue with Henry Pelling's claim, in *The British Communist Party* (London, 1958), p.158, that, 'there is no doubt that this trouble was fomented and in several cases directly instigated by the party or by Communists from overseas.

8 RETHINKING LABOUR HISTORY: THE IMPORTANCE OF WORK

Richard Price

The mid-1960s in Britain saw the emergence of what might be called the underside of the British labour movement. By the end of the first year of the second Wilson government, it was becoming increasingly clear that the corporate bargain between industrial labour and the state which dated from the Second World War was breaking down, and no amount of appeals to the 'Dunkirk spirit' could bandage it up. The dimensions of this new, twentieth-century version of the 'labour question' were many and varied. At one level, it was part of a much wider cultural crisis in the society which reflected the end of a formal imperial role (Aden was evacuated only in 1968) whose passing encouraged the widespread sense that old class conventions and structures were musty, irrevelant relics which deserved (as they undoubtedly did and do) to be consigned to the dustbins of history. There was talk on the left of new opportunities and new openings for socialism. And, as a counterpoint to the collection of attitudes and values associated with the Establishment which was now on the defensive, the working classes became fashionable again in a way that they had not been since the 1930s. There was no greater status symbol amongst university students of that period than to claim a working-class paternity; and should that be impossible, then an imagined style of working-class dress or accent would do. At another level, and clearly related to the popularity of attacks upon ruling-class convention, was the recognition that Britain could no longer afford to coast along, basking in the warm afterglow of the Second World War and protected by the nuzzling-up nature of the special relationship with the United States. The world was changing rapidly and, although the 1950s had generally concealed the fact, by the mid-1960s it was clear to every thinking person that Britain's sliding economic performance could not be allowed to continue. Modernisation was proclaimed to be the key; Harold Wilson talked confidently of a white hot technological revolution, of harnessing the new computer science to a dynamic socialist management of the economy to produce a second – or was it a third? – industrial revolution. Enough of us were sufficiently impressed to give him a tentative hold on power in 1964 which was affirmed eighteen months later.

But there remained the working class and it was on that stolid and formidable reef that things came to grief long before the disastrous descent into an inflationary world recession. For any modernisation of Britain's ancient industrial base depended upon the ability of the state and the employers to cope with the collection of customs and practices that had grown up since 1945 and which posed a considerable barrier to the reorganisation of industry and the economy. In very simple terms, worker power at the workplace had grown (especially in the strategically important industries like automobiles and engineering) to such an extent that there were serious questions about management's ability to manage. To this problem the official labour movement really had no answer and it was left to the state and employers to invent a series of devices which ranged from productivity bargaining to 'In Place of Strife' in an attempt to bring labour at large to heel.

Today we are intimately familiar with the elements that composed this phenomenon of labour's influence and control over the labour process. Its distinctive features have been investigated by a large body of industrial sociologists and even by a Royal Commission. All of these studies affirmed that since the end of the Second World War, a structure of 'informal' workshop bargaining had emerged which, it was explained, filled the voids left by the national negotiating structures. To service this informal system, a whole network of shop stewards had also blossomed, especially in the 1950s, whose place and position depended not upon the 'responsible' channels of industrial procedure and authority, but upon the democratic wishes of their rank-and-file constituents. The practice of this system was turning notions of hierarchy and authority in industry upside down. Restrictive practices flourished, not only in the old established 'craft' industries, but also amongst the 'unskilled' dock and automobile workers. The dockers' ganger possessed locally the same sort of influence as the venerable 'father' in the printing chapel. Even in places like Chemco, where unionisation had been imposed as part of a conscious managerial strategy to incorporate the workforce, covert forms of resistance extended to workers devising their own system of job rotation.[1] In addition, this informal system was militant in disturbingly new ways. The wave of strike activity which began in 1968 and peaked in 1972 was not confined to Britain. But in Britain it represented not so much the 'explosion' that it did elsewhere in Europe as the climax to persistent trends first noticeable in the 1950s of 'unofficial' strikes which tended to be more concerned with issues of authority and control at work than they did with pure wage or economic issues.

There was, it seemed, a new willingness to assert worker demands on issues like redundancy which challenged the rights of management to operate according to the impersonal dictates of market pressures.[2] Not only had labour succeeded – consciously or unconsciously, by design or default, it hardly mattered – in extending its frontier of control at the workplace, but it was also willing to challenge the state head on. Both Labour and Conservative governments found to their cost the enormous negative power of the trade unions to impede and ultimately to destroy industrial relations policy and legislation. But it is interesting to note that although the union leaderships were opposed to 'In Place of Strife', the militant initiative derived almost entirely from the rank and file.[3]

It is not the purpose of this chapter to treat in any detail the nature and consequences of the post-1945 growth of informal bargaining structures and the expansions of the 'frontier of control' that this represented, but it is important to note that because the field has been left largely to the industrial sociologist, with occasional forays by political scientists, it has generally lacked an historical perspective. Only James Cronin and Keith Middlemas have approached the industrial conflict and politics of those years as historians: Cronin as part of a wider examination of strike waves and Middlemas to trace the changing patterns of the 'corporate bias' of the state in relation to labour and industry since the First World War. Of course, many industrial sociologists are far from ignorant of history: on the whole, they are more conscious of its relevance to their discipline than historians are aware of the significance of industrial sociology. Practitioners as different as Hugh Clegg and Richard Hyman consistently bring a *sense* of history to their work and some, especially Flanders and Fox, occasionally go beyond that to explore the historical roots of contemporary developments.[4] But even in those cases, the predominant emphasis is on the uniqueness of the post-Second World War developments, and most other investigators are totally presentist in their perspective. Thus, the growth of informal bargaining tends to be treated as a distinctly new phenomenon, as an instrumental response to economic opportunities such as tight labour markets, or as the product of the inadequacy of the national bargaining structures to cope with changing industrial structures and the immediate needs of the workplace. In a similar vein, the militancy of the late 1960s is often seen as a response to the sharpening inflationary pressures which stiffened employer resistance to demands which the new, affluent workers had been accustomed to securing with ease over the previous

25 years. The radicalism of that militancy — the way it demanded various forms of work control — is also seen solely within a limited time frame of the post-war era, its newness is emphasised by the genuinely new factor of an increase in white-collar militancy.[5] Other aspects of sociological study have reinforced these tendencies. The now largely discredited assumptions and findings of Goldthorpe's affluent worker series, for example, claimed that the 'modern' vanguard of the working class had broken with the class conscious attitudes of its forefathers and viewed its work and politics solely through an instrumental perspective whose goals conformed to the values of the consumer society and whose aspirations were close to those of the middle class. Indeed, many did believe in the end of this particular kind of traditional class conflict and in the mid-1960s one could be forgiven for believing that the cloth cap working class was to be found only in the cartoon character of Andy Capp.

There was something to all of this. When class conflict of a traditional kind revived it was not simply a replay of the heroic days of Featherstone or the General Strike. The memory of the depression, the overall security provided by full employment and the Welfare State had provided the basis for a shift in consciousness, but it was a shift, as we shall see, grounded in historical tradition. The demand for the right to work, the refusal to accept the inexorability of redundancy were new in this period only in the confident aggressiveness with which they were asserted. In addition, changes in the industrial and occupational structures, most particularly the huge growth of the service sector, had created 'white-collar proletarians' often well educated and socially conscious, whose work situation and militancy was intimately related to their sense of political priorities.

But to admit this is to immediately suggest that it is inadequate to regard the 'challenge from below' simply as a product of transient local factors, peculiar to the 1950s and 1960s. Those factors were undeniably important and they can and do explain the moment of militancy and the prominence of its forms and structures. But it is equally the case that the nature of post-war industrial relations is composed of a distinct set of identifiable historical traditions whose significance transcends and informs the particular forces that conditioned and aroused its emergence in the 1960s. This chapter is concerned to explore the meaning of these traditions and the place they occupy within the dynamics of labour history.

One of the central indictments made against 'unofficial' labour in the 1960s was the widespread presence of restrictive practices which even the popularity of productivity bargaining failed to remove to any appreciable extent. The Donovan Commission generally confirmed the more politically inspired indictment of *The Restrictive Society* by John Lincoln whose appeal for the reinstatement of the common law doctrine of restraint of trade does not now appear so crankily right wing as it must have done when published. Both Donovan and Lincoln, however, agreed that rigid demarcation lines, various forms of overmanning, unnecessary overtime, the pegging of output and other more specific practices like 'welting' and 'spelling' in the docks and shipbuilding were common to much of industry. The Donovan research paper also noted, but did not elaborate upon, the fact that many of these practices were of long standing and appeared to be impervious to dislodgement by high unemployment. It was also noted that restrictive practices were not the sole province of skilled craftsmen — although some of the most highly developed were naturally to be found amongst this group — but were also to be found amongst the semi-skilled or unskilled. The impetus to restriction of production, was both general and widespread, but of central interest from our point of view is the seeming permanence of these practices.[6]

Virtually every example that Lincoln and Donovan gave could be matched from earlier periods. Since the 1930s, there have been three extensive surveys of restrictive practices in Britain and the most remarkable feature of them all is how relatively little had changed. When Zweig conducted his investigation in 1950 he remarked upon the many specific similarities he found with John Hilton's more partisan study of 1935, *Are Trade Unions Obstructive?*, and Hilton himself made the same point. Hilton's study was flawed by its excessive reliance upon trade union rule books (generally the last place to look for evidence of restriction of output), and its failure to seriously enquire into the vaguer employer's evidence (which was more suggestive of the informal nature of restrictive rules) allowed him to legitimately claim that the 'obstructions to industrial efficiency and improvement set up by the trade unions are nothing like so serious as is commonly alleged'.[7] It is hard to make specific comparisons between the three books because they all had slightly different purposes and varied in the amount of information they provided for particular industries. Furthermore, I have not traced back in a systematic way a set of restrictive practices in a variety of trades — although such a task is both feasible and worthwhile. However, certain examples do stand out.

Thus, in building, both Hilton and Lincoln noted the strict enforcement of similar demarcation boundaries, and amongst the masons it is evident that the question of worked stone, so prominent in the nineteenth century, was still very much alive in the 1930s.[8] Printers and dockworkers also stand out in the evidence and in these cases, it is clear that the practices have a long history. In the London newspaper sector of printing, for example, precisely the same complaints about the rigid conditions imposed upon the machines were being made in the 1960s as in the 1930s and 1890s. From the beginning the men had refused to allow counters on the machines to check the amount of copy, the output had been adjusted so that the machines were run at well under capacity, and dating back even further, the LSC had insisted on being paid for made-up copy as if it were being set for the first time.[9] As the recent struggle at Thomson Newspapers has illustrated, such issues remain central to industrial relations in London printing. Because of the market structure in printing, it so happens that these restrictions were by no means as serious as they would be in other industries. Indeed, their persistence over such a long period (and there is little doubt that similar practices go back even further) owes not a little to the fact that they did not generally hamper profit margins. Provincial newspapers and printers did not, at least in the 1930s, see themselves unduly hampered by such restrictions, partly, no doubt, because they were weaker outside of London. But it was clear that their main effect was both to obstruct the technological development of the industry (and thus to set the scene for the periodic and intense struggles in the industry) and to move provincial standards closer to London levels. In the Webbs' limited terms, then, these rules served a purpose of maintaining and improving the standard rate and minimum conditions.

The same kind of tradition may be found in dockwork — where the presence of restrictive customs *was* more of a brake upon employers' freedom. Thus, the list of restrictions that were placed before the Devlin Inquiry could be matched almost exactly with that presented to the Shaw Inquiry of 1920. In the meantime, the depression had evidently failed to temporarily remove the over-manning in London and Liverpool where twelve men were employed to do the work of six; nor had it prevented a strict restriction of overtime working by the imposition of severe financial penalties which involved the employment of the whole gang when part of it would do and the payment for a whole night's work even if only three hours were actually worked. The practice of 'welting' provides a specific example of the entrenchment of such a restrictive custom. Its origins seem to lie in the First World War — which period, of course, saw the conditions for such an exercise of dockers' work control power — when the practice arose of allowing men who worked in the frozen meat holds one hour on and one hour off with full pay. Interestingly enough, this custom may be found in many of the major ports of the world, but in Liverpool and Glasgow by the 1930s, at least, it had rapidly expanded beyond the frozen meat jobs into chilled meats and beyond. Although concentrated efforts were made to buy out the practice under the stimulus of the Devlin modernisation, it proved remarkably resilient and 'on ship' welting still occurred in the early 1970s.[10]

Restriction of output then, is by no means limited to skilled workers either in contemporary or historical terms. It is important to emphasise this because there is always a tendency in labour history to assume that efforts to exercise some control over working conditions are only characteristic of craft or skilled trades. It remains true, of course, that the ability to impose control is conditioned by factors of skill just as it is conditioned by the structure of product markets, the state of the labour market, the method of payment, and other factors. We may also assume that the degree of skill plays a prime role in the ability of workers to retain an historical continuity of restrictive practices, although the case of dockworking should remind us of the difficulties in defining skill which remains a fluid category changing as the division of labour is altered. There is an obvious need for more detailed, local research which alone would reveal the conditions and contours of restrictive practices among the less skilled. But the fact of such efforts is not in doubt.

As Nichols and Beynon found in their study of Chemco, 'skill is not essential to control. It is possible for unskilled workers, subdivided into routine repetitive jobs, to use their collective strength to oppose capital'. Chemco is a particularly apposite example because its workforce was conventionally unmilitant and broken into small groups whose work routine paralleled the nineteenth-century labourer's fetching and carrying. Nor, it seems, was this case atypical either of its time or occupational strata. Writing at the same time, both Hilton in Britain and Mathewson in the United States came to the conclusion that restriction of production was as common amongst unorganised workers as it was amongst the organised — although we may be sure that the latter could be both more confident and bolder in their assertions than could the former. By way of further example, we might note the Leeds gas workers in 1891 — who were only just organised — but who, like the craft printers, refused to accept weighing machines to measure their supposed quota of coal to be carbonised each day.[11]

A second of the traditions of resistance to be addressed is the matter of informal organisation. Although some industrial sociologists recognise the historical precedents for the prominent role that the 'unofficial system' of industrial relations played in the 1950s and 1960s, most would tend to agree with Hawkins' emphasis upon the novelty of the situation:

> Workgroups are either ignoring or directly challenging the rules and restraints imposed from above. This new pattern of behaviour has revealed itself . . . in a growing dissatisfaction with the traditional methods of making decisions.[12]

But the tradition of informal organisation has both linear and cyclical patterns of historical development. Its modern roots go back to the 1890s when it grew as a clear response to the pressures towards incorporation that were manifested in the burgeoning systems of conciliation and arbitration procedures. In that sense, informal organisation must be seen as directly descended from the traditions of autonomous regulation in both union government and in relations with employers whose whittling away began in the 1860s and reached a climacteric in the 1890s. On the other hand, a firm institutional continuity is harder to trace, and less meaningful anyway. Assertions of rank-and-file authority and the revival of oppositional movements as their expression will recur at each point where a cycle of incorporation seems to be operative. This, for example, is the significance of the revolt of Halewood workers in July 1968 against their shop stewards which was marked by the election of an unofficial strike committee and where a major theme was the control over negotiating issues by the rank and file. Until 1967 there was a fairly close concordance between the stewards and the shop floor, but in that year a new grading agreement was adopted which destroyed the role of the stewards as arbiters of the men's grievances and replaced them with a computer at Worley into which the grievances were fed to see if they conformed to the agreement. Thus, ironically, an agreement designed to undercut the powerful informal organisation of the rank and file and the stewards in order to ensure a more effective subordination to management only resulted in reviving a tradition and form of resistance that possessed even older historical roots.[13] This example should also serve to remind us that informal organisation cannot simply be seen as an oppisitional response to union bureaucratisation — many militants in the 1890s, for example, recognised the need for more complete organisational forms in the face of a growing concentration of capital — but more as a rejoinder to the priorities of that bureaucracy. It is for this reason that the 1890s saw the beginnings of the modern tradition of informal organisation, for it was then that the implications of bureaucratic organisation for the traditions of rank-and-file authority were first clearly apparent.

The creation of national procedures of collective bargaining went hand in hand with the growth of union executive authority. I have recently examined this process in some detail for the building trades, but it was a common theme of the period and extended over a wide range of industries and trades. Whenever systems of industrial relations were created we may note a close connection between their workings and the growth of informal organisation, not only to fill the gaps created by systems which emphasised national negotiation (although that was a factor in some industries like engineering) but also as a response to the denial of rank-and-file responsibility.[14] In the boot and shoe industry, for example, the growth of rank-and-file militancy and organisation (the details of which are unclear) was a response not only to problems created by the changing division of labour in the trade, but also to the fact that the method of resolving those problems virtually denied the rank-and-file a voice. At the 1892 conference between the union and the employers an arbitration system had been erected in an explicit attempt to 'strengthen the union's national leadership and ... increase its authority over the membership'. Significantly the issue had not been put to the vote. Militancy was now given a specific focus and, as was the case elsewhere, the delays that arbitration imposed in settling contentious issues and its inability to actually diminish the threats facing the rank and file only served to stimulate and develop oppositional organisation. In London, for example, which with Bristol, Leicester and Northampton was a centre of such activity, these two themes came together when meetings called to discuss withdrawal from the arbitration system were denied the right to elect their own chairmen by the executive who insisted upon officials leading the meetings. Indeed, on one notable occasion, the executive and General Secretary unilaterally invited employers to address the gathering in order to buttress their pro-arbitration sentiments. By 1894 such tensions had led to the abandonment of seven of the regional conciliation boards. The general failure of the system to mitigate rank-and-file militancy was the critical factor in the employers' decision to embark on the national lockout of 1895.[15]

The same connections may be seen elsewhere. On the railways, the 1907 conciliation system — adopted again without consultation with the rank and file — was designed to fracture the all-grades sentiment which had grown since the 1890s and to reinforce the sectional divisions that characterised the industry. In fact, its effect was probably the opposite. The workings of conciliation served to boost militancy and accentuate the desirability of an all-grades movement, thus providing a stimulus to the pressure from below that contributed so greatly to the formation of an 'amalgamated' NUR in 1911.[16]

Amongst the printers, too, the transformation of autonomous regulation into informal organisation occurred in the 1890s and was coincident with the expansion of executive authority demanded by such national negotiations and agreements as that between the Typographical Association and the Linotype Users' Association in 1898. In London, Vigilance Associations complete with their own publications and monthly meetings recur throughout the 1890s. Their purpose was to act as watchdogs on the executive of the London Society of Compositors which, like its national counterpart the Typographical Association, was revealing an increasing tendency to overrule or obstruct policy decisions laid down at the annual meetings. Although the issues of rank-and-file dissatisfaction were different in the TA — reflecting its more centralised organisation — the theme of the alienation of power and authority remained the same. On the Linotype Agreement, for example, it was pointed out by about a dozen major branches that the negotiating mandate of the Liverpool delegate meeting had been so widely breached that an agreement 'fraught with grave significance [for] . . . the future of the trade' should have been submitted to 'the final arbitrament of the rank and file'. Indeed, this issue precipitated a crisis in the government of the Association and a power struggle between the Representative Council (set up in 1892 with the specific purpose of controlling the Executive) and the Executive which, although ultimately resolved in favour of the latter, did nothing to prevent a revival of the same kind of militancy on the occasion of the next major conflict in the trade in 1911.[17]

Like most explosions of rank-and-file militancy, these examples did not finally decide the issues or organisational questions they addressed. They were significant more because they represented a tradition of alternative action and experience which, like the informal trade committees of the nineteenth century, were available when the formal structures were incapable of formulating an adequate response.

There are other links, too, with that older organisational form of the
Victorian period, and occasionally some that look forward to the
present day. Of the latter, we may note the Clyde Stewards in 1914
who, in defiance of their executive and the 1907 agreement, formed
an early example of a Combine Committee to take action against non-
unionists. Or, in the early 1930s, there were the calls emanating from
Minority Movement influenced engineers for Councils of Action to be
composed of union and non-union men to resist the recently negotiated
agreement which had accepted unfavourable revisions in overtime and
other working conditions.[18] On the railways, too, there is at least a
thematic link between the all-grades committees of the 1890s and early
1900s and the Vigilance Committees of the 1920s and 1930s whose
emergence was a response to the unions' acceptance of rationalising
policies which involved speed-ups and dismissals. Indeed once
research into the informal history of labour is further advanced, it
would be surprising if continuous links were not discovered. It is
already clear, for example, that the joint productivity councils of
the Second World War were based upon networks of informal
organisation, often composed of communist militants, which were
active in the 1930s. Furthermore, that pattern of transformation was
also reversible: the demise of the councils and the attack upon
workshop participation by management in the late 1940s were the
seedbed for the informal systems of the 1950s and 1960s.[19]

In engineering the tradition of workshop bargaining represents an
historical continuity that extends back to the modern beginnings of
the industry and its role was recognised by the tradition of loose
central control in the Amalgamated Society of Engineers. The changes
of the 1890s, however, both reinforced this tradition and established
threats to its autonomy which obliged it to adopt an oppositional
stance. On the one hand, new payment systems such as premium
bonus accentuated the need for local bargaining. In Manchester, for
example, the District Committee's traditional responsibility for piece
prices was now joined by the formal creation of workshop committees
empowered to negotiate with foremen and managers. The shop
stewards — recognised in the rules for the first time in 1896 — were a
clear response to this need. On the other hand, such a formalisation
of informal traditions provided the basis for the oppositional militancy
to the centralising forces of the various collective agreements that
followed the debacle of 1898 and whose climacteric role in the war
years has been analysed by James Hinton. Indeed, the growing
militancy and solidarity — expressed through the discussions of
amalgamation — of the pre-war years both anticipated that of 1915-18

and contrasted sharply with the internal chaos that marked the official organisation. The objects of that militancy were the Terms of Agreement originally negotiated in 1902 and re-affirmed in 1907 and which the ballot of 1912 voted against renewing. In a pattern that was all too familiar during these years, this decision was blandly ignored by the Executive which on the eve of war negotiated temporary terms of settlement with the employers to remain in force until union permission could be secured to negotiate a new procedure.[20]

Out of these experiences, and more particularly out of the better-known tensions and dynamic of the war, the habit and structures of informal organisation and bargaining were well-established by the 1920s. Just to skim the Organisers Reports in the AEU *Monthly Journal* in the early 1920s is to discover that the unofficial system of industrial relations, wages drift and the shop steward network are all phenomena that pre-date Donovan. Even though weakened by the depression, it is unlikely that this informal system was ever completely smashed. By 1923 it was true that previous centres of steward organisation and wartime militancy such as Beardmores, Dalmuir and John Brown's in Glasgow were without stewards because nobody could be found willing to risk taking the job, and 'those shops, once solidly organised are now about the worst in the district as far as membership is concerned'. But in London in the mid-1920s the informal system was capable of mounting an impressive campaign of resistance against rationalisation at Hoe's Engineering through the agencies of an overtime ban, a go-slow campaign and ultimately a stay-in strike. The whole action breached the sacred Procedure, the shop stewards did all the negotiating and the mass meeting acted as a sovereign body. Eventually, official union discipline was restored and not coincidentally the stewards were dismissed, payment by results introduced and the general speed-up sought by the company commenced. The point, however, is not to search for ultimate final victory, but to note the persistence of themes and issues that could be transposed without violence to their essence either into the 1890s or the 1960s.[21]

This tradition of informal, unofficial organisation, then, may be argued to derive not only from the spontaneous needs of any particular industrial context — although that is clearly important; nor may it be seen simply as a response to needs that are unmet in the system of industrial relations — although that, too, is obviously a significant component of its character. Were its meaning and significance encompassed by these relatively simple and obvious precepts, it is hard to see how its persistently oppositional features could be explained. The fact is that this tradition represents a resistance to the constricting denial of rank-and-file authority that the particular development of the industrial relations system in Britain has demanded. We might note here that there is no inherent contradiction between centralised, bureaucratised collective bargaining and authority structures that are responsible to the workshop level. The reasons why the main thrust of British industrial relations, procedures and organisations has not sought ways of more completely meshing the various levels of responsibility and authority is a complex question which cannot be entered into here. What is clear, however, is that the informal, unofficial tradition represents an alternative structure of authority in industrial relations which refuses to die, and in this respect, there are two aspects to that tradition of alternative authority structures that deserve a brief mention.

First, there is the theme of the assertion of rank-and-file sovereignty over negotiations which runs consistently through the history of the informal system. Historically, this strand must be traced back to the eighteenth and nineteenth centuries and it remained the dominant form of authority structure until the last third of the nineteenth century when it began to be systematically chipped away. It is often forgotten how hard this tradition died in its classical form amongst skilled workers. As late as 1912-13 the Scottish Typographical Association was grappling with the issue, connected as it always was to the shift from autonomous regulation to mutual negotiation in the trade. Similarly, when the Linotype Users' Association negotiated with the Typographical Association in the 1890s, they insisted that the union executive assume or secure plenary powers of negotiation.[22] Until the last part of the nineteenth century, this tradition posed no conflict to either the demands of capital or the structure of union government, but as those imperatives changed in symbiotic relationship, so the tradition itself became increasingly redundant. It found a new home, however, in the new forms of unofficial organisation that emerged in response to the changes in the structures of bargaining of the same period — although it is only fair to point out that its remnants are enshrined in some union constitutions by the device of referring back. The tradition of rank-and-file control over negotiations was also intimately connected to the notion of autonomous regulation, and this tradition, I would suggest, underwent an equal transformation once its legitimacy was denied by formalised structures of industrial relations which fed into and issued forth in the notion of workers' control. It is surely no coincidence that historically workers' control found its strongest support in those industries like engineering, mining and building where the traditions of site or workshop bargaining and organisation were most completely developed. This is hardly the place to embark upon a full-scale examination of the history of support for workers' control in British industry. It is only too clear that the notion is surrounded by many difficulties and weaknesses, the most serious of which has been the failure of its advocates to think deeply about its relation to politics, the state and the unions. We can readily admit that even at the moments of its greatest strength, the movement was confronted with enormous obstacles of an internal and external nature. But what is perhaps most significant is the hardiness of the idea itself. It is impossible to conduct even the most superficial examination of rank-and-file activity or literature at any point in the last seventy years without being continually confronted with the question. Only at moments of crisis, however, does the matter emerge into a wider public view and begin to receive the attention of thinkers like Cole and of politicians who then attempt to resurrect the panacea of schemes for greater participation and industrial democracy. The enduring nature of this tradition — half-baked though its formulations may be — clearly marks it as an important component of the traditions of resistance at the workplace to be found in British labour history.

The third of the traditions of resistance to be addressed is that of the struggle for control of overtime. As with the previous examples, I do not wish to deny that this question touches more aspects of the labour experience than I shall here address. But, once again, there are two points of central importance for our argument. First, there is the persistence of the issue. Whilst it is clear that the general character of overtime was transformed from a disincentive to the employer, to an incentive for the men during the nineteenth century — at differing times for different industries — it is also the case that there has been no cessation of efforts by workers to make overtime serve their purposes. Secondly, this continuity can best be conceptualised not as a simple economist struggle — although it can be that — but as a further illustration of resistance to subordination at the workplace. To restrict or control overtime is to restrict the employer's freedom to deploy his capital resources according to the priorities of the market or production. If, as at Fawley, the docks, or the auto plants in the 1950s, overtime was totally controlled by the men and used to maximise earnings then this does mean that a substantial area of employers' authority was diminished.

It is for this reason, for example, that in each of the celebrated engineering conflicts of 1852, 1889, and 1922 the overtime issue occupied a central role. In the first of these struggles the question of whose discretion should determine overtime working was part of a wider contest between autonomous regulation by the men or the singular authority of employers which accompanied the decisive shift away from craft-organised production to that of the heavily capitalised, mechanical workshop. Systematic overtime, which first emerged as an important issue in the mid-1840s, reflected the employers' need to cheapen the cost of working and possess the flexibility to respond quickly to immediate economic and market pressures. On this issue, questions of economy and authority were inextricably mixed, for the customary concept of overtime as part of the property of labour posed an explicit challenge to the imperatives of a tightened sphere of employer perogative:

> In the settlement of this question [i.e. when overtime was to be worked] employers can scarcely claim to have a voice . . . for we conceive that a workman who has completed his working day in a satisfactory manner, has no right to be called upon to bind himself to the performance of extra work, or at all events that such should be entirely optional on his part.

This spirit did not die with the defeat of 1851-2; indeed, it loomed large in each of the periods surrounding the subsequent major conflicts in the industry. Thus, the regulations proposed by the men in May 1851 (and for a while reluctantly acquiesced in by the employers) stipulated that permission for overtime working be secured from the District Committee: exactly the same requirement was enforced in Lancashire in the summer of 1920, so that employers' complaints about the veto exercised by the men on overtime were equally similar.[23] Collective bargaining tended to make the issue of overtime restriction into an unofficial one and in the agreements of 1898 and 1922 the union explicitly recognised employer control of overtime. This was even the case when defeat could not be used as an excuse. The overtime agreement of 1920 was resented by the rank and file because the cases where overtime was not to be considered systematic were claimed to be so wide as to cover virtually every eventuality. Although the agreement failed to address the issue of union consultation, the localities immediately began to assert this unilaterally and the Executive was drawn to support this interpretation by pressure from below, but readily abandoned it in the negotiations of January 1922 – that is three months *before* the lockout of March. Although this formally resolved the issue until 1976, resistance to employer control of overtime recurred throughout even the depression years to become one of the notable successes of the unofficial system of industrial relations in the 1950s and 1960s.[24]

Control of overtime could serve two practical, and related purposes. In times of prosperity and boom, it could be used to organise the work day so as to maximise earnings; in times of depression, restrictions on its working served to mitigate the effects of unemployment by a wider distribution of the workload. It thus contributed to, and was a part of, the fourth and final tradition of resistance I wish to address: that of job security.

Since the Second World War, the notion of property rights in a certain job has been recognised to be an important feature of labour's militancy. Although this has been explained in the cases of the auto industry and the docks as a reflection of the historical seasonality and casuality that marked those industries, such reasoning (whilst not incorrect) fails to appreciate the historical tradition which this represents.[25] The desire to spread and share the work underlies much of the activity of nineteenth-century workers in their hours agitations, demarcation rules and restriction of production. Indeed, the recent enshrinement of a somewhat qualified job security in the 1976 Employment Protection Act may be seen as a triumph of this particular tradition of resistance to capitalist freedom, for official unionism has historically shown little interest in pressing this demand.[26] Workers of course did not then articulate these demands in the explicit way that modern workers do, but we might note a not too fanciful parallel in the way large strikes in the post-war auto industry coincided with slumps and the equally 'irrational' winter strikes of the masons before 1900, both of which can be seen as attempts to spread the workload and maximise job security. By the late nineteenth-century, however, perhaps because of the influence of socialist ideas, expressions of the right to work began to appear. James Samuelson, for example, was quite shocked to report that the Cleveland iron miners' response to mechanisation in the 1890s was to demand that those displaced by machinery be found other work. The equivocating silliness of his reply is worth noting:

The patentee or inventor may be a foreman [sic], or he may have run through all his property before he has perfected his machine,

or many other circumstances may make it unfair or impossible for
him to find employment of displaced labour. And labouring men
must not forget that the employment of machinery may be a necessity, and that the establishment . . . must either modernize . . . or . . .
shut up shop.[27]

These demands tended to be made, it would seem, mainly by workers
whose means of protecting their jobs were limited in scope. The first
demands by engineers for full maintenance by industry of those it
employed come in the early 1920s when, in fact, it was a commonplace
assumption. But the idea that 'every worker ought to have the right
of security of employment' was to be found amongst transport workers
in 1912 and, as Bean has shown, the Liverpool dock strike of 1890
was primarily about job regulation to ensure security even though
union negotiation concentrated solely on the wage demand. In the
years immediately preceeding the First World War the question of job
security was a major component of the syndicalist spirit and there was
an explicit willingness to strike on the issue, the most famous examples
being the Knox and Richardson cases on the railways.[28] During the
war, a vast expansion of the control over dismissals was achieved.
Although this was mainly of an informal nature, it was in some places
included within the procedures and the purview of Works Committees.
The Commissioners on Industrial Unrest for South Wales went so far
as to recommend that every employee be guaranteed security of tenure
and be subject to dismissal only with the agreement of his fellow
workers. With the worsening of conditions in the mid-1920s, the
largely informal nature of this control made it vulnerable to removal,
but the notion retained a furtive if usually ineffective presence even
(or perhaps one should say especially) in the 1930s. Hilton found it
in the docks. The TUC discussed the right to maintenance in the early
1930s. There was the occasional active resistance to redundancy which
pre-figured the widespread militancy on the issue of the 1940s through
to the 1970s. Thus, in 1933 the refusal of a driver and fireman to do
the work of discharged coal tippers led to the latters' reinstatement,
although a similar attempt to enforce the re-hiring of 70 Somerstown
railwaymen by work-to-rule was ignored by Unity House and
abandoned after a week. These examples, scattered and sporadic though
they are, suggest that the prominence of the issue from the late 1940s
was not merely a response to expectations that derived from the
wartime experience of a closely regulated labour market. That
experience was certainly important because it legitimised (at least in
the workers' eyes) the notion that redundancy did not lie unilaterally

within the sphere of managerial prerogatives. Even before the war ended the shop stewards' movement in engineering was demanding full consultation and alternative work for those made redundant by the return to peacetime production. With the failure to secure any formal gains in this area, the issue retreated to the province of the informal system where it was enormously successful. Strikes against management's right to hire and fire at will were a prominent — if little noticed — feature of engineering in the late 1940s and early 1950s, and demands for negotiations on numbers and the provision of alternative work were a consistent feature throughout the period.[29]

The best example of this tradition as manifested in the 1950s was at Standard Motors where the workers had secured informal rights to consultation over redundancy during the war as part of a broader expansion of their control. A deliberate managerial policy of 'relative autonomy' encouraged these developments, but worker control over redundancy was never explicitly recognised by management and had to be enforced several times by strike action in the early 1950s. Indeed, the issue provided the major obstacle to the rationalising plans of the company in the mid-1950s and was the most serious cause of the strike of 1956. This strike was significant because it opened a new phase of conflict in the industry, as it struggled to rationalise and mechanise the production process to meet the challenge to its world market position. It is a story that demands to be told in full because the failure of the auto industry to cope successfully with worker resistance is central not only to the economic decline of that industry but suggestive of the wider story of British capitalism as a whole since the mid-1950s. The basic element in this history was the struggle of management to re-assert a control over the line that had been lost since the war. Amongst the managerial strategies in this effort were speed-up, measured day work, the destruction of the gang system and the efforts to formalise the role of the stewards. Under these threats of increased mechanisation and insecurity, an industry-wide campaign against redundancy was generated in the mid-1950s; strikes over the issue were frequent; it formed a central part of the consciousness of auto workers throughout the whole period and broadened enough to contribute to the Labour government's legislation on employment protection in 1965 and 1976.[30]

This fairly cursory examination of four of the most significant aspects of the tradition of resistance has drawn attention to the fact that the labour militancy of the recent past can be seen as part of an historical continuum whose roots lie in the 'informal' history of labour's post-industrial revolution experience. But to chart the themes of this resistance is, in a sense, the lesser of the tasks to be addressed; of more importance is to make some assessment of how we should theorise them and where they should be located within the wider context of labour history. The first thing to note is that these traditions cannot be regarded as the product of purely instrumental factors such as incomplete bargaining systems, or the sense of security that derived from post-war affluence. A consideration of continuity alone precludes that kind of analysis which, in reality, only points to the conditioning factors that permit these traditions to achieve success or confines them to narrow limits. Indeed, that very continuity suggests a deeper, more fundamental determinant which may be seen to lie in the productive process itself. As we have already suggested, it is as resistance to capitalist domination of the labour process that these traditions must be viewed, for this provides them with their unity and continuity and explains the prominent place they occupy in managerial rhetoric when they obstruct the flexible re-arrangement of the forces of production.

The labour process under industrial capitalism can only be understood as a struggle for authority and control; the technical and material elements in the labour process, important though they are in closing off or opening up the potential for resistance, are in the final analysis subsidiary to the imperatives of authority. Indeed, although we should beware of any kind of reductionism, even the adoption of a particular kind of technology itself cannot be divorced from this context.[31] As Marx pointed out, the logic of industrial capitalism is flawed by the essential paradox that the kind of obedience demanded at work is not reflected in the supreme cultural values of individualism and freedom that accompany capitalist enterprise. More than in any other previous economic and social formation, industrial capitalism depends upon authority over the labour process: without industrial discipline, the very foundations of capitalism are threatened. Of course, there are very broad limits of tolerance at work here. If, for example, the traditions of resistance contributed in some measure to undermining the profitability of British capital by the late 1960s, it was equally true that capitalism was capable of accommodating those traditions for nearly thirty years. Nevertheless, the problem of authority and control could not be ignored indefinitely and the necessity to re-assert the primacy of capitalist control over the labour process was the central aspect of industrial policy in Britain from the late 1960s. And this merely translated into 'crisis' proportions (and not for the first time) the essence of social relations at the labour process: that in order to achieve valorisation and profit maximisation, capital must strive to subordinate labour to its control. The logic of the automaton *is* the logic of industrial capitalism. But, of course, history is not necessarily logical and the symmetry of the labour process is continually disturbed by resistance from the workforce which is driven by the nature of the labour process itself to deny its mutation into the 'living tools' of Taylorist fantasy. The pressure of these traditions of resistance, then, serves as a constant brake upon, and can develop into a challenge to, subordination at the labour process. There is at all points, both between industry and over time, a space between the formal subordination of labour and the extent to which this is measured by real subordination. The presence of this space of resistance has not been properly appreciated by historians who have tended to dismiss its efficacy as marginal and minor because it fails to measure up to an idealised standard of how the working class *should* behave.

To understand this it is necessary to appreciate that resistance and subordination are neither mutually exclusive, not autonomously separable from each other. Within working-class culture as a whole, there is a constant and uneasy tension between acquiescence and dissent. At different times and within different levels of experience, one may predominate over another, but both are continually present not as a predetermined, static relationship, but as a constantly changing and shifting dynamic. As recent studies of the labour aristocracy have shown, the acceptance of mid-Victorian hegemony was always qualified and fractured in ways that allowed for the option of an escape into the wider dissenting tradition of socialism at the end of the century. It is, therefore, necessary to reconcile the mutuality of resistance and subordination and we can only begin to do this at a theoretical level by appreciating the nature of the labour process.

In order to realise itself, capital has to surrender to workers the actual use of the means of production. Thus, in spite of the best efforts of Henry Ford and Frederick Taylor, the only certain subordination that the assembly line and division of labour impose is a formal subordination through the wage relationship. The rest is a matter of 'negotiation'. But, equally, labour can only live and struggle by gaining access to the means of production through the sale of its labour power and accepting formal subordination. At this level, then, both capital and labour have an inherent interest in a co-operative relationship which was reflected in the prominence of the idea of the mutuality of 'capital and labour' amongst the mid-Victorian labour aristocracy. The visibility of this mutuality was reinforced during that particular period by the wider security that British capitalism held within the world economy; a security that was, perhaps, unparalleled in the history of the world and which permitted the demand for 'real subordination' at the labour process to be only weakly pressed once the general principle of capitalist authority had been achieved through the struggles of the 1830s and 1840s. Once that situation altered, however, the notions of mutuality flipped over. For it is also the logic of the labour process that in order to achieve maximum valorisation, capital is driven to continually extend and effect labour's subordination. It was only in the latter years of the nineteenth century that this logic fully entered the history of British capitalism, but in any case, labour will resist such efforts (and frequently oblige management to modify or abandon them). Workers are able to do so precisely because they 'actually control the detail of . . . performance of their tasks, and the importance of this, although it varies with the productive process, never disappears altogether'. In the words of an unskilled line worker, 'we've always got the last card because we're running the job'. The value of this last card varies enormously, but it is never entirely worthless and its value and play determine the extent of real subordination. Thus, the immediate choice for labour in the labour process is *not* between autonomy or subordination, resistance or incorporation, but the balance (which varies between and within historical periods) between these two that allow for the 'form of bargain that labour makes with capital'.[32] Two further points follow: to understand and analyse resistance (or, for that matter, subordination) we cannot adopt absolutist categories which imply a settled, determined and foreclosed character; and secondly, we cannot assume that these traditions of resistance are at most marginal and at best 'economist' aspects of labour's history. Let us illustrate these contentions by a closer examination of the dynamics of resistance.

The first person to investigate empirically the extent and nature of workers' resistance at the workplace, and who coined the phrase the 'frontier of control' was Carter Goodrich. Goodrich was writing in the heady days of the early 1920s, most of his examples were taken from the war years and his book lacked any real historical perspective. As a political scientist attempting to come to grips with the phenomenon of workers' control, Goodrich proposed a set of conceptual distinctions which revolved around a series of opposites: customary control or contagious control, enforced or reactive, and positive or or negative. Although he seems to have glimpsed the danger in such an analysis (claiming at one point that 'the right to say yes or no shades very easily into the right to say which or what') it is this series of absolutes that have continued to dominate our perception of worker resistance. The distinctions rested primarily upon the *intent* with which control was exercised. Customary control was associated with the struggles of old crafts to preserve ancient privileges, assumed a conservative hue and possessed no capacity for extending beyond its own traditionally established boundaries. Enforced control was superior to reactive control because it signified independent initiative rather than aquiescence to employer rights. Finally, positive control was distinguished from negative control by, for example, 'the right to say not *under what* conditions machinery might be introduced but actually *where* it *should* be introduced'. These distinctions, therefore, emphasise the narrow limitations which confine most acts of workers' control, and they have continued to exercise a subterranean but important influence on the literature. The main thrust of a recent American work, for example, is to emphasise how the techniques and area of resistance compose a 'game' workers play to countervail monotony and are actually encouraged by management as part of the process of 'manufacturing consent' to subordination. Elsewhere, the same author has argued that the intensification of struggle created by piecework leads to a reinforcing of subordination by a rigid concentration on 'looting' or 'making out' games.[33]

The problem with this kind of analysis and that which Goodrich followed is two fold. First, it dictates that most resistance be relegated to a marginal role — a position adopted by many industrial sociologists.[34] Secondly and more importantly, it implicitly ascribes to the labour process a static quality which disguises the dynamic relationship between resistance and subordination. Of course, certain kinds of control demands are laden with greater potential than others, but the determinants of this have less to do with the original intent of the demand and more to do with the relationship between its presence and the nature of efforts at subordination. There is nothing inherently and absolutely conservative or negative about old-style craft control (which, anyway, is very hard to define empirically) and should that control be challenged extensively enough or widely enough, it is perfectly capable of shedding its conservative features and assuming broader implications. Thus, the craft compositors were 'driven to socialism' by the threats of the 1890s; the craft engineers were, equally, driven to at least a strong flirtation with workers' control by the challenges of the First World War. Neither of these developments could have occurred without the solid basis of a negative or conservative conception of control. In other words, the dynamic of the struggle for control is such that a negative posture may be converted into a positive reaction depending on the opportunities that are opened up by efforts to ensure real subordination. Two specific examples may be taken to illustrate this.

First, piecework which Marx saw as the form of wages payment most appropriate to capitalism. It is not hard to see why he thought this was the case, and formally he was correct; but what he did not consider was the possibility that workers might so regulate piecework as to turn it from an instrument of subordination into one of resistance. We do not know precisely how successfully workers regulated piecework in the nineteenth century, but it is clear that in engineering and shipbuilding they were able to exercise some control either through the effort bargain or through direct negotiations. Platers, for example, 'negotiated' piece prices by the gang remaining outside the yard gates until they secured the price demanded. It is indisputable that in the post-war era, piecework was captured largely by the workers. Even the ordering of individual piecework was found to reflect collective regulation, and in many places the rules governing piecework were both tenacious and restrictive. William Brown catalogued them: the prevention of stop watches or work study controls over the speed of machines; rules prohibiting wage rates from changing even if the job changed or the men moved to other machines; the maintenance of a certain rate for the job no matter who performed it. It should be noted that all of these rules were directly contrary to the written agreements in the trade which expressed the formal subordination of the workers. Hugh Scanlon pointed to the ambiguities of piecework in 1967 when he remarked that although most of the ills of engineering could be blamed on piecework, engineers fight to retain it because 'with piecework you have the man on the shop floor determining how much effort he will give for a given amount of money'.

Protection of piecework lay at the heart of the myriad of customs and practices that tunnelled through British industry in the 1950s and 1960s, but it is important to appreciate that those customs and practices cannot be seen, therefore, simply as the product of unilateral worker regulation. They were the results of precedents granted or extended from various levels of management because they were in no position to refuse or because of accidental decisions whose consequences were unforeseen, or because of a general policy of relative autonomy. This provides a particularly apt example of the mutality of resistance and subordination. In theory, piecework should act as an instrument of subordination and, indeed, it can act in this way. In reality, it would seem that workers are typically able to get some control over it and it thus becomes the basis for a set of customs and practices whose growth is not necessarily stimulated by the overt desire to challenge managerial authority and may, in fact, originate from a 'defensive' posture, but which is capable of transcending those limitations. As Brown has pointed out, the inevitable tendency of this matrix is 'to drift towards increasing worker control over work'.[35]

A concerted effort was made from the early 1960s to wrest control over piecework away from the men by the introduction of measured day work and technology that removed the need for worker initiative in production. Measured day work was designed to restore managerial control over the productive process by removing the ability of workers to use the effort bargain to secure better conditions. But its effects were not one-dimensional, for it obliged the men to reconsider and renew their strategies of resistance and led in the automobile industry and coal mining to a higher degree of practical unity since management now confronted them with a unified system. Indeed, measured day work, uniformly applied across the coalfields, went a long way to overcoming sectional divisions and differences. The tradition of resistance to redundancy was the key to understanding the reaction to measured day work because the method promised reductions in manning and speed-ups; the worker's argument at the shopfloor level in automobiles shifted from money to men and the effort had to be placed on not 'losing men to push your earning up but to man the tracks to the highest condition'. In that way, too, measured day work became a unifying force and

> we carried over from the piecework days the control we had got into standard day work [by including] ... in our agreements a measure of mutuality [which] ... appeared not to be very great [but] ... which was sufficient for us to exercise the same sort of control ... by ensuring that each track was manned to a reasonable level. [36]

There is a dynamic to the struggle between resistance and subordination at the shop floor which ensures that the results and consequences of a particular strategy are never foreclosed. Thus, in their investigation of

Chemco, Nichols and Beynon found an extensive if covert system of largely negative 'counter-planning' controls exerted by unskilled workers within the context of a system of formal subordination which was designed to deny any space or legitimacy to shopfloor bargaining. A threatened disruption of this system by the introduction of a new grade of operators, legal within the procedure, transformed this negative control into a more positive direction. The men refused to do any filling in on this new category, made the lives of the new operators difficult (in the process radicalising some of them, so that one became a steward), and most importantly learned to use the formal procedure as an adjunct to these activities by forcing a complaisant union to fight the matter through to an eventual victory. This whole experience did *not* lead to revolutionary consciousness, but it did lead 'them to assess trade unionism and its potential in a way that was quite at odds with the established practices'. It also led to 'conflicts *within the union* [over] ... what trade unionism *should* be about' and to a consideration of alternative authority structures: 'I think the union should try and get *everything* under control. You know, control it.' As the authors conclude, out of a context in which formal subordination was assured, and real subordination effective, arguments evolved which reflected the presence of a quite different set of traditions within the working class to those that are characteristic of a pure and simple labourism.[37]

This leads us to a final aspect of our conception of resistance at the workplace, which is the tendency to see this struggle as primarily economist whether in the sense that it is simply concerned with wage determination, or in the Leninist sense that it is incapable of generating a political resistance to capitalism. To take the Webbian notion first, it should be obvious from what has gone before that it is totally inadequate to reduce these struggles to a matter of upholding the standard rate or maintaining minimum conditions. As has been shown elsewhere, that tendency is the function of official trade unionism within the bargaining structures. The Webbs, however, can hardly be blamed for failing to see much beyond that perspective; they failed to take account of the unofficial traditions of labour action (although their manuscript notes reveal that they collected plenty of information on it) because they really believed them to be irrelevant and moribund, important only to the decentralised world of the past. Since it is impossible to separate the political Webbs from the scholarly Webbs, and since both these aspects of their lives were devoted to fostering a corporatisation of society in which various estates of representative democracy would compete co-operatively in the search for greater efficiency, the values and activities of workers which impeded those virtues could be quite legitimately relegated to residual forms which time would ultimately destroy. It is clear that they were wrong, although labour history has yet to learn the lesson fully; and they were wrong because they failed to understand the multi-dimensional nature of social relationships at the workplace which are linked not so much by economic ties as by those of power. Today the notion that worker action at the labour process is simply a matter of money, is no longer widely held. Brown for example showed how 'money matters can become apparently inextricably entangled with wider questions of the control of work. The pursuit of more stable and predictable earnings led [for example] to workers . . . gaining control over their mobility between gangs and over the speeds at which their machines were run.' But the point is not simply one of a progressive development from money to control, both are or can be present in any particular issue or dispute because both are inherent to the social relations of production. Stonemasons who prohibited worked stone had excellent economic reasons for doing so, but the extent of their ability in this respect was both a reflection and an expression of their power to restrict the full exercise of employers prerogatives and authority. There is, therefore, no contradiction between economic demands or control demands and, indeed, it is frequently impossible to delineate where one leaves off and the other begins. Thus, 'every aspect of work is a control problem' and, as a car worker remarked

> Workers' control is not something to be fought for or dreamt of as a far-off goal. It is a factor inherent in every bargaining situation . . . Control is a matter of degree — the more we have the less for them. It's a commodity in limited supply in every given situation — and its marginal utility doesn't diminish.[38]

But there is a further, more constraining, implication to the notion of the economism of contests over control of the labour process in which the Webbs join company with Lenin. This view, which pervades much of the literature, holds that contests at the point of production are to be viewed as essentially separate from the generation of political consciousness; that because these struggles do not overtly challenge capitalistic ownership, they reveal the limitations of all the self-activity of the working class. Although many have implicitly or explicitly rejected this orthodoxy, and accept that there is some relationship between political consciousness and the labour process, they are usually unclear as to what the exact relationship is and what it portends.[39] It is important to realise that this view, which has bedevilled Marxist theorising about labour action ever since Lenin formulated it in the early twentieth century, is a logical extension of Marx's own analysis of the actual details of the labour process. Although Marx only addressed this question in fragments of his writings (which have only recently become available in English), he assumed the unproblematic nature of the subordination of labour at the point of production once machinery had been successfully harnessed to productive activity – a view that underlies the fullest contemporary treatment of this question. Thus, in *Grundrisse*, Marx wrote with a clear sense of the abstract power of machinery and capitalist organisation within the new system of industrial capitalism:

> The productive process has ceased to be a labour process in the sense of a process dominated by labour as its governing unity. Labour appears, rather, merely as a conscious organ, scattered among the individual living workers at numerous points of the mechanical system; subsumed under the total process of the machinery itself, as itself only a link of the system, whose unity exists not in the living workers, but rather in the living, active machinery, which confronts his individual, insignificant doings as a mighty organism. In machinery, objectified labour confronts living labour within the labour process itself as the power which rules it.[40]

Marx did not forsee, therefore, that resistance to capitalist control of the labour process could make much of an impact. Rather, he envisaged that the powerlessness of the working class at the productive process would force them into the separate realm of revolutionary political activity. By Lenin's time, however, it was evident that things were not working out that way and it was necessary to more fully accommodate the trade union struggles of the working class within Marxist theory. In fact, this accommodation – undertaken in the context of intra-party factionalism – has proved to be an impediment, understanding either the theory or the practice of resistance at the point of production because it falsely separates the economic from the political. It imposes a bias which conveys an inadequate image of the mechanism by which political ideology is generated within the working class.

Marxism was formulated through an examination of the self-activity of capitalism and that starting point has determined its attitude towards the self-activity of the working class. The questions historians have asked concerning the failure of the working class to act as a class for itself have tended to reflect this bias, concentrating either on the internal weaknesses of the class, or upon the external constraints that ensure that it acts only as a class in itself. None of these categories, however, are adequate to explain quiescence, because they are all admitted to be incomplete and qualified. An internal constraint like 'sectionalism' possesses elements both of quiescence and dissent, of fragmentation and unity. Whilst it may explain one particular episode or incident, it may not be elevated into an absolute category because it is capable of inversion and of being transcended.[41] A further problem is that to use such a term always involves an implicit comparison with an alternative and unrealistic ideal of 'unity' which serves only to accentuate the force of the original accusation of sectionalism's disintegrating power. We should also note that the 'fractures' that are recognised to exist within capitalism are seldom endowed with the heavy analytical burden of explaining its failure to make the world thoroughly conform to its wishes. Similarly, the notion of Anderson and Nairn, that the hegemony of bourgeois culture has been so complete as to allow no model for working-class dissent to copy and follow, is inadequate because it dismisses the fact and content of working-class resistance and ignores the imperviousness of working-class culture. Were Anderson and Nairn correct, the presence of a counter-ideology amongst the working class would be inconceivable.[42] In like manner, analyses that emphasise the incorporative tendencies of labourism fail to explain how it is that the hegemony of official labourism has never been unproblematic and may not, therefore, be taken as the inevitable representation of working-class politics. From the very moment of its inception, official labourism has been challenged by policies and programmes that lie much closer to the self-activity of the working class. The central historical problem is to explore the struggle that labourism has constantly fought against those alternatives. Incorporation is not a pre-determined quality. Agencies of incorporation have a curious way of opening up spaces for counter-acting forces to emerge.[43] But it is clearly *not* the case that these kinds of factors are of no account; it is obvious that they do describe certain levels of reality and, in particular cases, it may be that their role is determinant. What impresses one most forcibly however, is the way these categories implicitly determine the (pessimistic) conclusions that are subsequently drawn from them and that their analytical power flows not from a realistic understanding of working-class self-activity but from the erection of external ideal standards against which labour action and behaviour is measured and judged.

This, I suspect, derives from the fact that the theory of working-class action has not allowed its assumptions to be altered and changed by the actualities of working-class self-activity. In other words, the limitations of working-class resistance are taken to reflect the inadequacies of the particular situation of the class itself, rather than the theories that are adduced to explain that activity. Castoriades pointed to the traditional dilemma that Marxism has created in this respect when he remarked how the 'historical role of the proletariat exists only in so far as the proletariat does what the theory knows and predicts it must do'. As a consequence, the traditions of working-class self-activity and resistance are relegated to marginality and we are driven to the conclusion that 'for over a century [the proletariat] has fallen prey to tenacious illusions and [has manifested] ... an outstanding capacity to believe in directions hostile to its own interests'. The requirement that the only proper struggles are those which explicitly question the authority of the established power dismisses the fact that even a coffee break strike challenges or undermines the 'foundations [of the] ... capitalist definition of reality'. That such struggles have compromised or helped to alter capitalism indicates that they are not without political implications. Indeed, a large part of the story of post-war British capitalism is precisely its vulnerability to this kind of 'marginal' labour pressure.[44]

But, it could be replied, such pressure is never enough to actually transform capitalist social relations. It is true that the traditions of resistance are by themselves incapable of generating an effective political ideology, but there are two things to be said about this. First, to argue in this way is to impose a false separation between economics and politics which does not describe reality and is to imply that in some way the productive process may be separated from other spheres of social and cultural activity. If this were the case, then it would be impossible for productive activity to generate anything but the valorisation of capital. This is as absurd as conceiving of intellectuals advancing thought apart from a constant interaction with the material realities of their surroundings. As we have seen, the logic of resistance and subordination may lead in many different directions, none of which may be characterised as purely economic or, for that matter, as purely political. Secondly, and more important, Marxism has generally failed to integrate working-class self-activity into its own theoretical assumptions, and this failure has compounded the absence of an intellectual and political ideology that either rests upon the basis of that activity, or is close enough to it to provide a viable explication of its social, political and cultural dimensions. In this context, the hegemony of labourism is hardly surprising since it provides the closest fit between the material situation of the working class and the expression of that situation within a political vocabulary.

The historical mechanism of developing political consciousness amongst the working class is too complex to explore fully here. But it is broadly the case that such consciousness moves when an ideology, or set of prescriptive values, attains a relevance in explaining or understanding the material dilemmas and challenges that face the working class in society. The bedrock origins of these forces are industrial, but they obviously link into and are part of a wider set of cultural traditions and contemporary cultural debates. Thus, Chartism, the growth of labourist socialism and later, syndicalism, all emerged from such a context to express the political consciousness and programmes of sizeable sections of the working class. What should also happen is that these 'ideologies' engage in a 'dialogue' with the traditions of working-class self-activity and resistance that fostered them in order to become more relevant in answering mass needs. But in Britain, at least, this has not happened, mainly because there was no place within the dominant intellectual tradition for such a process to occur. Where that interaction has occurred, it has done so within the boundaries that could comfortably be legitimated by other sources of authority. Thus, the emergence of labourist socialism at the end of the nineteenth century was markedly influenced by the fusion between the religio-ethical tradition of social criticism and the cultural attitudes and biases of the labour aristocracy. There was no space for a similar catalytic reaction between 'culture' and the traditions of resistance to capitalist control over the labour process which were firmly entrenched within the labour aristocracy. Syndicalism itself was almost totally a product of these traditions, but its uncertainty in Britain (well-expressed by Cole's description of it being more of a sentiment than a hardcore ideology) reflected the absence of that juncture. Of course, given their 'craft' history, the traditions of resistance could be verbalised and expressed to a certain extent by labourist socialism, but that formulation could not contain the dynamic of those traditions at a time when the definitions of hierarchy and authority themselves were being widely challenged and by 1910, or so, the limits of labourism in this respect were clearly visible.[45]

It may not be the case, then, that the limitations of labourism reflect the internal flaws of the traditions of working-class resistance. Indeed, it is important to appreciate that those traditions are not merely an empty ideological shell waiting to be filled with the potion of correct theory. Within the industrial perspective, those traditions contain a pre-figurative political ideology which is far distant from Leninist prescriptions and whose key element would include anti-centralism, the accountability of leaderships, mandated responsibility, and collectivist notions of democracy which reject the individualism of the secret strike ballot. Working-class action and even to an extent working-class institutions like the trade unions contain, then, the striving towards alternative authority and organisational systems which occasionally receive a 'quasi-ideological' expression in such concrete ways as the *Workers' Report on Vickers*. But if the working class does possess a well-established tradition of dissent which, in its industrial perspective, is revealed by resistance to real subordination at the labour process, the confinement of dissent to a tendency as opposed to an ideology may not be attributed solely to the inherent nature of the tradition itself. We have also to consider the absence of a visible cultural, intellectual, or political tradition within which that tradition could be conceptualised and realised as an ideology.

In this respect, it is striking how efforts to generalise the patterns and traditions of worker self-activity into a coherent set of political and ideological principles have been typically transient reactions to worker militancy at periods when a general reorganisation of the basis of subordination in industry was in progress. The widespread discussion of syndicalism, guild socialism and workers' control that bracketed the First World War and the revival of a similar set of ideas in the mid-1960s reflect that relationship. But neither the internal weaknesses characteristic of such formulations, nor the fact that both periods ended (or in the contemporary case seem about to end) in the successful assertion of a new basis of subordination in industry, fully explain the absence of a developed ideology or theory that could build upon or endeavour to extend those traditions of resistance. The achievements of British syndicalism were by no means as meagre as they have traditionally been portrayed, but its inability to produce native versions of Gramsci, Pouget, Sorel or De Leon was its most revealing failure. It was true that intellectuals like G.D.H. Cole, Guy Bowman and William Mellor for a time gave official labourism a good run for its money, but in the long run they proved incapable of distilling any lasting theoretical generalisations from the experience of those years, and soon lapsed into the more secure environment

of the dissenting tradition. We need only note the banality of much
of the contemporary analysis of the pre-1914 'labour-unrest' to
understand the cultural and intellectual desert in which British
syndicalism had to operate. As a consequence, no cultural or
intellectual monuments of that period remain within the British
experience — not even a body of songs like those of Joe Hill in the
USA.[46] What did remain, and it was of no little significance, was the
practical lesson of an organised shop stewards' movement. It may be,
then, that the internal weaknesses of the working class have less to do
with its traditions and more to do with the voids that exist in the
culture and the available ideologies.

Thus, in addition to the 'normal' constraints with which the
working class in Britain (and elsewhere) have to cope, there is the
poverty of theory. The logic of the Leninist position that working-
class and self-activity is relatively insignificant has fitted well with the
dominant cultural (and institutional) traditions in Britain. But these
traditions of resistance within the working class are not to be
dismissed or denigrated so easily. From an historical perspective, their
persistence and tenacity is striking, and their character may not be
understood within categories of analysis such as economism,
marginality or spontaneity. Equally, none of this should be taken as
a romanticisation of worker activity; my purpose has been to suggest
the continuities of the traditions of workplace action, the necessity
to view them as integral to the dynamic of labour history, and the
inadequacies that derive from the categories into which they are usually
placed. It is important to understand sectionalism, the divisions within
the working class, the power of elites and the rest, but it is also
important to integrate the persistence of resistance into our efforts
to theorise and conceptualise labour history. That cannot be done
if we are to resist modifying or rejecting those parts of the Marxist-
Leninist analysis that labour action has historically shown to be
false. Conceptualising labour history requires that we move the self-
activity of the working class to centre stage and proceed from there,
rather than arrive at that activity with a bundle of Webbian, Leninist
or labourist categories and expectations into which it is then placed
and judged.

Notes

1. Theo Nichols and Huw Beynon, *Living with Capitalism* (London, 1977),
pp.113, 135, 141.

2. James Cronin, *Industrial Conflict in Modern Britain* (London, 1979), pp.141-4; Colin Crouch, 'The Intensification of Industrial Conflict in the United Kingdom', in Colin Crouch and Alessandro Pizzorno (eds.), *The Resurgence of Class Conflict in Western Europe since 1968*, vol. 1 (London, 1979); Pierre Dubois, *Sabotage in Industry* (Harmondsworth, 1979); Kevin Hawkins, *The Management of Industrial Relations* (Harmondsworth, 1979), pp.26-8, 31, 35-44.

3. Leo Panitch, *Social Democracy and Industrial Militancy* (Cambridge, 1976), p.179; Keith Middlemas, *Politics in Industrial Society* (London, 1979), p.440.

4. H.A. Clegg, *The Changing System of Industrial Relations in Great Britain* (Oxford, 1979); Richard Hyman, 'Industrial Conflict and Political Economy', in *The Socialist Register*, 1973 (London, 1974); Richard Hyman, *Industrial Relations. A Marxist Introduction* (London, 1975); Richard Hyman, *The Workers' Union* (Oxford, 1971); Alan Fox and Allan Flanders, 'The Reform of Collective Bargaining: From Donovan to Durkheim', *British Journal of Industrial Relations*, vol. 7, 1969.

5. For example see, Hawkins, *Management of Industrial Relations*, pp.22, 26; Clegg, *Changing System of Industrial Relations*, p.80; Crouch, 'The Intensification of Industrial Conflict', pp.208, 211, 215-18.

6. John A. Lincoln, *The Restrictive Society* (London, 1967); Royal Commission on Trade Unions, 1965-68, *Research Paper, No. 4* (HMSO, 1966).

7. F. Zweig, *Productivity and Trade Unions* (Oxford, 1951), pp. 8-9; John Hilton, *Are Trade Unions Obstructive?* (London, 1935), pp.309, 334.

8. Hilton, *Are Trade Unions Obstructive?* pp.21-2; Lincoln, *Restrictive Society*, p.100.

9. Lincoln, *Restrictive Society*, pp.104-7; Linotype Users' Association, *Monthly Circular*, May 1899, p.2, May 1900, p.7; *Webb Collection*, B, vol. LXXIV, f.41, pp.4-5 for a privately circulated memo from the Linotype Company which pointed to the disparity between American operators who set 20-27,000 ens per hour and the London Society of Compositors' claim that the maximum rate was 7000. The average output on the *Daily Telegraph* at this time was claimed to be 3000 ens per hour. For the similarity of conditions in the 1930s see Hilton, *Are Trade Unions Obstructive?* pp.231-6.

10. David Wilson, *Dockers, The Impact of Industrial Change* (London, 1972), pp.212-15; Hilton, *Are Trade Unions Obstructive?* pp.96, 106, 109.

11. Nichols and Beynon, *Living with Capitalism*, p.108; Stanley Mathewson, *Restriction of Output Among Unorganised Workers* (New York, 1931); *Journal of Gas Lighting*, 17 March 1891, pp.403, 409.

12. Hawkins, *Management of Industrial Relations*, p.13.

13. Huw Beynon, *Working For Ford* (Harmondsworth, 1973), pp. 164-73. We should also note that this led to efforts to overcome divisions between the various plants at Halewood which eventually resulted in the emergence of the Parity campaign in 1971. This episode also suggests that the post-Donovan efforts to incorporate the stewards' organisation that Richard Hyman has analysed as potentially destructive of informal organisation and militancy will not be free of countervailing tendencies. See Richard Hyman, 'The Politics of Workplace Trade Unionism', *Capital and Class*, no. 10, Summer 1979.

14. Richard Price, *Masters, Unions and Men: The Struggle for Work Control in Building and the Rise of Labour 1830-1914* (Cambridge, 1980). It should be pointed out that the argument here is not that informal organisation was always and necessarily an oppositional force: we are not dealing in absolutes, only tendencies, and it is clearly the case that it could also complement national structures and systems. This was certainly the case in engineering and probably elsewhere. The point is, however, that it was not integrated into the official structures and there was always an inherent oppositional element to informal organisation which stood ready to emerge whenever the need arose.

15. Alan Fox, *National Union of Boot and Shoe Operatives 1874-1957* (Oxford, 1958), pp.155-7; National Union of Boot and Shoe Operatives, *Monthly Reports*, May 1893, pp.25-6, 38, 44; Elizabeth Brunner, 'The Origins of Industrial Peace: The Case of the British Boot and Shoe Industry', *Oxford Economic Papers*, no. 1, 1949, p.255.

16. Charles Watkins, 'Conciliation or Emancipation', in *The Industrial Syndicalist*, May 1911; Fred Henderson, *The Labour Unrest* (London, 1912), pp.23-6.

17. See, for example, *Vigilance Gazette*, May 1888-February 1889; *London Printers' Circular*, May 1889-May 1890; *Print*, May 1896-October 1896; *Typographical Circular*, February 1899, pp.4-5, March 1899, pp.1-5, 8-9, April 1899, p.6, June 1899, pp.4-9, July 1911, pp.2, 4, 6; A.E. Musson, *The Typographical Association* (Oxford, 1954), pp.124-5.

18. *The Socialist*, July 1914, p.84; Amalgamated Engineering Union (AEU), *Monthly Journal*, August 1931, pp.4-5, 7.

19. *Railway Vigilant*, January 1933; Arthur Exell, 'Morris Motors in the 1930s', parts I and II, *History Workshop Journal*, no. 6, Autumn 1978, no.7, Spring 1979; James Hinton, 'Coventry Communism: A Study of Factory Politics in the Second World War', *History Workshop Journal*, no. 10, Autumn 1980; Ken Coates and Tony Topham (eds.), *Workers' Control* (London, 1970), p.197; *Metal Worker*, August 1948, p.4.

20. Amalgamated Society of Engineers (ASE), *Monthly Journal*, April 1899, p.60; *The Socialist*, July 1914, p.84.

21. AEU, *Monthly Journal*, December 1923, p.24, March 1926, pp.9-17, April 1926, pp.10-12, May 1926, p.45, September 1926, p.35.

22. For the Scottish Typographical Association see the fascinating account of a conference with employers in the early part of 1913 where the issues of mutual responsibility and union accountability were the central issues. *Scottish Typographical Journal*, January 1913, p.14, February 1913, pp.36, 41-3, 47, 55; Linotype Users' Association, *Monthly Circular*, December 1898, pp.1-3, October 1899, p.1.

23. *The Operative*, 12 April 1851, p.234, 24 May 1851, p.333; Keith Burgess, 'The Influence of Technological Change on Social Attitudes and Trade Union Policies of Workers in British Engineering Industry 1780-1860', unpublished PhD thesis, University of Leeds, 1970, p.254; ASE, *Monthly Journal*, June 1920, p.32; *Engineering*, 17 March 1922, p.330.

24. AEU, *Monthly Journal*, November 1920, p.76, May 1921, pp.14-15, January 1922, pp.60-61, February 1922, p.12, July 1923, p.27, March 1934, pp.6, 11. For control of overtime in the 1950s and 1960s see Seymour Melman, *Decision-Making and Productivity* (New York, 1958), p.52; Alan Flanders, *The Fawley Productivity Agreements* (London, 1964), Ch.6.

25. H.A. Turner, Garfield Clack and Geoffrey Roberts, *Labour Relations in the Motor Industry* (London, 1967), pp.115, 332; Dennis Butt, 'Men and Motors', *New Left Review*, no. 3, May-June 1960, p.14.

26. For the unofficial roots of the demand for control over redundancy see, for example, *Metal Worker*, April 1959, p.4.

27. James Samuelson, *Labour-Saving Machinery* (London, 1893), pp.60-2.

28. ASE, *Monthly Journal*, April 1920, p.47, August 1930, pp.50-1; *Humberside Transport Workers' Gazette*, June 1912, pp.2-3; R. Bean, 'The Liverpool Dock Strike of 1890', *International Review of Social History*, vol. XVIII, pt. 1, 1973; Philip Bagwell, *The Railwaymen* (London, 1963), p.339.

29. Carter L. Goodrich, *The Frontier of Control* (London, 1975), pp.104-10; Hilton, *Are the Trade Unions Obstructive?* p.323; *Railway Vigilant*, March 1933, p.11. April 1933, p.4; *New Propellor*, October 1944, p.7; *Metal Worker*, May

1949, p.1, February 1950, p.3, August 1950, p.1, April 1959, p.4, November 1960, p.1.

30. Melmann, *Decision-Making and Productivity*, pp. 178, 180-3; Andrew Friedman, *Industry and Labour. Class Struggle at Work and Monopoly Capitalism* (London, 1977), Cronin, *Industrial Conflict*, p.62.

31. See the very suggestive piece by Stephen Marglin, 'What Do Bosses Do?' in Andre Gorz (ed.), *The Division of Labour* (Hassocks, 1976).

32. Peter Cressey and John MacInnes, 'Voting for Ford: Industrial Democracy and the Control of Labour'. *Capital and Class*, no. 11, Summer 1980, pp.14-15; Nichols and Beynon, *Living with Capitalism*, p.145.

33. Goodrich, *Frontier of Control*, pp.254-64; Michael Burawoy, *Manufacturing Consent. Changes in the Labor Process Under Capitalism* (Chicago, 1979); 'The Politics of Production and the Production of Politics,' in *Political Power and Social Theory*, vol. I, 1980. Burawoy emphasises the generation of consent (or subordination) that is one aspect of the capitalist labour process but it is only fair to point out that at certain moments he does recognise the equal presence and power of resistance. Of course, he is dealing with the American working class where the traditions of resistance are almost certainly much weaker than they are in Britain. See Burawoy's critique of Braverman which includes a recognition of the presence of resistance: 'Toward a Marxist Theory of the Labour Process: Braverman and Beyond', *Politics and Society*, vol. 8, nos. 3-4, pp. 266, 273, fn. 61.

34. See, for example, John Purcell and Robin Smith, *The Control of Work* (London, 1979).

35. William Brown, *Piecework Bargaining* (London, 1973), pp.60, 88, 91, 98, 111, 114, 115; see also his 'A Consideration of Custom and Practice', *British Journal of Industrial Relations*, vol. 10, no. 1, March 1972; Geoff Brown, *Sabotage* (London, 1977), p.314.

36. For measured day work in the coalfields see Brown, *Sabotage*, pp.326-39; for autos see John Bloomfield, 'Interview with Derek Robinson', *Marxism Today*, March 1980.

37. Nichols and Beynon, *Living with Capitalism*, pp.111, 113, 135, 141, 143-5. For a similar example of extensive counter-planning, combined with a high level of organised sabotage, see Bill Watson, 'Counter-Planning on the Shop Floor', *Radical America*, vol. 5, no. 3, May-June 1971.

38. The Webbs' understanding of labour action is most fully explained in *Industrial Democracy* (London, 1897); Brown, *Piecework Bargaining*, p.114; Coats and Topham (eds), *Workers' Control*, p.426.

39. See, for example, Michael Mann, *Consciousness and Action Among the Western Working Class* (London, 1973); John Foster, *Class Stuggle and the Industrial Revolution* (London, 1974) which represents a bold attempt to ground this Leninist viewpoint in empirical data. Interestingly enough, Gareth Stedman Jones' equally impressive critique of Foster implicitly emphasises even more strongly the economism of autonomous labour action and consciousness by its argument that the central struggle of this period was over the ultimately successful assertion of real subordination. See his 'Class Struggle and the Industrial Revolution', *New Left Review*, no. 90. This kind of argument possesses a profoundly pessimistic tone about the nature and potential of labour action seen especially in Alastair Reid, 'Politics and Economics in the Formation of the British Working Class: A Response to H.F. Moorhouse', *Social History*, vol. 3, no. 3, October 1978. Furthermore, it is an argument which ignores the fact that Lenin's distinction between trade union and revolutionary consciousness just will not hold at the level of workplace action and it thus leaves us encased within the Leninist conclusion that socialist consciousness must be brought to

the workers from agencies that are essentially outside their experience. See Laurie Clements, 'Reference Groups and Trade Union Consciousness', in Tom Clark and Laurie Clements (eds.), *Trade Unions under Capitalism* (Hassocks 1978) and Cornelius Castoriades, 'On the History of the Workers' Movement', *Telos*, no. 30, Winter 1976-7; V.I. Lenin, *What Is to Be Done?* (New York, 1973), pp.31-2, 40, 78.

40. Karl Marx, *Grundrisse* (New York, 1973), p.693; *Capital*, vol. 1, (Penguin edition, Harmondsworth, 1976), Appendix: Results of the Immediate Process of Production; Harry Braverman, *Labor and Monopoly Capital* (New York, 1974).

41. Thus the reinforcement of sectionalism by the 1969 grading agreement at Halewood actually encouraged the workers to campaign for parity between all the plants. Benyon, *Working for Ford*, pp.172, 211, 263, 289.

42. This counter-ideology needs to be examined more seriously by historians than has hitherto been the case. See C.W. Chamberlain and H.W. Moorhouse, 'Lower-Class Attitudes Towards the British Political System', *Sociological Review*, vol. 22, no. 3, August 1974; and the same authors' 'Lower-Class Attitudes to Property: Aspects of the Counter-Ideology', *Sociology*, vol. 8, no. 3, September 1974; Perry Anderson, 'Origins of the Present Crisis', *New Left Review*, no. 23; Tom Nairn, 'The English Working Class', *New Left Review*, no. 24.

43. David Coates, *Labour in Power? A Study of the Labour Government 1974-1979* (London, 1980); Panitch, *Social Democracy and Industrial Militancy;* Stephen Yeo's religion of socialism represents the first such challenge, Bennism the latest. See Stephen Yeo, 'A New Life: The Religion of Socialism in Britain 1883-1896', *History Workshop Journal*, no. 4, Autumn 1977.

44. Castoriades, 'History of the Workers' Movement', pp.4, 27-8, 34, 38.

45. The crisis in the ILP in 1908-9 over the relationship between its parliamentary tactics, its increasingly centralised focus and the definition of socialism may be seen in this context. See Stanley Pierson, *British Socialism. The Journey from Fantasy to Politics* (Cambridge, Mass., 1979), pp.158-68.

46. See, for example, Henderson, *The Labour Unrest*; William Mellor, *Direct Action* (London, 1920). We might also note in this respect how it took a Russian scholar to uncover and publish the rich collection of Chartist poems see Yuri Kovalev, *An Anthology of Chartist Literature* (Moscow, 1956).

NOTES ON CONTRIBUTORS

James Cronin is Associate Professor of History at the University of Wisconsin-Milwaukee. His publications include *Industrial Conflict in Modern Britain*.

Lynn Hollen Lees is Associate Professor of History at the University of Pennsylvania. Her publications include *Exiles of Erin*.

Richard Price is Professor of History at Northern Illinois University. His publications include *An Imperial War and the British Working Class* and *Masters, Unions and Men*.

Jonathan Schneer is Assistant Professor of History at Yale University. His publications include the forthcoming *Ben Tillett: Portrait of a Labor Leader*.

Charles Tilly is Professor of Sociology and History, and Director of the Center for Research on Social Organization at the University of Michigan. His publication include *The Vendée, The Rebellious Century* (with Louise and Richard Tilly) and *Strikes in France, 1830-1968* (with Edward Shorter).

Peter Weiler is Associate Professor of History at Boston College. His publications include *The New Liberalism: Liberal Social Theory in Great Britain, 1889-1914*.

Joe White is Associate Professor of History at the University of Pittsburg. His publications include *The Limits of Trade Union Militancy*.

INDEX